Traute Scharf studied law an[d] science at Vienna Universit[y] degrees of Dr. iur. and Dr. rer. [...] and 1962. Her thesis dealt with [...] Problems in Developing Countr[ies]. From 1964-1966 the author [...] socio-economic problems of [...] countries in the Institute for Ad[vanced] Studies (Ford Institute) in Vienna, after which she was engaged for two years on research work and lecturing to IDEP at Dakar in Senegal.

In addition to three years' study of ethnology, the author has travelled to Greece, the United Arabic Republic, Turkey, Morocco, Tunisia, the Near East and Mexico and the outcome of her researches is apparent in over thirty publications.

Traute Scharf was Associate Industrial Development Officer of UNIDO, Vienna from 1968-1969 and took up her present position of Project Economist at the Asian Development Bank, Makati in 1969. On her missions she travelled extensively in Asian countries, in Korea, Japan, Taiwan, Malaysia, Singapore, Hongkong, India, Afghanistan, Nepal and Pakistan.

Majur Chandrashekar Shetty obtained his B.A. and M.A. degrees in economics at the Bombay University, where he spent a further two years' research work on the problems of industrial location and decentralized industrial growth.

His subsequent assignments concerned rural economic problems, specializing in applied and policy-oriented studies related to household and small-scale industries and agro-economics, as well as industrial extension problems. He wrote two books covering these issues in 1962 and 1963 and several articles. During this period he taught industrial economics at the postgraduate level in the Vallabhai University, India.

Majur Shetty is at present with the ICICI, an outstanding development bank, where he supervises Development and Training Activities. At varying periods his services were seconded to UNIDO, Vienna and the Asian Development Bank, Manila as consultant on industrial development and development financing. Aside from his current work, the results of his world-wide researches throughout this time have been recorded in three books, which were published in 1968, 1969 and 1972.

DICTIONARY OF
DEVELOPMENT BANKING

From the same Publisher:

DICTIONARY OF DEVELOPMENT ECONOMICS
English, French, German

GLOSSARY OF ECONOMICS
English/American, French, German, Russian

GLOSSARY OF FINANCIAL TERMS
English/American, French, Spanish, German

DICTIONARY OF INTERNATIONAL RELATIONS AND POLITICS
German, English/American, French, Spanish

ELSEVIER'S BANKING DICTIONARY
English/American, French, Spanish. Italian, Dutch, German

Complete catalogue is available on request.

DICTIONARY OF DEVELOPMENT BANKING

A compilation of terms in English, French and German with definitions in English

COMPILED AND ARRANGED BY

TRAUTE SCHARF

Asian Development Bank, Makati, Rizal, Philippines

and

MAJUR C. SHETTY

The Industrial Credit and Investment Corporation of India Limited, Bombay, India

ELSEVIER PUBLISHING COMPANY

Amsterdam London New York

1972

ELSEVIER PUBLISHING COMPANY
335 Jan van Galenstraat
P.O. Box 211, Amsterdam, The Netherlands

AMERICAN ELSEVIER PUBLISHING COMPANY, INC.
52 Vanderbilt Avenue, New York, New York 10017

Library of Congress Card Number: 72-83212

ISBN 0-444-41028-7

Printed in The Netherlands

INTRODUCTION

Development Banking is a nascent, albeit emerging discipline. Many trace its origin to the post-Second-World-War years; some, however, go farther back in economic history and associate the concept with the activities of merchant banks and financial companies of yore. This surely is an area of research best left to economic historians. What is of importance is that development banking is of relatively recent origin the world over, and more significantly a fairly new technique in the developmental armoury of the newly industrializing countries of Asia, Africa and Latin America.

Thanks largely to the pioneering efforts of the World Bank and the other international and regional institutions engaged in providing developmental assistance, the newly industrializing countries all over the world have come to look upon development banking as an effective and potent instrument in their developmental efforts. This fact is borne out by the numerical strength of these institutions. A publication of the OECD* identified three hundred and forty development finance institutions in the developing countries in 1966. Since then, scores of new institutions have been, and continue to be, added to the list.

However, as is characteristic of an emerging discipline, the supply of professional expertise, as also the requisite supporting literature on concepts, techniques and operational tools relevant to the discipline, do not appear to have kept pace with the rapid growth of development finance institutions. The authors, having been involved in developmental and development financing operations over the years, have felt this inadequacy a serious handicap in their various assignments; and they are sure this is an experience shared by most institutions, professionals and research workers connected with economic development in general and development finance in particular. The present compilation is offered, in a spirit of humility, as a modest beginning in an effort to stimulate larger and more significant contributions from practitioners and research scholars in this new and emerging discipline.

The concepts, techniques and tools relevant to development banking have a multi-disciplinary bearing. Essentially, development banking combines and adapts the basics of a variety of disciplines including engineering, economics, finance, commerce, accountancy, management, marketing, agronomy, social psychology, behavioural science and extension techniques. Inevitably, therefore, the terms and concepts basic to these disciplines form the mainstay of development banking. It needs to be emphasized, however, that in their usage in development banking these terms and concepts assume a different and unique significance, compared to their

---

*J.D. Nyhart, E.F. Janssens: A Global Directory of Development Finance Institutions in Developing Countries; The Development Centres of OECD, Paris, 1967.

original and traditional usages. The present compilation, therefore, represents an earnest attempt at defining traditional terms and concepts in their new usage and import.

This compilation incorporates over 1200 terms. These are organized under three broad sections: (1) the Environmental Frame, (2) Development Banking, and (3) Development Bank. Each of the sections is further subdivided into convenient sub-sections. No finality is claimed about the rationale underlying the organization of terms under the respective sections or sub-sections. The main objective has been to facilitate location of specific terms in the context of their relevance. However, difficulties could still be experienced in locating terms in their context. This, despite utmost care, was found unavoidable. To alleviate difficulties on this score, a general alphabetical index of terms in English is provided.

A dictionary concerning a discipline such as development banking, which derives its basic tools and techniques from a variety of social, economic and technical disciplines, will inevitably draw on similar existing works in these disciplines. The present work is no exception to this. While, therefore, grateful acknowledgement is proffered to various glossaries and dictionaries in economics, commerce and accounting, too numerous to be acknowledged individually here, the authors would like to mention that the responsibility for specific definitions in the present compilation is entirely theirs.

The authors would like to express their appreciation to Mrs. Flor Angel Z. Suaco for her devoted secretarial work.

The authors would also like to emphasize that this work, being a modest attempt towards providing conceptual and terminological precision concerning an emerging discipline, will doubtless need upgrading from time to time. Suggestions in this regard will be gratefully acknowledged and considered for incorporation in any future revisions.

TRAUTE SCHARF
MAJUR SHETTY '
Manila
December, 1971

CONTENTS

Introduction   v

Language Indication viii

PART ONE. ENVIRONMENTAL FRAMEWORK
    I. Economic and industrial background – Fond économique et industriel – Wirtschaftlicher und industrieller Hintergrund . .   3
    II. Governmental, monetary, fiscal and legal aspects – Aspects gouvernementaux, monétaires, fiscaux et juridiques – Regierungs-, Währungs-, Steuer- und legale Aspekte 15
    III. Capital market and banking – Marché de capital et opérations banquaires – Kapitalmarkt und Bankwesen 27

PART TWO. DEVELOPMENT BANKING
    IV. Development institutions and agencies – Institutions et agences de développement – Entwicklungsinstitutionen und Einrichtungen . 49
    V. Objectives, policies and activities – Objectifs, politiques et activités – Zielsetzung, Politik und Tätigkeiten 61
    VI. Project evaluation aspects and techniques – Aspects et techniques d'évaluation de projet – Gesichtspunkte und Techniken der Projektbegutachtung 76
    VII. Pre- and post-financing aspects – Aspects d'avant- et d'après-financement – Gesichtspunkte der Vor- und Nachfinanzierung . 97

PART THREE. DEVELOPMENT BANK
    VIII. Capitalization – Capitalisation – Kapitalstruktur 113
    IX. Organization, management and staff – Organisation, administration et personnel – Organisation, Verwaltung und Personal 123
    X. Professional expertise and training – Expertise professionnelle et formation – Berufliche Fachkenntnis und Ausbildung 133
    XI. Financial aspects – Aspects financiers – Finanzgesichtspunkte . 147

English Index 159
French Index 177
German Index 195

LANGUAGE INDICATION
LANGUES
SPRACHEN

f	French	français	Französisch
d	German	allemand	Deutsch

PART ONE
ENVIRONMENTAL FRAMEWORK

I.
ECONOMIC AND INDUSTRIAL BACKGROUND
FOND ECONOMIQUE ET INDUSTRIEL
WIRTSCHAFTLICHER UND INDUSTRIELLER HINTERGRUND

1   AREA DEVELOPMENT;
      REGIONAL DEVELOPMENT
Regions or smaller geographic
areas within regions, earmarked
for concentration of developmental
efforts, including those of development banks.

f   Développement d'une région;
      Développement régional
d   Regionalentwicklung

2   AREA, BACKWARD
Referred basically to industrial
development deficiencies and in
most developing countries, preferred for industrial development
for reasons such as provision of
gainful employment opportunities;
normally, such areas have lagged
in development on account of
deficiencies in social and economic
overhead facilities conducive to
the location of industrial enterprises; promotion of development
projects in such areas forms an
important promotional obligation
of development banks.

f   Région arriérée
d   Unterentwickeltes Gebiet;
      Rückständiges Gebiet

3   BACKWASH EFFECTS
Generally associated with the
phenomenon of accentuated
differential in development between
underdeveloped and developed
countries as a result of exclusive
emphasis on promotion of primary

exports from the former to the
latter. Similar situation has
been observed to develop within
a developing country as between
regions, sectors and areas.

f   Effets de remous
d   "Backwash" Effekte;
      "Backwash" Wirkung

4   BALANCE OF PAYMENTS
      DEFICIT
A situation wherein a country's
import obligations exceed that
of export earnings; characteristic
of most developing countries.

f   Déficit de la balance des
      paiements
d   Zahlungsbilanzdefizit

5   BALANCE OF TRADE
The relationship between the
money values of a country's
visible imports and exports.

f   Balance commerciale
d   Handelsbilanz

6   BLACK MARKET
The process of buying or selling
of goods at prices above those
fixed statutorily; in many
developing countries - because
of import restrictions - several
commodities of necessity to
consumers and of basic intermediate goods are supplied by
a process of rationing and price
regulation, thus giving rise to

3

such type of dealings.

f   Marché noir
d   Schwarzer Markt

7   BOOM
A period of expansion of business
and economic activity where all
factors of production are employed
to near full-employment level.

f   Hausse rapide
d   Schneller geschäftlicher Aufschwung

8   CAPITAL FLIGHT
A situation where capital seeks
investment outlets outside of the
country; a phenomenon generally
observed in most developing
countries for a variety of reasons,
e.g., uncertainties associated with
new national philosophies,
nationalization, repatriation
restrictions, lack of incentives,
policies tending to restrict profit
levels, high levels of taxation, etc.

f   Fuite des capitaux
d   Kapitalflucht

9   CAPITAL FORMATION
The process of creating various
types of productive assets, through
savings from industrial, household,
corporate and government sectors.
In most developing countries, this
is sought to be achieved by
augmenting savings by curtailment
of consumption at various levels.

f   Formation du capital
d   Kapitalbildung

10   CAPITAL INFLOW
Process of inducting foreign
capital through various means such
as unilateral, bilateral, multi-
lateral aid, private investment
capital by providing various incentives such as repatriation facilities, controlling interests
in enterprises, infra-structure
facilities, helpful fiscal and

monetary policies. Development
banks are expected to play a
vital role in this behalf. (See:
Resource mobilization 566)

f   Afflux des capitaux
d   Kapitalzufluss

11   CAPTIVE UNIT
A manufacturing, processing or
servicing unit, the output of
which is used entirely by a
parent company, instead of
being sold to the public.

f   Unité captive
d   "Gefangene" Produktionseinheit

12   CENSUS OF INDUSTRIAL
       PRODUCTION
A periodic survey of output and
related aspects of various
sectors of industry, commerce
and services undertaken annually
by a department of the Government; aspects covered include
information on fixed capital formation, stocks carried and other
items of importance for national
statistics.

f   Recensement de la production
    industrielle
d   Zensus der industriellen
    Produktion;
    Industrieproduktionszensus

13   CONSUMER COUNCILS
Organization of consumers
set-up, voluntarily or statutarily,
to protect consumers against
unhealthy or monopolistic
practices of producers or
distributors.

f   Conseil de consommateurs
d   Konsumentenberatung

14   COOPERANT FACTORS
The elements complementary
to capital necessary for promotion of economic development,
such as a labor force with the

appropriate skills, entrepreneur-
ship, management know-how,
economic, commercial and financial intelligence, institutional incentives, etc. (See: Investment
adsorptive capacity 71)

f   Facteurs coopérants
d   Zusammenwirkende Faktoren

15   DECENTRALIZED INDUSTRIAL
      DEVELOPMENT
      Process of dispersal of industrial
      location to bring about a more or
      less balanced development of
      various regions or areas in a
      country; one of the developmental
      obligations enjoined on development
      banks.

f   Développement industriel
      décentralisé
d   Dezentralisierte industrielle
      Entwicklung;
      Dezentralisierte Industrie-
      entwicklung

16   DEFLATION
      A condition characterized by
      rapidly falling prices and dull
      business. Normally, it takes place
      when the amount of goods produced
      far exceeds the ability or willing-
      ness of people to buy.

f   Déflation
d   Deflation

17   DEVELOPING COUNTRIES
      Countries which historically
      lagged in economic and industrial
      development; normally applicable
      to the newly independent or
      emerging nations of Asia, Latin
      America and Africa.

f   Pays en voie de développement
d   Entwicklungsländer

18   DEVELOPMENT AREAS
      Specified areas or regions in a
      country where favorable terms
      are offered for location of industrial

units in order to encourage
development.

f   Régions de développement
d   Entwicklungsgebiete

19   DEVELOPMENT SCHEME
      Individual programs for develop-
      ment evolved for implementation
      within the overall frame of
      development plans.

f   Plan de développement
d   Entwicklungsprogramm

20   DISINFLATION
      The removal of inflationary
      pressure from the economy in
      order to maintain the value of
      the monetary unit.

f   Anti-inflation
d   Anti-Inflation

21   DIVERSIFICATION,
      INDUSTRIAL;
      DIVERSIFICATION, PRODUCT
      Process of enlarging the in-
      dustrial base of the economy by
      promoting a variety of industries;
      also manufacturing activities of
      a firm into related products or
      services with a view normally
      to obtain economies of scale.
      This forms an important policy
      objective of most developing
      countries.

f   Diversification industrielle;
      Diversification des produits
d   Erweiterung der industriellen
      Aktivitäten;
      Vervielfältigung der Industrie-
      produkte

22   ECONOMIC DEMOCRACY
      Objectives aspired for by most
      developing countries where
      citizens will have equal
      opportunities for pursuing
      activities of production, con-
      sumption and employment:
      consists of, among other things,

5

enlarging opportunities for gainful economic pursuits and reduction in disparities in income. Another facet of the same objective consists in the prevention of undue privileges accompanying wealth in the hands of individuals, or groups of individuals.

f   Démocratie économique
d   Wirtschaftliche Demokratie; Wirtschaftsdemokratie

23   ENTERPRISE, FREE
An economic system under which property of all kinds can be privately owned and in which individuals, alone or in association with one another, can own productive resources and undertake production. (See: Enterprise, private 442)

f   Liberté d'entreprise; Liberté d'entrepreneur
d   Unternehmensfreiheit; Unternehmerfreiheit

24   ENVIRONMENTAL ENGINEERING
Activities related to the provision of facilities against pollution of waterways, industrial effluent, air, water refuse, sewage, etc.

f   Facilités d'anti-pollution
d   Anti-Pollutionsvorkehrungen

25   EXPORTS, FOREGONE
The value of goods produced domestically which in fact could be exported, but which actually are used instead, domestically.

f   Exportations manquées; Exportations renoncées
d   Verzichtete Exporte

26   EXPORT UNIT REALIZATION
An important consideration in the industrialization programmes of developing countries to raise export earnings through increased realization per unit of commodity exported. Such increases in unit realization are brought about by increase in the value added content of exported commodities by raising the proportion of manufactured exports in the total exports.

f   Réalisation d'une unité d'exportation
d   Exportrealisierungseinheit

27   EXTERNAL ECONOMY
Positive or negative benefits of a project which are not reflected in the profitability calculation. These are pecuniary and technological in nature.

f   Economie externe
d   Externe Wirtschaftseffekte

28   EXTERNAL ECONOMY, PECUNIARY
The effects of externalities are pecuniary, when these are transmitted through the price system, as by lowering the market prices of certain products or factors. (See: External economy 27)

f   Economie externe pécuniaire
d   Pekuniäre externe Wirtschaftseffekte

29   EXTERNAL ECONOMY, TECHNOLOGICAL
The externalities are technological when the stimulating or spread-effects of a project affect other producers or consumers directly, one way or the other. (See: External economy 27)

f   Economie externe technologique
d   Technologische externe Wirtschaftseffekte

30   FACTOR PROPORTIONS
The relative volumes of input of different factors of production

for a given volume of output depending on the factor endowment situation in a country; e.g., when labor is abundant and capital relatively scarce, the combination of factor inputs normally tends to substitute capital by labor, and vice-versa.

f   Proportion des facteurs
d   Faktorenverhältnis

31   FOREIGN EXCHANGE
      RESERVES, DEPLETION OF
One of the main constraints in the industrial development programmes in developing countries; consists in the constant draw-down of foreign currency resources.

f   Epuisement des réserves en
     devises
d   Verminderung der Devisenreserven

32   FREE TRADE ZONE
A measure intended to promote exports in the context of measures to control imports and exports. Normally, forms an earmarked geographic area where manufacturing units are supplied with duty-free imports of inputs exclusively for being processed and exported.

f   Zone de libre-échange
d   Freihandelszone

33   GOODS, CAPITAL
Economic goods used in the production of other goods; normally consist of plant, machinery and . equipment.

f   Biens d'équipement
d   Kapitalgüter

34   GOODS, CONSUMER
Manufactured products used primarily for personal consumption.

f   Biens de consommation
d   Konsumgüter

35   GOODS, INTERMEDIATE
Goods that enter into the production of other goods.

f   Biens intermédiaires
d   Halbfertigprodukte;
     Halbfertigfabrikate

36   GROWTH-ORIENTED POLICY
Refers to policies aimed at providing incentives for increasing production, rather than emphasizing on restrictive or redistributive policies. Also refers to policies aimed at building upon existing facilities such as additional investment in industries already fairly developed, in areas and sectors already developed, as against new industries, new centers of location and new sectors.

f   Politique orientée au développe-
     ment
d   Wachstumsorientierte Politik

37   INCOME DISTRIBUTION
The manner in which personal income is distributed among the various income classes in an economy; one of the important objectives of planned development in most developing countries is to reduce the gap in the pattern of distribution.

f   Distribution des revenus;
     Distribution des émoluments
d   Einkommensverteilung

38   INDEX OF INDUSTRIAL
      PRODUCTION
A series of data compiled to measure changes in the volume of production.

f   Indice de la production
     industrielle
d   Industrieproduktionsindex

39· INDEX OF PRICES AND
      OUTPUT

7

A computation of series of prices, values of output for industry, agriculture, and so on, measuring relative changes in each series, with or without the use of deflators.

f   Indice des prix et de la production
d   Preis- und Produktionsindex

40   INDEX NUMBER
Computation used as a basis to measure the relative level of prices of commodities, securities, money or currency supplies.

f   Nombre indice;
    Chiffre indicateur
d   Indexzahl;
    Kennziffer

41   INDUSTRIAL DESIGN CENTRE
A publicly sponsored institution for evolving designs for industrial products which may subsequently be produced by private entrepreneurs on commercial basis.

f   Centre de dessin industriel
d   Industrieentwurfszentrum

42   INDUSTRIAL EDUCATION
Training designed to impart skills and disciplines required in modern industrial enterprises.

f   Formation industrielle
d   Industrielle Ausbildung;
    Industrieerziehung

43   INDUSTRIAL ESTATE;
     INDUSTRIAL PARK
Centre for location of industrial units, fully provided with basic overhead facilities, such as power- and water supply, communication-, transportation- and transshipment facilities and, in some instances, industrial sheds.

f   Parc industriel
d   Industriepark;
    Industriegelände

44   INDUSTRIAL ESTATE,
     ANCILLARY
Fully developed industrial location area, housing units producing ancillary components and parts required by parent industrial units.

f   Parc industriel subordonné;
    Parc industriel annexe
d   Annexer Industriepark

45   INDUSTRIAL ESTATE,
     FUNCTIONAL
Fully developed industrial location area, housing units specializing in certain specific processes of a composite product, or specific products for an integrated industrial line.

f   Parc industriel fonctionnel
d   Funktioneller Industriepark

46   INDUSTRIAL ESTATE,
     SINGLE-TRADE
Fully developed industrial location area, housing units specializing in one product or trade.

f   Parc industriel spécialisé à un seul commerce
d   In einem einzigen Handelsgewerbe spezialisierter Industriepark

47   INDUSTRIAL LICENSING
A mechanism through which realization of plan targets for industrial development is regulated amongst individual projects and entrepreneurs, through official sanctions.

f   Licence industrielle
d   Industrielle Konzessionierung

48   INDUSTRIAL MIGRATION
The movement of industrial establishments from one region to another within a country; the migration may be on account of

a drastic shift in the demand for the firm's product, in the supply of resources it needs, or in wage differentials, or tax benefits.

f Migration industrielle
d Industriebedingte Wanderbewegung

49 INDUSTRIAL PROMOTION AGENCY
An organizational arrangement designed primarily for attracting industrial ventures into a country or any specific area therein, by providing economic intelligence services and sometimes overhead- and infra-structure facilities, such as industrial estates, industrial parks and industrial housing facilities.

f Agence de promotion industrielle; Agence d'encouragement industriel
d Industrieförderungsinstitut

50 INDUSTRY, AGRO-
Industries related to, or based on agriculture; the relationship may be one of supplying manufactured inputs, or of processing agricultural produce or products.

f Industrie agronome; Industrie agronomique
d Agrarindustrie

51 INDUSTRY, BY-PRODUCT
Industries based on the utilization of by-products arising from main processes or products.

f Industrie de produits secondaires; Industrie de sous-produits
d Nebenproduktindustrie

52 INDUSTRY, CAPITAL-INTENS-IVE
An industry that uses large amounts of capital equipment in relation to its labor force or its output; normally deferred for a later stage in the process of industrial development by most developing countries.

f Industrie intense en capital
d Kapitalintensive Industrie

53 INDUSTRY, CAPITAL-LIGHT
An industry that uses relatively less capital and less sophisticated techniques for a given volume of output and employment; normally preferred in the early stage of development by most developing countries.

f Industrie non-intense en capital
d Kapitalleichte Industrie

54 INDUSTRY, COTTAGE; INDUSTRY, DOMESTIC; INDUSTRY, HOME
An avocation where the production activities are conducted in the place of residence of the artisan, using mostly family labour, primarily on manual power and where the market does not extend beyond the locality.

f Industrie à domicile
d Heimindustrie; Hausindustrie

55 INDUSTRY, EXPORT
A priority item in the industrialization programme of most developing countries is to develop industries geared to an export market; development banks are expected to give preference to such projects.

f Industrie d'exportation
d Exportindustrie; Exportgüterindustrie

56 INDUSTRY, FEEDER
An industry whose development is supported on the ground that the products emanating would sustain a cluster of related industries; examples are a

naphthacracking unit, sustaining a host of down-stream petro-chemical industries.

f Industrie d'embranchement
d Zubringerindustrie

57 INDUSTRY, INFANT
A nascent industry which may not be able to weather the initial period of experimentation and financial stress because of strong foreign competition. With a grace period, where initial protection is granted. the industry is expected to develop economies of scales and technological efficiency.

f Industrie dans son enfance
d Industrie in den Kinderschuhen; Glashausindustrie

58 INDUSTRY, KEY
An industrial field which has an important bearing on a nation's economic activity and so designated for developmental priorities.

f Industrie-clef
d Schlüsselindustrie

59 INDUSTRY, MARKET-ORIENTED
An industry, where a predominant number of units of manufacture is influenced for locational considerations by proximity of market for their products.

f Industrie orientée au marché
d Marktorientierte Industrie

60 INDUSTRY, REGULATED
Industry whose profits, prices, and in some cases distribution policies, are officially regulated on account of its strategic importance for public life. Another category of industry is also so designated because of reservation of entry for various reasons only to the public sector.

f Industrie réglementée
d Regulierte Industrie; Kontrollierte Industrie

61 INDUSTRY, SKILL-ORIENTED
An industry where a predominant number of units of manufacture is influenced for locational considerations by the availability of specialized skills.

f Industrie orientée à la compétence technique
d Auf professionelle Fertigkeit ausgerichtete Industrie

62 INDUSTRY. SMALL-SCALE; SMALL BUSINESS
A business that is owned and operated by relatively few persons, has a relatively small sales revenue, and has relatively small capital investment.

f Petite exploitation; La petite industrie
d Kleinbetrieb; Kleingewerbe

63 INDUSTRY CENTRE, PROTOTYPE
One of the common methods employed to disseminate new processes, techniques, blueprints and technologies appertaining a new industry; consists in setting up centres where these aspects are demonstrated, blueprints provided, and additional information disseminated and experiments conducted for the benefit of entrepreneurs in a locality or region for being used in commercial production. Such centres help to multiply the prototype on a commercial basis.

f Centre d'industrie prototype
d Prototyp Industriezentrum

64 INDUSTRY STATUS, PIONEER
A process of granting recognition
to an individual enterprise for
being first of its kind, or for being
in the list of priority industries;
recognition as pioneer industry
entitles the enterprises, in several
developing countries, to various
promotional facilities and
concessions, such as preference in
foreign currency allocation for
importation, concessional rates
of taxation, among others.

f   Statut d'une industrie pilote
d   Industrie mit Pionierrang

65 INFLATION
A condition characterized by
rapidly rising prices, when profits
tend to be high in monetary terms
but purchasing power of money
steadily diminishes.

f   Inflation
d   Inflation

66 INFLATION, HYPER-;
INFLATION, RUNAWAY;
INFLATION, GALLOPING
The rapid rise of prices without
limit, with the resultant disruption
of normal economic inter-relation-
ships, a significant depreciation in
the value of currency, and the
eventual disruption of the entire
monetary system.

f   Inflation en cours
d   Galoppierende Inflation

67 INFLATIONARY GAP
A term used to describe the
excess of investment over savings
under full employment conditions;
it is the value of excess demand
for goods and services over the
goods and services that can be
produced with full employment.

f   Ecart inflationniste
d   Inflationslücke

68 INFRA-STRUCTURE;
SOCIAL OVERHEAD CAPITAL
An economy's capital in the
form of roads, railways, water
supplies, educational facilities,
health services, etc., without
which investment in factories,
machinery, etc. cannot be fully
productive. The absence of
infra-structure restrains the
rate of economic growth of
developing countries.

f   Infrastructure
d   Infrastruktur

69 INFRA-STRUCTURE,
FINANCIAL
Institutional arrangements in
an economy, providing safe
media for investment of savings,
and for borrowings, to meet
normal needs of production,
trading and consumption.

f   Infrastructure monétaire
d   Finanzinfrastruktur;
Finanzielle Infrastruktur

70 INVESTIBLE FUNDS
Resources including individual
and institutional savings,
seeking new investment outlets.

f   Fonds investibles
d   Investierbares Kapital;
Investierbare Geldmittel

71 INVESTMENT ABSORPTIVE
CAPACITY
The volume of investment
expressed as a percentage of
GNP, required to sustain a rate
of growth commensurate with
availability of complementary
factors or inputs of production.

f   Capacité d'absorption des
investissements
d   Absorptionsfähigkeit von
Investitionen

72   INVESTMENT CLIMATE
An atmosphere conducive for infusing investor confidence; consists in creating the necessary atmosphere for free flow of investible resources in productive priority channels by appropriate fiscal, monetary, and labor policies.

f   Climat d'investissements
d   Investitionsklima

73   INVESTMENT PRIORITIES
A schedule of projects ordered according to priority of development as between sectors, and within the same sector; normally formulated in terms of periodic planning programs.

f   Priorités d'investissements
d   Investitionsprioritäten

74   INVESTMENT, AUTONOMOUS
Investment that is independent of rising economic activity, and occurs as a result of introduction of new products or processes.

f   Investissement autonome;
    Placement autonome
d   Autonome Investierung;
    Autonome Kapitalanlage

75   INVESTMENT, INDUCED
Investment that occurs in response to actual or anticipated increases in outlays on existing products or projects.

f   Investissement induit
d   Induzierte Investierung

76   INVESTOR CONFIDENCE
Particularly applicable to developing economies basing their development program on market principles; consists of policies directed towards stability in economic, financial and social spheres; private sector investment from within and without the country,

assumes crucial significance for achieving development targets.

f   Confiance de capitaliste
d   Kapitalanlegervertrauen;
    Investorvertrauen

77   LINKAGE
The ability of one industry to induce the establishment and growth of other industries; it develops through the interdependence of inputs (raw materials) and outputs (semi-finished or finished goods).

f   "Linkage"
d   "Linkage"

78   LINKAGE, BACKWARD
The process whereby an industry seeks to buy inputs that can be made by other domestic industries instead of manufacturing it within its own factory.

f   "Linkage" en arrière
d   Rückwärts "Linkage"

79   LINKAGE, FORWARD
The process whereby an industry seeks to sell its output to other domestic industries for use in production.

f   "Linkage" en aval
d   Vorwärts "Linkage"

80   OUTLAYS, PRIVATE
Volume of investment envisaged to be forthcoming from the private sector including corporate sector resources, for financing development programs during a given period.

f   Dépenses privées
d   Private Auslagen

81   OUTLAYS, PUBLIC
Volume of investment envisaged to be forthcoming from the budgetary resources of the

government for fulfilling developmental targets during a given plan period.

f   Dépenses publiques
d   Öffentliche Auslagen

82   PARITY, INDIRECT
The rate of exchange between currencies as calculated through a third centre.

f   Parité indirecte
d   Indirekte Parität

83   POPULATION EXPLOSION
A rapid upsurge in the growth rate of population.

f   Explosion démographique;
    Explosion des naissances
d   Bevölkerungsexplosion

84   PUBLIC SECTOR
The sector of the economy, usually forming the entrepreneurial activities of the Central Government, local authorities, the nationalized industries and other public owned corporations.

f   Secteur public
d   Öffentlicher Sektor

85   PUBLIC UTILITY
A business organization such as gas, electricity, water and transport facilities, which performs an essential service for the public.

f   Entreprise de service public;
    Corporation d'utilité publique
d   Öffentlicher Versorgungsbetrieb

86   PUBLIC WORKS
Government-sponsored development projects or programmes with the main objectives of creating public utility facilities, such as roads, minor irrigation works, land development programmes. Some developing countries emphasize such

programmes for providing employment avenues.

f   Travaux publics
d   Öffentliche Arbeiten

87   SAVINGS RATIO
A measure of current savings to current disposable income.

f   Taux de l'épargne
d   Sparrate

88   SECTORS, ORGANIZED
Sectors of activity in an economy which is characterized by modern management techniques and organizational methods.

f   Secteurs organisés
d   Organisierte Sektoren

89   SECTORS, UNORGANIZED
Sectors of activity in an economy where modern management know-how is found to be absent; include sectors such as small industries, agriculture and farming, rural and cottage industries, agro-based industries.

f   Secteurs non-organisés
d   Unorganisierte Sektoren

90   SKILL FORMATION
     FACILITIES
Policies aimed at imparting training in various trades, vocational and professional spheres.

f   Facilités de formation de compétence professionnelle
d   Fertigkeitsausbildungsmöglichkeiten

91   SPREAD EFFECT OF
     INDUSTRIALIZATION
Rapid industrial growth which will give a decisive growth impetus to the rest of the economy.

f   Effet de propagation industrielle

d   Verbreitungseffekt der
    Industrialisierung

92 STAGFLATION
    A situation where inflationary
    conditions are witnessed alongside
    of recessionary situations.

f   Stagflation
d   Stagflation

93 SUB-CONTRACTING SYSTEM
    A system whereby enterprises
    manufacturing composite products
    farm out orders for the supply of
    standardized components and
    parts to smaller manufacturing
    establishments.

f   Système de sous-traitant
d   Zulieferersystem;
    Unterlieferantsystem

94 SUBSIDIZED CAPITALISM
    A transfer of resources from a
    poor taxpayer or consumer to an
    investor who is usually a man or
    a group of men of means.

f   Capitalisme subventionné
d   Subventionierter Kapitalismus

95 TECHNOLOGY, CAPITAL-
    INTENSIVE
    A process of manufacture requiring
    sophisticated technology and
    relatively high rate of capital per
    unit of output. Apart from the high
    capital/output ratio involved in the
    process, the factor endowment
    situation generally obtaining in
    developing countries makes the
    introduction of such technologies
    inappropriate in most industry
    lines. (See: Technology, labor-
    intensive 97)

f   Technologies d'intensité de capital;
    Technologies intenses en capital
d   Kapitalintensive Technologien

96 TECHNOLOGY, INTERMEDIATE
    A strategy for industrialization

seeking to match the compuls-
ions of productivity and competitiveness (at the national and
international market) with the
socio-economic needs of
optimum labor intensity. One
concrete policy measure sought
to be adopted in the strategy is
application of different intensity
of technology for different stages
of production and sections of
activity.

f   Technologies intermédiaires
d   Zwischentechnologien

97 TECHNOLOGY, LABOR-
    INTENSIVE
    A process of production in which
    there is a considerable use of
    labor in relation to the amount
    of capital equipment per unit of
    output.

f   Technologies d'intensité de
    travail
d   Arbeitsintensive Technologien

98 TRANSFER EARNINGS
    The amount that any factor of
    production could earn in the
    best paid alternative use.

f   Revenue de transfer
d   Transfereinkommen

99 UNIT, ANCILLARY
    A relatively small enterprise
    receiving orders from the
    parent unit in a sub-contracting
    system.

f   Unité d'annexe
d   Annexbetrieb

100 UNIT, PARENT
    A relatively large enterprise
    farming out orders in a sub-
    contracting system.

f   Unité centrale
d   Mutterbetrieb

14

II.

GOVERNMENTAL, MONETARY, FISCAL AND LEGAL ASPECTS
ASPECTS GOUVERNEMENTAUX, MONETAIRES, FISCAUX ET JURIDIQUES
REGIERUNGS-, WÄHRUNGS-, STEUER- UND LEGALE ASPEKTE

101 BUDGETARY CONSTRAINTS
The situation where the resource
raising capacity of the government, relative to demand for
resources, is restricted.

f Contraints budgétaires
d Budgetbeschränkungen;
Etatbeschränkungen

102 CAPITAL RATIONING
The process of allocation of
available capital resources
amongst high priority projects,
priority being determined from
the point of view of financial,
economic and social return.

f Rationnement de capital
d Kapitalrationierung

103 CONTRACT NOTE
An agreement, either oral or in
writing, whereby one party
undertakes certain obligations of
payments, delivery or services to
be performed, or otherwise, for
the other party to the contract.

f Bordereau d'achat;
Bordereau de courtage
d Kaufnote;
Schlussschein

104 CONVEYANCE
The procedures and processes
prescribed under law for the
transfer of title to property from
one person or body to the other.

f Disposition de biens;

Transfert de biens
d Vermögensübertragung

105 COUNTERPART FUNDS
Proceeds in local currency for
commodities obtained from
one government by another as
gift, aid or on other concessional terms; typical example is the
local currency funds resulting
from the PL 480 Law of the
U.S. Government to various
developing countries.

f Fonds de contre-partie
d Counterpartgeldmittel

106 COVENANT, FINANCIAL
Codes of conduct regulating the
dealings of financial institutions
amongst one another on the one
hand, and as between these and
their clients on the other; sometimes sanctified by law of the
country.

f Convention financière;
Contrat financier
d Finanzabkommen

107 COVENANT, RESTRICTIVE
A contract for purpose of
restricting use of patents or
distribution rights, or marketing areas; normally found to be
imposed by foreign participants
in joint ventures.

f Convention restrictive;
Contrat restrictif
d Einschränkende Abmachung

108   CREDIT CONTROL
Regulation of the flow of credit into the economy, either to curb inflationary pressures or to help stimulate economic and industrial activity.

f   Contrôle de crédit
d   Kreditkontrolle

109   CREDIT CONTROL, SELECTIVE
A policy of credit control designed to purvey volumes and costs of credit, in a discriminatory way, as between sectors or amongst unit, in each sector, depending on the objectives in view.

f   Contrôle sélectif de crédit
d   Selektive Kreditkontrolle

110   CREDIT CREATION
The power of the central monetary authorities to add to the flow of credit through the banking system, either through quantitative measures or other regulatory systems. Commercial banks themselves can also be creators of credit within limits.

f   Création de crédit
d   Kreditschöpfung

111   CREDIT FACILITIES
Arrangements available in the economy for meeting the genuine credit requirements of industry, trade, households and individuals.

f   Facilités de crédit
d   Kreditmöglichkeiten

112   CREDIT INFLATION
A situation of uncontrolled rise in price levels attributed largely to the rise in the levels of credit.

f   Inflation de crédit
d   Kreditinflation

113   CREDIT GUARANTEE

A system whereby institutional credit to desired sectors, or industries, or borrowers, who otherwise would not have been entitled to such credits, is guaranteed by government-sponsored or private organizations or agencies.

f   Garantie de crédit
d   Kreditgarantie

114   CREDIT RESTRICTION, QUANTITATIVE
A policy which aims at reducing total bank lending.

f   Restrictions quantitatives de crédit
d   Quantitative Kreditbeschränkungen

115   CREDIT SHIFT
The regulation of the flow of credits amongst sectors.

f   Déplacement de crédit
d   Kreditverschiebung

116   CREDIT SQUEEZE
A policy of across the board restriction on bank credit.

f   Limitation de crédit; Restriction de crédit
d   Kreditknappheit

117   CURRENCY APPRECIATION
A rise in the value of a currency in terms of others in the foreign exchange market.

f   Revaluation de la monnaie; Revalorisation
d   Währungsaufwertung

118   CURRENCY CONVERTIBILITY
The privilege extended to a holder of a nation's currency to exchange his holdings at the prevailing rate of exchange, for the currency of another nation for any purpose.

f   Convertibilité de devises

d   Währungskonvertierbarkeit

119   CURRENCY, HARD
A currency that is freely convertible into gold or into the currencies
of other countries.

f   Devise forte;
Monnaie forte
d   Harte Währung

120   CURRENCY, OVER-VALUED
Situation wherein the established
par value of a currency, in
reference to gold and other
"reserve" currencies, is reckoned
to be higher than is warranted by
its current market value.

f   Monnaie surévaluée;
Monnaie surestimée
d   Überwertete Währung

121   CURRENCY, SOFT
A currency with a relatively un-
stable or declining value in
international exchange.

f   Monnaie faible
d   Weiche Währung

122   CUSTOMS TARIFF
Schedule of rates applicable to
different imported commodities,
from time to time. (See: Duties,
customs 127)

f   Tarif douanier;
Tarif de douane
d   Zollsatz;
Zollverzeichnis

123   DEFICIT FINANCING
The process of resorting to creation of unbacked currency to meet
budgetary requirements. Most
governments of developing
countries resort to this device
when they are confronted with the
dilemma of current developmental
outlays exceeding their revenues
and other receipts.

f   Financement par déficit
budgétaire
d   Defizitäre Finanzierung

124   DEVALUATION
The determination of a lower
fixed exchange rate for a
currency; or the downward
adjustment in the par value of
the country's monetary unit in
reference to its value for gold,
and hence to other currencies.

f   Dévaluation de la monnaie;
Affaiblissement de la monnaie;
Dépréciation des changes
d   Geldentwertung;
Geldabwertung;
Währungsabwertung

125   DISINFLATIONARY POLICY
Refers to a situation where
the government adheres to a
policy of balancing the budget,
that is, restricting outlays to
the volume of receipts, particularly when the economy is
experiencing inflationary
situations.

f   Politique désinflationniste
d   Desinflationistische Politik

126   DUTIES, COUNTERVAILING
A situation whereby an indigen-
ously produced article is sub-
jected to a rate of excise duty
corresponding to the rate of
customs duty levied on
competitive imported products.

f   Droit compensateur;
Tarif douanier compensateur
d   Ausgleichszoll

127   DUTIES, CUSTOMS
A tax on the importation (and
sometimes on the exportation)
of particular goods, levied by
a national government and
payable to it when the item
crosses the nation's customs
border.

f   Tarif douanier
d   Zolltarif

128   DUTIES, EXCISE
Duty imposed on home-produced
goods and domestically provided
services.

f   Droit de consommation
d   Verbrauchssteuer;
Verbrauchsabgabe;
Akzise

129   DUTIES, IMPORT
Taxes imposed on goods entering
a country, the purpose being either
to protect home producers of the
commodity by making the imported
article dearer, or to increase the
State's revenue.

f   Taxe à l'importation;
Droits d'entrée
d   Importsteuer

130   EXCHANGE CONTROL;
FOREIGN EXCHANGE CONTROL
Control of rates of exchange of
currencies by a Government. It
may be utilized in support of the
following objectives: to keep exchange rates stable; to keep the
currency undervalued to stimulate
exports; to keep the currency over-
valued to handicap exports and
reduce costs of imports.

f   Contrôle de taux du change;
Contrôle de cours de change
d   Wechselkurskontrolle

131   EXCHANGE MANAGEMENT
Any form of regulating the country's
inflow and outflow of foreign exchange by the monetary authorities.

f   Administration de devises
d   Devisenverwaltung

132   EXCHANGE RESTRICTIONS
Regulated rationing of foreign
currency outflows.

f   Restrictions imposées au
mouvement des devises
d   Devisenbeschränkungen

133   EXCHANGE STABILITY
A situation wherein the par
value of a national currency in
reference to gold and the
currencies of other countries
has remained more or less
constant.

f   Stabilité de cours de change
d   Wechselkursstabilität

134   EXPENDITURE, DEVELOP-
MENT
Outlays on account of asset-
forming projects or programs.

f   Dépenses de développement
d   Entwicklungsausgaben

135   EXPENDITURE, GOVERN-
MENT
Outlays on current consumption
or assets creating developmental
projects, made by the government or government-sponsored
agencies.

f   Dépenses gouvernementales
d   Regierungsausgaben

136   EXPORT BONUS
Incentives provided to exporters,
for earning foreign currency,
normally by way of import
entitlements, at a higher rate of
local currency equivalent per
unit of foreign currency earned
than the current official rate.

f   Gratification pour l'exportation
d   Exportprämie

137   EXPORT CREDIT
GUARANTEE
An arrangement whereby a
development bank or other agency
offers exporters, against a fee,
insurance against bad debts incurred as a result of sales to

foreign buyers.

f Garantie de crédits à
   l'exportation
d Exportkreditgarantie

138 EXPORT CREDIT INSURANCE
     Arrangement to protect the risks
     of primary lending agencies in
     their credits or guarantees to
     exporters.

f Assurance de crédit de
   l'exportation
d Exportkreditversicherung

139 EXPORT INCENTIVES
     Various promotional measures
     initiated by a government on
     specified products, enterprises or
     industries in order to increase
     exports of these products.

f Stimulants de l'exportation
d Exportanreize

140 EXPORT LICENSE;
     EXPORT PERMIT
     Official permission authorizing
     manufacturers, individuals or
     agencies to export from the
     country, manufactured goods or
     other articles and commodities,
     to specified areas.

f Licence d'exportation;
   Certificat de sortie;
   Permis d'exportation
d Ausfuhrlizenz;
   Exportlizenz

141 FISCAL POLICY
     The taxation policy adopted by a
     government for raising revenue to
     meet expenditure and for influenc-
     ing the levels and directions of
     industrial and commercial
     activity.

f Politique fiscale
d Steuerpolitik;
   Finanzpolitik

142 FOREIGN TRADE POLICY
     Governmental measures in-
     tended to regulate, stimulate
     and promote exports and im-
     ports.

f Politique de commerce
   extérieur
d Aussenhandelspolitik

143 IMPORT BAN
     Policies designed to prohibit the
     imports of stated articles and
     goods for various reasons, such
     as promotion of indigenous
     manufacture, curtailment of
     foreign exchange outflows, etc.

f Prohibition d'importation;
   Interdiction d'importation
d Importverbot;
   Importsperre

144 IMPORT QUOTA
     The maximum amount of a
     commodity, fixed by the
     Government, that can be im-
     ported into a country by an
     enterprise, individual or other
     entity during a specified period.

f Contingent d'importation
d Importkontingent

145 INDENTURE;
     TRUST INDENTURE;
     DEED OF TRUST
     An agreement between a
     corporation and a trustee that
     governs the conditions under
     which bonds are issued and
     empowers the trustee to act
     for all bondholders.

f Engagement contractuel
d Vertragliche Verpflichtung

146 INSTITUTIONAL FINANCE
     Arrangements existing in an
     economy, for provision of
     credit facilities through
     specifically created agencies
     to promote general development

or development of desired industries, sectors and areas.

f Financement institutionel
d Institutionelle Finanzierung

147 INVESTMENT GUARANTEE
Legal protection granted by
national governments, mostly to
foreign investors against political
and other social risks.

f Garantie d'investissement
d Investitionsgarantie

148 INVESTMENT INCENTIVES
Facilities, concessions and inducements provided by a Government to
increase the flow of investment in
priority industries, sectors and
areas.

f Stimulants d'investissement
d Investitionsanreize

149 ISSUE, TAP
The issue of bills and securities
by the Finance or Treasury
Department, direct to various
government departments and
agencies and other buyers at a
special price, without going
through the market.

f Emission directe du Gouvernement
d Direkte Regierungsemission

150 LAW ENFORCEMENT
      PROCEDURES
Processes and procedures
statutorily provided for in the
legal set-up of a country for
enforcing court decisions.

f Procédures d'exécution de la loi
d Gesetzesdurchführungsverfahren

151 LAW OF CONTRACTS
Legal enactments provided for
statutory covenants governing
contractual transactions between
individuals and other corporate
entities.

f Loi sur les contrats
d Vertragsgesetzgebung

152 LAW OF PARTNERSHIP
Statutorily laid down and
enforcible covenants governing
various partnership deeds,
relationships and transactions.

f Loi sur l'association et
    participation
d Gesetz über Beteiligung und
    Partnerschaft

153 LAW, BANKING
Legal covenants and statutorily
recognized customary relationships and procedures governing
banking transactions in a country.

f Loi sur les banques
d Bankgesetz

154 LAW, BANKRUPTCY
Statutorily laid down processes
and procedures governing
insolvency, bankruptcy and
other related situations.

f Droit de faillite;
    Législation sur les faillites
d Konkursordnung;
    Konkursrechtliche Bestimmungen

155 LAW, BLUE-SKY
Laws enacted by various States
to regulate the issuance of
securities, the sale of a
particular block of securities,
or the business of dealing in
securities.

f Loi sur les titres et actions
d Wertpapiergesetzgebung

156 LAW, COMPANY
A body of law, consolidated in
the Companies Acts, governing
the formation, registration and
operation of companies and
setting out legal requirements
regarding the appointment of
directors, the issue of shares

and debentures, etc.

f   Loi sur les sociétés
d   Gesetz über die Gesellschaften

157   LAW, FOREIGN CAPITAL
      INVESTMENT
Statutorily laid down provisions,
processes and procedures governing
investments by foreigners in a
country. The covenants normally
are so designed as to, on the one
hand, provide an inducement for
foreigners to bring in capital
and related technical and technological know-how into fields of
activities and lines of industry
accorded highest priority and,
on the other, to protect and
promote existing and new indigenous entrepreneurs and industries.

f   Loi sur l'investissement du
    capital étranger
d   Auslandskapitalinvestitionsgesetz

158   LAW, MERCANTILE
Body of covenants statutorily
provided for or recognized by
custom, governing the operation
of, and transactions amongst,
entities belonging to trade, commerce, industry and finance.

f   Droit commercial
d   Handelsgesetz

159   LEGAL AID
Statutorily provided legal
measures of assistance available
in a community for the aggrieved
to seek redress.

f   Assistance juridique
d   Juristische Hilfe

160   LEGAL IMPEDIMENTS
Loop-holes inherent in the
existing legal set-up, either
conceptual or procedural, which
act as a damper for new investments or fresh economic activities; often the lengthy and in-

volved procedures and processes
defeat the purposes and objectives of law which frustrate the
aggrieved.

f   Empêchements légales
d   Gesetzliche Hindernisse

161   LEGISLATION, INCENTIVE
Enactments providing for
specific inducements for new
investments in preferred
sectors, areas or industry lines,
by way of income and corporate
tax concessions, duty drawbacks,
liberal allocation of foreign
exchange resources, exemptions
or rebates in local duties, a
higher depreciation allowance,
among others.

f   Législation stimulante
d   Stimulierende Gesetzgebung

162   LEGISLATION, PIONEER
      INDUSTRY
Enactments regulating facilities
provided for industries and
activities which are recognized,
for development purposes or
pioneering efforts; such legis-
lations seek to provide incentives, concessions and facilities
for inducing fresh investments
in sectors, areas or industries
which are accorded high
priority for development in an
economy.

f   Législation pour l'industrie
    pilote
d   Pionierindustriegesetzgebung

163   LETTER OF
      HYPOTHECATION
A letter from an exporter to
his bank authorizing the latter,
in the event of the importer
failing to accept or pay a bill
of exchange, to sell the goods
exported and remit the proceeds
less expenses.

f   Certificat d'inscription
     hypothécaire
d   Hypothekenbrief

164   LIEN
     A charge against a property, for
     the purpose of exacting settle-
     ment of a debt.

f   Droit de rétention;
     Privilège de rétention
d   Pfandrecht

165   LIQUIDITY PREFERENCE
     The desire to hold cash or
     checking accounts rather than
     assets, such as stocks and bonds,
     that earn a return and are less
     easy to convert to cash.

f   Préférence de liquidité
d   Liquiditätspräferenz

166   MONETARY POLICY
     The policy governing creation
     and regulation of the flow of
     currency, bank credit, levels of
     interest rates and other related
     banking and credit activities,
     adopted by the monetary author-
     ities of a country.

f   Politique monétaire
d   Währungspolitik

167   MONEY, CHEAP;
     MONEY, EASY
     A situation where bank rate and
     other rates of interests are
     relatively low so that borrowing
     is cheap.

f   Argent abondant
d   Flüssiges Geld;
     Billiges Geld

168   MONEY, DEAR;
     MONEY, TIGHT
     A situation where bank rate and
     other rates of interests are
     relatively high, so that borrowing
     is expensive.

f   Argent cher
d   Teueres Geld

169   MONEY, HOT;
     MONEY, FUNK
     Volatile movements of capital
     from one country to another;
     such movements are not
     directly connected with trade
     between countries, but are
     rather a reflection of some loss
     of confidence in the country
     from which the money is being
     withdrawn.

f   Argent "chaud"
d   "Heisses" Geld

170   MORTGAGE
     A legal transfer of ownership,
     but not possession of property,
     from a debtor to a creditor.

f   Hypothèque;
     Gage hypothécaire
d   Hypothek;
     Hypothekenpfand

171   MORTGAGE, CLOSED
     A mortgage covering indebted-
     ness on a property which cannot
     be further increased.

f   Hypothèque fermée
d   Von der Höhe der Forderung
     und dem Umfang des belasteten
     Grundstücks unabhängige
     Hypothek

172   MULTIPLIER
     A ratio indicating the effect on
     total employment or on total
     income of a specified amount
     of a real capital investment.
     The multiplier applies equally
     to expansion as well as to
     contraction.

f   Multiplicateur
d   Multiplikator

173   NATIONALIZATION
     The process of acquiring

privately-owned enterprises or activities into public hands, with or without compensation. This has often proved to be an impediment to new investments, both local and foreign, in developing countries.

f   Nationalisation
d   Nationalisierung

174   OPEN MARKET OPERATIONS
The buying or selling of Government bills and notes in the open market by the Central Bank for the purpose of making the bank rate more effective in regulating the volume of credit.

f   Opérations du marché ouvert
d   Offenmarktgeschäfte

175   PARITY
In foreign exchange, the value of one currency in terms of another is determined by their respective gold backing. In commodities, the price level at which two delivery points are equalized, after expenses of shipping, interest, and insurance have been adjusted. When there is a disparity between the two, one is referred to as being above parity or below parity.

f   Parité
d   Parität;
      Paritätskurs

176   PRICE CONTROL
The mechanism whereby the Government statutorily fixes either a maximum price for a product in order to protect consumers against high prices, or a minimum price in order to protect producers against uneconomic prices.

f   Contrôle des prix
d   Preiskontrolle;
      Zwangswirtschaftliche Preisbildung

177   PRICE STABILIZATION
The process of bringing about relative and individual prices to a level, where the overall price level, over a period of time has secular and favorable effect on economic activity.

f   Stabilisation des prix
d   Preisstabilisierung

178   PROTECTION
The adoption by the State of special measures to protect an industry from competition of imported products generally, and from indigenous manufactures, at times. Measures of protection include import ban or reduction, tariff imposition, differential rates of customs and other taxes.

f   Protection;
      Patronage
d   Protektion

179   RATE, BANK
The official minimum rate at which the Central Bank will discount first-class bills. The bank rate is the main instrument used by Central Banks to control interest rates, and thus the volume of credit, in general.

f   Taux d'escompte bancaire;
      Escompte officiel
d   Banksatz;
      Bankrate;
      Bankdiskontsatz;
      Diskontsatz

180   RATE, DISCOUNT;
      RATE, REDISCOUNTING
The margin Central Banks charge for loans to commercial banks on notes, acceptances, and bills of exchange. The rate varies according to conditions in the money market and is changed by the Central Bank

whenever it believes bank credit
should be tightened or relaxed.

f Taux d'escompte;
Taux de réescompte
d Wechseldiskont;
Diskontsatz;
Neudiskontierungssatz

181 RATE OF EXCHANGE,
FLEXIBLE
A rate of exchange governing
foreign currencies in relation to
the local money unit which, though
controlled broadly, is allowed to
fluctuate within a given groove.

f Cours du change flexible
d Flexibler Wechselkurs

182 RATE OF EXCHANGE, FIXED
A rate of exchange governing
foreign currencies in relation to
the local money unit which is
officially fixed and controlled.

f Cours du change fixe
d Fixer Wechselkurs

183 RATE OF EXCHANGE, FREE
Exchange rates which depend
upon the supply and demand for
a currency on the foreign exchange market.

f Cours du change libre
d Freier Wechselkurs

184 RATE OF EXCHANGE,
MULTIPLE
A situation wherein the exchange
value of a country's currency is
differentially fixed according to
the purpose for which it is
allocated.

f Cours du change multiple
d Mehrfacher Wechselkurs;
Multipler Wechselkurs

185 REVALUATION;
REVALORIZATION
The upward change in a currency's
value, relative to gold or other
currencies.

f Revalorisation
d Aufwertung

186 SAVINGS, CORPORATE
Undistributed profits of the
corporate sector redeployed
into productive purposes, either
within the same enterprise or
in related enterprises.

f Epargnes corporatives
d Ersparnisse von Körperschaften

187 SAVINGS, FORCED;
SAVINGS, COMPULSORY
A situation where individual
entities in an economy are
compelled, by various means,
such as high rate of taxation
and other compulsory means of
savings arrangements, to curtail
current consumption.

f Epargnes forcées
d Zwangssparen;
Zwangsersparnisse;
Zwangssparbeträge

188 SAVINGS INVESTMENT GAP
A situation where the investment needs of an economy are
found to be higher than the
available volume of domestic
savings. This gap is normally
bridged by foreign assistance.

f Décalage entre épargnes et
investissements
d Spar-Investitionslücke

189 SURETY BOND;
DEED OF SURETYSHIP
A contract between a principal
and a responsible third party,
the surety, which makes the
surety responsible for the
principal's fulfillment of an
obligation to the obligee.

f Acte de caution;
Contrat de garantie

24

d   Garantieerklärung;
     Bürgschaftsurkunde

190   SURTAX
     An additional tax levied on a tax
     base after a normal tax has been
     applied.

f   Surtaxe
d   Steuerzusatz

191   TAX CREDIT;
     TAX CONCESSION;
     TAX RELIEF
     A legal provision permitting tax-
     payers to deduct from their
     taxable incomes certain specified
     sums for stated activities; norm-
     ally investment in economically
     and socially desirable projects, or
     in industries where prospects of
     relative returns and other invest-
     ment features are less attractive.

f   Exemption d'impôts;
     Immunité fiscale;
     Franchise d'imposition
d   Steuerbefreiung

192   TAX HAVEN
     Some developing countries, by
     virtue of the various concessions
     and relief in taxation, particularly
     to foreign investors, are regarded,
     in reference to home country
     levels, as places where invest-
     ment is more lucrative and
     rewarding.

f   "Ciel d'impôt"
d   "Steuerhimmel"

193   TAX INCENTIVE
     Tax measures designed to provide
     positive encouragement to
     individuals and businesses to help
     achieve higher rates of economic
     activity for the nation.

f   Stimulant fiscal;
     Motif fiscal
d   Steueranreiz

194   TAX, CAPITAL GAINS
     A tax that is paid upon the profit
     made from the buying and
     selling of assets.

f   Impôt sur l'accroissement de
     fortune;
     Impôt sur la fortune acquise
d   Vermögenszuwachssteuer

195   TAX, CORPORATION
     A tax on company profits.

f   Impôt sur les sociétés
d   Körperschaftssteuer

196   TAX, DEVELOPMENT
     A levy imposed by government
     or local authorities on enter-
     prises or others who have
     benefited from the developments
     effected; also levied for
     promoting improvements, on
     taxpayers and others, who may
     not directly enjoy the benefits
     of development.

f   Impôt de développement
d   Entwicklungssteuer

197   TAX, INTEREST
     EQUALIZATION
     A levy collected from corporate
     bodies or enterprises to form
     a pool out of which enterprises
     or sectors requiring concessional
     finance or help are provided for;
     the term also indicates levies
     on enterprises to offset subsid-
     ized finance received earlier.

f   Impôt de péréquation d'intérêts
d   Zinsangleichssteuer

198   TAX, UNDISTRIBUTED
     PROFITS
     A tax imposed on enterprises
     which accumulate retained
     earnings beyond the reasonable
     needs of business.

f   Impôt sur les bénéfices non
     distribués

d   Steuer auf nicht ausgeschüttete
    Gewinne;
    Steuer auf nicht verteilte Gewinne

199   TAXABLE CAPACITY;
     TAXABILITY

The extent to which an individual
or a corporate body can be taxed
without impeding, in some way, the
power or capacity to produce, or
saving as a disincentive.

f   Capacité contributive
d   Steuerkraft;
    Besteuerungsfähigkeit

200   TAXATION, DOUBLE
A situation, wherein a corporation
is taxed on its total earnings, as
also on that part of its earnings,
it distributes as dividend to stockholders. Tax on the latter amount
is normally borne by the stockholders, but all the same, the
same block of earnings is taxed
twice.

f   Double imposition;
    Double taxation
d   Doppelbesteuerung

201   TAXATION, MULTIPLE
A levy imposed by two or more
authorities on the same person
or unit on the same ground.

f   Multiple imposition;
    Taxation multiple
d   Mehrfachbesteuerung

202   TAXES, INDIRECT
Taxes on goods or services, as
distinct from taxes on income.

f   Contribution indirecte;
    Impôt indirect
d   Indirekte Steuer

203   TRANSFER DEED;
     TITLE DEED
A legal document by which
ownership of stocks or shares
is transferred from a holder
to a purchaser.

f   Acte translatif de propriété
d   Eigentumsübertragung

204   TREASURY BILL
The shortest-term security
issued by the Government, sold
to the public.

f   Billet du Trésor à court terme
d   Kurzfristiger Schatzwechsel

205   TREASURY NOTE
A government security issued
by the Treasury Department
with a medium maturity period.

f   Billet du Trésor
d   Schatzschein;
    Darlehenskassenschein

206   UNDERVALUATION
Refers to a situation wherein
a currency is given a lower
value externally than internally,
that is, a lower value than it
would have in a free market. The
effect of this is to make imports
dearer and exports cheaper,
and thus, to stimulate exports.

f   Sous-évaluation
d   Unterbewertung

III.
CAPITAL MARKET AND BANKING
MARCHE DE CAPITAL ET OPERATIONS BANQUAIRES
KAPITALMARKT UND BANKWESEN

207   ACCUMULATION
The process of acquiring, without tending to give publicity or affect market prices, a significant volume of shares or securities, as a profitable investment outlet, as opposed to acquiring management control.

f   Accumulation
d   Ansammlung;
Anhäufung

208   ARBITRAGE, STOCK
The process of taking advantage of price differentials in two markets for a given security or share, by buying in the one, where the price is relatively lower, and by selling in the other, where the price is relatively higher.

f   Arbitrage sur valeurs;
Arbitrage en bourse
d   Börsenarbitrage

209   AT PAR
A situation where shares, stocks and bonds of an enterprise or a development bank are quoted at the same value as the nominal or face value.

f   Au pair
d   Zur Parität;
Zum Nennwert

210   AT THE MARKET
Practices where a customer authorizes his broker to deal in shares and stocks on his behalf in the stock exchange.

f   Au marché
d   Auf dem Markt

211   AUTHORIZED CLERK
A stock broker's assistant who is authorized to deal on the floor of the stock exchange.

f   Clerc autorisé
d   Bevollmächtigter Angestellter eines Börsenmaklers

212   AVERAGING
The process of buying additional shares, stocks or debentures, at a time when prices of these are falling, in order to reduce the average cost of the holdings of such shares, stocks or debentures.

f   En moyenne
d   Im Durchschritt

213   BACKWARDATION
A payment made by a bear to a bull for arrangements to defer delivery of shares transacted; opposite of contango payments.

f   Transaction de déport
d   Deportgeschäft

214   BANK CREDIT
Credit created by a bank by increasing the size of the account of a depositor, e.g.

when making an advance; or when buying a security, or commercial bill at a discount.

f   Crédit bancaire;
     Crédit de banque
d   Bankkredit

215   BANK DISCOUNT
The difference between the volume of a bank loan and the amount credited to the borrower.

f   Escompte de banque;
     Escompte commercial
d   Bankdiskont

216   BANK DRAFT;
     BANKER'S DRAFT
A cheque drawn by a bank on behalf of its customers; differs from ordinary cheque being in the nature of cash, and regarded as such.

f   Traite
d   Banktratte;
     Bankwechsel

217   BANKING SYSTEM
A group of financial institutions fostering mobilization of savings and flow of credit to individuals, industry, trade and commerce.

f   Système bancaire
d   Banksystem

218   BEAR
An operator in a stock exchange who, in anticipation of fall in prices, sells short in the hope of buying them back again at a lower price. (See: Selling short 339)

f   Baissier;
     Joueur à la baisse
d   Baissespekulant;
     Baissier

219   BEAR RAID
A situation where a bear undertakes heavy selling of a scrip to bring about a sudden fall in its price.

f   Attaque du découvert;
     Attaque des baissiers
d   Auf Baisse gerichtetes Börsenmanöver

220   BID AND OFFER
The respective prices proffered by prospective buyers and prospective sellers for shares and securities.

f   Demande et offre
d   Nachfrage und Angebot

221   BILLS, DISCOUNTED
Notes, acceptances and other bills discounted by a bank.

f   Effets escomptés
d   Diskontierte Wechsel;
     Diskontwechsel

222   BILL, ACCOMMODATION-
A type of clean, short-term advance by way of a promissory note which, after being drawn and endorsed, can be discounted; this type of bill does not arise as a result of actual transaction of goods. (See: Trade bill 224)

f   Papier de complaisance;
     Billet de complaisance
d   Gefälligkeitsakzept

223   BILL, TIME-
A bill of exchange with a fixed date of maturity.

f   Effet à terme
d   Zeitwechsel

224   BILL, TRADE-
A commercial bill used in transactions actually involving goods. (See: Accommodation bill 222)

f   Effet de commerce;
     Papier commercial

d   Warenwechsel;
    Handelswechsel;
    Kundenwechsel

225   BLUE CHIPS
      Common shares of a corporation
      that is well established, high
      dividend yielding and with stable
      dividend records; usually such
      shares are quoted at relatively
      high prices. (See: Gilt-edged
      investment 278)

f   Titres de priorité
d   Erstklassige Wertpapiere;
    Spitzenwerte

226   BOND
      A certificate of indebtedness of
      an international organization, a
      national or local government,
      public body or a company,
      bearing on it details of interest
      rate, dates and conditions of
      maturity.

f   Certificat d'obligation;
    Titre d'obligation
d   Schuldverschreibung

227   BOND YIELD
      The rate of return on an invest-
      ment in bonds.

f   Rendement d'un titre d'obligation
d   Ertrag einer Schuldverschreibung

228   BONDS, ADJUSTMENT-
      Bonds issued in the reorganization
      and restructuring of the existing
      indebtedness of a corporation,
      seeking to bring about uniformity
      in the terms and conditions in-
      cluding maturity dates of various
      existing debt instruments.

f   Obligations d'adjustement
d   Angleichsschuldverschreibungen;
    Im Zuge einer Sanierung aus-
    gegebene Schuldverschreibungen

229   BONDS, BABY;
      BONDS, PIGGY

Bonds issued in smaller
denominations in order to
attract investors of comparatively small means.

f   Bons de petite épargne
d   Kleinobligationen;
    Kleinaktien;
    Volksaktien;
    Wertpapiere mit geringem
    Nominalwert

230   BONDS, BEARER
      A bond that does not bear the
      name of the creditor; can be
      negotiated as a bearer instru-
      ment. (See: Coupon bonds 233;
      Registered bonds 246)

f   Obligations au porteur;
    Titres au porteur
d   Inhaberschuldverschreibungen

231   BONDS, CALLABLE-
      Bonds which may be redeemed
      by the issuing company prior
      to the maturity date.

f   Obligations remboursable sur
    demande
d   Kündbare Schuldverschreibungen;
    Kündbare Obligationen

232   BONDS, COLLATERAL
      TRUST-
      Bonds which are secured by
      collateral, such as assets, other
      bonds and stocks and shares.

f   Obligations garanties par des
    effets
d   Durch Effektenlombard
    gesicherte Schuldverschreibungen

233   BONDS, COUPON-
      Bonds not registered in the name
      of the holder, but having coupons
      attached to them which can be
      cashed as they mature. (See:
      Bearer bonds 230)

f   Valeurs à revenu fixe
d   Festverzinsliche Schuld-

verschreibungen;
Pfandbriefe;
Inhaberschuldverschreibungen

234 BONDS, CONVERTIBLE
Bonds which can be converted
after a stated period into
equities at the option of the
owner and/or issuer.

f Obligations convertibles;
Obligations de conversion
d Wandelobligationen;
Wandelschuldverschreibungen;
Konversionspapiere

235 BONDS, FUNDING
Bonds issued for the creation of
specified funds or facilities.

f Obligations de consolidation
d Fundierungsschuldverschreibungen

236 BONDS, GENERAL MORTGAGE
Bonds which have as security
second mortgage claims or
properties already having prior
charges.

f Obligations garanties par une
hypothèque de seconde priorité
d Durch Gesamthypothek gesicherte
Schuldverschreibungen

237 BONDS, GUARANTEED
Bonds whose principal and/or
interest are guaranteed by a
party other than the issuer.

f Obligations garanties
d Garantierte Schuldverschreibungen;
Garantiescheine

238 BONDS, INCOME
Bonds where the interest payments
are dependent on the earnings of
the investments made of the
proceeds of the bonds.

f Obligations de profit
d Gewinnobligationen

239 BONDS, JUNIOR;
JUNIOR LIEN BONDS
Bonds whose claims for interest
and repayment of principal
rank last amongst other issues
of a company.

f Obligations nouvelles
d Durch im Range nachstehendes
Pfandrecht gesicherte Schuldverschreibungen

240 BONDS, LEGAL
Bonds with high ratings,
recognized by the Government
as suitable outlets of investments for public or official
institutional investors.

f Obligations légales
d Mündelsichere Schuldverschreibungen

241 BONDS, MORTGAGE
Bonds secured by a mortgage of
specific fixed assets. Holders
of these bonds, in the event of
default, have the right to
realize their investments by
liquidating such assets.

f Lettres de gage;
Titres hypothécaires
d Hypothekenbriefe;
Hypothekenscheine

242 BONDS, OPEN-END
Mortgage bonds in which the
amount issuable under the mortgage is left indefinite, the mortgage permitting subsequent
issue.

f Titres hypothécaires ouvertes
d Noch nicht bis zum Höchstbetrag in Anspruch genommene
Hypothekenscheine

243 BONDS, PARTICIPATING
Bonds which, in addition to
being entitled to a stated rate
of interest, also share in excess
profits of the issuing company.

f   Titres de participation
d   Schuldverschreibungen mit
     Gewinnbeteiligung

244   BONDS, PERPETUAL
     Bonds which have perpetual life
     for redemption.

f   Titres perpétuels
d   Rentenanleihen

245   BONDS, REDEEMABLE
     Bonds which are repayable at par
     at a future date, or over a stated
     period in the future.

f   Obligations amortissables;
     Obligations remboursables
d   Einlösbare Schuldverschreibungen;
     Rückzahlbare Schuldverschreib-
     ungen

246   BONDS, REGISTERED;
     BONDS, NON-NEGOTIABLE
     Bonds bearing the name of the
     owner; such bonds are not
     negotiable or transferrable until
     endorsed by the original owner.

f   Titres nominatifs;
     Obligations nominatives
d   Auf den Namen lautende Schuld-
     verschreibungen

247   BONDS, SERIAL
     A method of phasing of debt-
     retirement, whereby portions of
     the total bond issue are made due
     for payment at regular pre-set
     periods.

f   Titres en séries;
     Obligations en séries
d   Serienanleihen

248   BONDS, TAX EXEMPT
     Bonds mainly issued by govern-
     ments, or local authorities, or
     Government sponsored institut-
     ions which are exempt from
     certain taxes, either wholly or
     partly.

f   Titres exempt de taxe
d   Steuerfreie Wertpapiere

249   BROKERAGE
     A commission calculated as a
     percentage of the value of
     shares and securities trans-
     acted, charged by brokers to
     their clients.

f   Courtage;
     Commission de placement
d   Maklergebühr;
     Maklerprovision

250   BUCKET SHOP
     A dishonest brokerage house in
     which orders placed by a
     customer are not executed but
     are held on, in the hope that
     the customer is wrong.

f   Bureau d'un courtier marron
d   Büro eines Schwindelmaklers;
     Winkelbörse

251   BULL
     A trader who has purchased
     securities in anticipation of a
     rise in value; he is a prospect-
     ive seller.

f   Spéculateur à la hausse;
     Haussier
d   Haussespekulant;
     Haussier

252   CARRY-OVER;
     CONTANGO;
     CONTINUATION
     Process of settlement of
     dealings in a stock exchange,
     postponed to a future day,
     carrying a charge for such
     postponement. (See:
     Backwardation 213)

f   Réport;
     Prix de réport
d   Reportgeschäft;
     Aufgeld

253 CATS AND DOGS
A stock market term referring
to securities of doubtful value
which cannot be used as collateral
for a loan and which are held as
an acknowledged speculation.

f   Titres marrons;
    Titres de spéculation
d   Spekulationspapiere

254 CERTIFICATE OF DEPOSIT
Short term deposit receipts with
banks, which carry low interest
rates; normally serve as
negotiable instruments.

f   Récépissé de dépôt
d   Depotschein

255 CERTIFICATE OF
    INDEBTEDNESS
Unsecured short term notes
issued by Government or official
agencies.

f   Certificat d'endettement
d   Schuldschein

256 CLEARING
The volume of checks and drafts
processed for collection by the
banks in a given period. (See:
House, clearing 447)

f   Liquidation d'un compte
d   Saldierung eines Konto;
    Glattstellung eines Konto

257 COMMISSION
Charges to be paid to bankers or
brokers for handling transactions
on behalf of customers.

f   Commission;
    Droit de commission;
    Courtage
d   Provision;
    Kommissionsgebühr

258 CONSOLS;
    FUNDED GOVERNMENT
    SECURITIES

A government bond with
perpetual status of maturity,
periodically replaced and
consolidated; a term usually
applied to British Government
notes of this type.

f   Fonds consolidés;
    Rentes consolidées
d   Fundierte Staatsanleihen

259 CONTRACT
A legal document related to the
sale and purchase of shares
containing complete details of
the contract, such as names of
sellers and buyers, number of
shares transacted, the unit
price of transaction, name of
the company to which the
shares belong, and so on.

f   Contrat;
    Traité
d   Vertrag;
    Kontrakt;
    Abkommen

260 CORNERING THE MARKET
The buying-up of the whole or
larger part of particular shares
and stocks in the exchange
with a view to either gaining
control of the management of
the enterprise or rigging up
prices to realize higher profits.

f   Accaparement du marché
d   Aufkaufen des Marktes

261 COUPON PAYMENT
Interest accruals on bonds paid
at periodic intervals.

f   Paiement de coupon d'intérêt
d   Zahlung des Zinsscheines

262 DEBENTURE;
    DEBENTURE BONDS
Long-term debt secured by the
assets and general credit of
the borrower.

f   Certificat d'obligation
d   Pfandbrief

263   DEBENTURE, CONVERTIBLE
A certificate issued by a
corporation as evidence of debt
that can be converted at the option
of the holder into other securities
- usually common stock or preferred stock - of the same
corporation. (See: Rights, conversion 853)

f   Obligation convertible;
Obligation de conversion
d   Wandelschuldverschreibung;
Konversionspapier

264   DEBENTURE, FIXED
A type of mortgage debenture
secured by some particular
specified assets.

f   Obligation fixe
d   Feste Schuldverschreibung

265   DEBENTURE, IRREDEEMABLE
Debenture with no undertaking as
to its retirement; generally liable
to be redeemed for defaults in
payment of interests.

f   Obligation non amortissable;
Obligation irremboursable
d   Nicht einlösbare Schuldverschreibung

266   DEBENTURE, MORTGAGE
Debenture which is issued on the
security of the company's assets.
(See: Debenture, naked 267)

f   Obligation hypothécaire
d   Hypothekenpfandbrief

267   DEBENTURE, NAKED;
DEBENTURE, SIMPLE
A term used for unsecured
debenture as distinct from mortgage debenture.

f   Obligation chirographaire
d   Ungesicherte Schuldverschreibung

268   DEBT INSTRUMENTS
Commercial documents representing debt obligation of given
denomination (debentures,
bonds) normally negotiable and
traded in the capital market.

f   Instruments de dette
d   Schuldinstrumente

269   DEPOSIT, TERM;
DEPOSIT, FIXED
A type of borrowings resorted
to by development banks or
enterprises from the public or
from other institutional investors, maturing after a given
period of time, carrying fixed
interest rates, not backed by
any security, and ranking
lowest in terms of repayment.

f   Dépôt à terme;
Dépôt à terme fixe
d   Einlage auf feste Kündigung;
Befristete Einlage

270   DILUTION
A situation where the earnings
per share is reduced as a result
of issuing additional new shares.

f   Dilution des titres
d   Wertpapierverwässerung

271   DISCOUNT;
TO STAND AT A DISCOUNT
To cash a bill before it matures,
or the difference between the
price at which a security was
issued and the price at which
it now stands, if the latter is
the lower. (See: House, discount
449)

f   Escompter;
Etre au-dessous du pair
d   Diskontieren;
Einen Verlust ausweisen

272   DISCRETIONARY ORDERS
Instructions to a broker to
transact business in a stock

exchange according to his judgment, but at the risk of the
customer.

f   Ordres à appréciation
d   Dem Ermessen überlassene
    Aufträge

273   DUE BILL
A notice of an amount due; as
used in the securities business, it
is signed by the buyer of a
security and specifies an amount
due the seller under certain
conditions.

f   Lettre d'une somme exigible
d   Mitteilung über einen fälligen
    Betrag

274   DUMMY
A term used for directors or stockholders who have no financial
interest or responsibility in the
company.

f   Homme de paille;
    Prêt-nom
d   Strohmann

275   EURODOLLARS
Dollar deposits or loans in a
European country.

f   Eurodollars
d   Eurodollars

276   FORWARD EXCHANGE
The purchase or sale of amounts
of a foreign currency for delivery
at a specified future date.

f   Changes à terme
d   Termingeschäft

277   FORWARD TRADING CONTRACT
A contractual right for sale and
purchase of shares and stocks
over a given time at stated prices.

f   Contrat de changes à terme
d   Vereinbarung über Wertpapier-
    termingeschäfte

278   GILT-EDGED INVESTMENT
Represents shares and
securities of highest quality;
consistency in dividend yield
and steady level of prices are
some of its characteristic
marks. (See: Blue chips 225)

f   Placement de père de famille;
    Valeurs dorées
d   Mündelsichere Wertpapiere

279   HEDGE
Transactions intended to even
out trading positions in stock
exchanges with a view to
minimizing anticipated losses.

f   Faire la contrepartie
d   Sich durch Gegentransaktionen
    sichern

280   INTEREST RATE, MARKET
The actual rate of interest
ruling in the market in the short
run; those charged by the banks.

f   Taux d'intérêt du marché
d   Marktzinssatz

281   INTEREST RATE, NATURAL
The rate which equates the
demand for loans with the
supply of loanable funds.

f   Taux d'intérêt naturel
d   Natürlicher Zinnssatz

282   INTEREST RATE, NOMINAL
Token charges levied by
development banks in administer-
ing interest free agency funds
for assisting specific preferred
sectors or industries in the
economy. Such charges may
represent the operating costs
of development banks in ad-
ministering such funds.

f   Taux d'intérêt nominal
d   Nominaler Zinssatz

283 INTEREST RATE, PRIME
The rate charged by commercial
banks for short-term loans to
their best customers.

f   Première de taux;
    Taux d'intérêt excellent
d   Bester Zinssatz;
    Primazinssatz

284 INTEREST RATE, PURE
The interest rate on capital funds
if all risks and administrative
costs were eliminated.

f   Taux d'intérêt net
d   Reiner Zinssatz;
    Nettozinssatz

285 ISSUE BY TENDER
The process of floating a fresh
batch of shares which have a
minimum price attached, but subscribers have to tender the price
at which they are prepared to buy.

f   Emission comme déterminée
    dans l'offre
d   Emission wie im Kostenanschlag

286 ISSUE, CONVERSION
The flotation of new shares or
debentures by Government or
corporate borrowers, offered in
exchange for an existing share or
debentures which are expected to
be due for repayment.

f   Emission de conversion
d   Konversionsemission

287 ISSUE, DEFENSIVE
Shares and securities with a record
of stable earnings and price
levels and which although may not
record substantial price gains in a
bull market, are however expected
to display stability in their prices,
in the face of selling pressures in
a bear market.

f   Emission défensive
d   Defensive Emission

288 ISSUE, HOT
A placement of ordinary shares
whose issue prices are considered by investors and traders
as being considerably lower than
their potential value.

f   Emission "chaude"
d   "Heise" Emission

289 JOBBER'S TURN
The spread between the buying
and selling price which a
specialist broker quotes.

f   Profit de marchand de titres
d   Gewinnspanne des Börsenmaklers

290 LEGAL LIST
The list of investments of high
quality, approved by government
for investment by official
agencies. (See: Securities,
trustee 336; Eligible papers
336)

f   Liste des valeurs dorées
d   Liste von hochwertigen Wert-
    papieren

291 MANIPULATION
A process by which prices of
shares and securities are
artificially pushed up or
brought down. (See: Rigging 325)

f   Manipulation
d   Manipulation

292 MARGIN, SAFETY
The extent to which the assessed
value of collateral securities
for a loan exceeds the amount
of the loan, measured as a
percentage.

f   Marge de sécurité
d   Sicherheitsspielraum

293 MARKET FOR SECURITIES
The volume of securities
issued for the first time, or in
subsequent market trading, that
can be sold.

f   Marché des titres
d   Wertpapiermarkt;
     Effektenmarkt

294   MARKET SERVICES, CAPITAL
Facilities of registering, trading
in all forms, brokerage, transfers
of shares, debentures and other
securities.

f   Services de marché du capital
d   Kapitalmarktdienste

295   MARKET, ACTIVE
A situation when particular shares
or stocks are regularly traded in
a stock exchange.

f   Marché actif
d   Aktiver Absatzmarkt;
     Aktive Börse

296   MARKET, BEAR
A situation where the influence
of bears is pronounced in a stock
exchange resulting in persistent
downward movement of prices.

f   Marché à la baisse
d   Baissebörse

297   MARKET, BUYERS'
A condition in a market where the
level of demand is below that of
supplies, with buyers tending to
have an upper hand in regard to
market prices.

f   Marché de l'acheteur
d   Käufermarkt;
     Vom Käufer beherrschter Markt

298   MARKET, CAPITAL
Institutionalized sources for
long-term funds for investment
opportunities. The market
comprises financial institutions
dealing in bonds, corporate stocks
and mortgage credit.

f   Marché du capital;
     Marché monétaire
d   Kapitalmarkt

299   MARKET, DISCOUNT
A market in commercial and
treasury bills and short-term
government notes.

f   Marché d'escompte
d   Diskontmarkt

**300   MARKET, FOREIGN
     EXCHANGE**
A market in which foreign
currency is bought and sold;
such market consists of foreign
exchange dealers and brokers
who are in touch with each
other and with other similar
markets elsewhere in the world.

f   Marché des changes;
     Marché des devises
d   Devisenmarkt

301   MARKET, MONEY
Denotes institutionalized
sources for short-term funds;
comprising financial institutions which handle the purchase,
sale and transfer of short-term
credit instruments.

f   Marché des monnaies
d   Geldmarkt

302   MARKET, MORTGAGE
All financial transactions
concerned with refinancing
mortgage credits or associated
with the marketing of mortgages; this is normally a
secondary market.

f   Marché hypothécaire;
     Marché des hypothèques
d   Hypothekenmarkt

**303   MARKET, NARROW;
     MARKET, THIN**
A stock market denoting light
trading in an issue in which
there are few bids and offers;
or a market in which there are
comparatively few offers to sell
or bids to buy.

f   Marché étroit
d   Enger Markt

304   MARKET, NEW ISSUE
The volume and the extent of
participation for new shares
and stocks. This market represents the direct means whereby
financing may be provided for
new or growing enterprises.

f   Marché de nouvelles émissions
d   Markt für Neuemissionen

305   MARKET, OVER-THE-
       COUNTER;
       MARKET, TRADING
A market for securities which
includes all transactions in
securities that are not made on
organized stock exchanges.

f   Marché libre;
     Marché hors cote;
     Marché après Bourse
d   Freiverkehr;
     Freiverkehrsmarkt

306   MARKET, SPOT;
       MARKET, CASH,
       MARKET, PHYSICAL
A market in which stocks, shares
and other commercial papers are
sold for cash and delivered
immediately.

f   Marché du comptant;
     Marché du disponible
d   Barverkehr

307   MONEY, CALL;
       CALL LOAN;
       MONEY AT CALL AND SHORT
       NOTICE
A loan that must be repaid on
demand; often the money is lent
on a day-to-day basis. Such type
of transactions occur amongst
commercial banks to tide over
immediate liquidity requirements,
or by speculative traders in the
market for the same purpose.

f   Argent à vue;
     Argent remboursable sur
     demande
d   Geld auf tägliche Kündigung

308   MONEY, NEAR
An asset whose value is fixed
in terms of money and which
can easily be converted into
money, yet which cannot be
spent directly, e.g. time
deposits, government bonds.

f   Titres d'une grande liquidité
d   Geldnahe Werte

309   NEGOTIABLE
A bill or other types of financial
instruments which can be
readily passed or endorsed from
one person to the other; this
must be in writing, payable to
the bearer at specified time and
must bear the name of the
drawer.

f   Bancable;
     Négociable en banque;
     Commerçable
d   Bankfähig;
     Übertragbar

310   NEGOTIABLE INSTRUMENT;
       NEGOTIABLE PAPER
Bills of exchange, cheques,
promissory notes and such other
financial instruments, the title
to which passes on delivery.

f   Titre négociable;
     Titre commerçable
d   Inhaberpapier;
     Verkehrspapier

311   NOMINEE
An individual or an institution
including a corporation holding
shares and securities on behalf
and for the benefit of the real
owner and where the securities
are listed in the name of the
nominee.

f   Candidat nommé;
    Candidat désigné
d   Vorgeschlagener Kandidat

312   NON-CUMULATIVE
      A preference share (preferred
      stock) on which dividend is
      payable only when the enterprise
      issuing such shares and stocks
      has achieved a level of operation
      and profitability to be able to
      pay a dividend and where unpaid
      dividends for previous years are
      not deemed to be accrued.

f   Non-cumulatif
d   Nichtkumulativ

313   PLACING
      A method of issuing shares or
      securities whereby the services
      of a stockbroking firm is enlisted
      to sell shares so issued to
      institutional and other investors.
      (See: Offer for sale 841)

f   Placement
d   Anlegung;
    Plazierung

314   PLACING, PRIVATE
      The process whereby a finance
      company provides additional
      funds to an enterprise by purch-
      asing new shares or debentures
      of the enterprise.

f   Placement privé
d   Private Anlegung;
    Private Plazierung

315   PREMIUM
      A situation where the market
      price exceeds the issue price of
      a share or security; the extent
      of difference to be referred as
      premium. (See: Discount 271)

f   Prime
d   Prämie

316   PRICES, CLOSING
      Prices of shares and securities

in a stock exchange at the
close of the day's business.

f   Cours de clôture;
    Dernier cours
d   Schlusskurs;
    Letzter Kurs

317   PRICES, COMING-OUT
      Prices at which new shares
      are issued.

f   Premier cours des obligations
d   Anfangskurs von Schuld-
    verschreibungen

318   PRICES, OPENING
      Prices at which business first
      commences on the floor of the
      stock exchange at the official
      opening time.

f   Prix d'ouverture
d   Eröffnungskurs;
    Erster Tageskurs

319   PROFIT TAKING
      The process whereby bulls
      undertake sales of shares and
      securities in a rising market
      to realize profit.

f   Tirer profit
d   Profitieren

320   PROMISSORY NOTE
      A document stating that a
      person promises to pay another
      a specified sum on or before
      a specified date.

f   Billet simple;
    Billet à ordre
d   Eigener Wechsel;
    Trockener Wechsel

321   PUNTER
      A person who buys and sells
      quickly, never holding a
      security for long.

f   Spéculateur
d   Spekulant

322 PYRAMIDING
Using paper profits as the basis
of additional margin with which to
finance the purches of more stock.
The term also applies to the
acquisition of several holding
companies.

f "Pyramiding"
d Verschachtelung

323 QUOTATION
A privilege granted to a company
by the Stock Exchange of having
the price of its shares listed in
the official list of share price.

f Cote;
Cotation;
Cours
d Preisnotierung;
Kursnotiz;
Börsennotiz

324 REDISCOUNT
The process of discounting an
instrument for the second time,
as e.g. when one bank calls upon
another bank, or the Central Bank
to discount instruments which it
has previously discounted for a
customer.

f Réescompter
d Neudiskontieren

325 RIGGING
Manipulating the prices of stocks
and shares in a stock exchange.

f Tripotage de bourse
d Börsenschiebung

326 ROUND LOT
The unit of trading or multiple
thereof, specified by the issuing
company or specified by a stock
exchange for shares and
securities traded by it.

f Tranche d'actions
d Aktienpaket

327 SCRIP
A capital market terminology for
traded shares. Also denotes
subscription certificates
provisionally provided to subscribers who have been allotted
shares and documents the
bearer of which is entitled to
receive stated privileges, such
as rights, allocation or bonus
shares.

f Action provisoire;
Certificat nominatif
d Zwischenschein;
Interimsschein;
Gutschein

328 SECURITIES
A document that establishes,
represents, or evidences a right
or rights to property as e.g. a
share, bond or debenture
certificates.

f Valeurs
d Sicherheiten;
Wertpapiere;
Effekten

329 SECURITIES, CONVERTIBLE
Bonds or stocks that may be
exchanged for other securities
of the issuing corporation,
usually common shares, at the
option of the holder. (See: Stock
conversion 363)

f Valeurs de conversion
d Konvertierbare Effekten

330 SECURITIES, DIGESTED
Securities which are owned by
investors who are expected to
hold on to these for a long time.

f Valeurs digérées
d Vom Markt aufgenommene
Wertpapiere

331 SECURITIES, GOVERNMENT;
GILT-EDGED BONDS
Securities issued by Government,

government-sponsored institutions,
or agencies, or by nationalized industries, guaranteed by the Government; traded in the Stock Exchange,
carrying the least amount of risk,
a fixed rate of interest, repayable
at par at a definite date or dates.

f   Valeurs de gouvernement
d   Regierungseffekten

332   SECURITIES, IRREDEEMABLE
Securities issued with no date of
redemption laid down.

f   Valeurs non amortissables;
Valeurs irremboursables
d   Nicht einlösbare Werte

333   SECURITIES, LISTED
A stock or bond that has been
registered with a stock exchange
and is eligible for trading on that
exchange.

f   Titres notés
d   Amtlich notierte Werte

334   SECURITIES, MARKETABLE
Securities which are traded on a
stock exchange.

f   Valeurs fungibles
d   Börsengängige Werte;
Fungible Effekten

335   SECURITIES, SECOND-HAND
Securities bought over by an
investor from an original owner.

f   Valeurs de seconde main;
Valeurs d'un tiers
d   Werte aus zweiter Hand;
Werte von dritter Seite

336   SECURITIES, TRUSTEE;
ELIGIBLE PAPERS;
SECURITIES, APPROVED
Securities declared by law to be
suitable for the investment of
money held in trust. Recognition
of shares, debentures and other
notes as a trustee security has

the advantage of certainty of
subscription as also relatively
lower rates of return to be
offered. Since many institutional investors such as
commercial banks, insurance
companies, unit trusts, trust
funds, pension funds, provident
funds, have the obligation to
invest a part of their resources
in trustee securities, a development bank which has the
privilege of its debentures and
bonds recognized as trustee
securities, finds it a great
advantage in augmenting its
working resources. (See: Legal
list 290)

f   Titres éligibles;
Valeurs éligibles
d   Mündelsichere Wertpapiere

337   SECURITIES, UNDIGESTED
Securities issued in an amount
too large to be absorbed by the
investment market.

f   Valeurs non digérées
d   Vom Markt noch nicht aufgenommene Wertpapiere

338   SECURITIES, UNLISTED
Securities that are not
registered with a stock exchange
but are traded in the over-the-
counter market.

f   Titres non notés
d   Amtlich nicht notierte Werte

339   SELLING SHORT
A bear who sells shares or
stocks in the market without
owning these shares. (See:
Bear 218)

f   Réalisation des actions
d   Verkäufe auf Baisse;
Blankoverkäufe;
Blankoabgaben;
Fixgeschäfte

340   SETTLEMENT DAY
The date on which a buyer must
pay for securities bought and the
seller must deliver the securities
he has sold.

f   Jour de liquidation;
Jour du réglement
d   Abrechnungstag;
Abrechnungstermin

341   SHARE CERTIFICATE
A document issued under the
official seal of the company,
showing ownership of shares in
the company.

f   Titre d'actions;
Certificat d'actions
d   Aktientitel;
Aktienmantel

342   SHARE OPTION
A contract which gives the
purchaser the privilege of buying
or selling a specified amount of
stock at a stated price within a
specified period.

f   Titre d'option
d   Wahlaktie

343   SHARES AND STOCKS
Individual portions of a company's
capital owned by shareholders.
These terms tend to be used inter-
changeably, but a special meaning
can be given to the term "stock"
to denote money lent to a government, local council, or a company
and involving a fixed rate of
interest.

f   Valeurs de bourse;
Titres de bourse
d   Wertpapiere;
Börsenwerte;
Effekten

344   SHARES, BONUS;
BONUS ISSUE
The process of distributing un-
impaired reserves amongst

eligible shareholders; requires
permission of shareholders and
company law authorities. (See:
Capitalization of reserves 902)

f   Action gratuite
d   Gratisaktie;
Bonusaktie

345   SHARES, CALLABLE
Equity or preferred shares
which have been subscribed in
part and the remaining values
of each of the shares to be paid
as and when called upon by the
issuing company. (See: Call
882)

f   Valeurs remboursables sur
demande
d   Kündbare Aktien

346   SHARES, CONVERTIBLE
Preferred shares which have the
right to be converted at the
option of the shareholder into
ordinary shares after a stated
period.

f   Valeurs convertibles
d   Wandelaktien;
Konversionsaktien

347   SHARES, CUMULATIVE
Preferred stocks or shares,
dividends on which, if not paid
in the first year, or in a series
of years, will have to be paid in
the cumulative amount at the
first opportunity.

f   Actions cumulatives
d   Sonderaktien

348   SHARES, CUMULATIVE
PREFERENCE
A type of stock ownership
bearing a fixed rate of dividend
and having preference for
payment over ordinary shares;
such dividends have to be
compulsorily paid.

f   Actions privilégiées cumulatives;
    Actions de priorité cumulatives
d   Sondervorzugsaktien

349   SHARES, DEFERRED
      A type of shares which rank after
      ordinary shares, for purposes of
      payment of dividends or for capital
      sum in the event of liquidation.

f   Actions différées
d   Nachzugsaktien

350   SHARES, DEFERRED
      MANAGEMENT
      Shares owned by original promoters
      which have to wait for their
      dividend until all other classes of
      shares have participated in the
      profit.

f   Tantièmes des administrateurs
d   Direktorentantiemen

351   SHARES, MULTIPLE VOTING
      A complex of shares issued by a
      company with varying voting rights;
      this device is sometimes employed
      when a small limited company
      wishes to expand and issues new
      shares to the general public with
      little or no voting rights in order
      to permit control of the business to
      remain in the hands of the few
      people who controlled it when it
      was small.

f   Actions avec droit de vote multiple
d   Multiple stimmberechtigte Aktien;
    Aktien mit multipler Stimm-
    berechtigung

352   SHARES, NO-PAR-VALUE
      Shares which, while issuing,
      carried no nominal value, these
      shares only have the value
      currently determined by the stock
      exchange.

f   Actions sans valeur nominale
d   Aktien ohne Nennwert

353   SHARES, ORDINARY;
      COMMON STOCK
      Equity capital of an enterprise
      which confers unconditional
      ownership rights in proportion
      to volumes of shares owned,
      but where the returns are the
      residuals after meeting all
      obligations including the
      returns for preferred stock-
      holders.

f   Actions ordinaires;
    Actions de capital
d   Stammaktien

354   SHARES, PAID-UP
      Shares whose full amount has
      been paid.

f   Actions libérées
d   Voll eingezahlte Aktien

355   SHARES, PREFERENCE;
      SHARES, PREFERRED
      Shares which rank for payment
      of dividend next to debentures
      and prior to ordinary shares.
      They carry a fixed rate of
      dividend.

f   Actions de préférence;
    Actions de priorité;
    Actions privilégiées
d   Vorzugsaktien;
    Prioritätsaktien

356   SHARES, PREFERENCE
      PARTICIPATING
      Preference shares which, in
      addition to a fixed dividend,
      are also entitled to an addition-
      al amount of bonus when the
      dividend to ordinary shares
      exceeds certain amounts.

f   Actions privilégiées de
    participation
d   Vorzugs-Beteiligungsaktien

357   SPECULATION
      The act of knowingly assuming
      above-average risks with the

hope of gaining above-average
returns on a business or financial
transaction.

f   Spéculation
d   Spekulation

358   SPIN-OFF METHOD
A method used by a corporation
to distribute stock that it owns
in another corporation to its own
stockholders; basically for tax
purposes.

f   Echange de titres;
d   Aktientausch

359   SPLITTING;
       STOCK SPLIT;
       SPLIT-UP
The process of dividing share
units into smaller denominations
to increase their marketability.
A situation where the par value
of a share is lowered, and the
number of shares increased, the
total capital remaining unchanged.

f   Fractionnement des actions;
     Partage des actions
d   Aktienspaltung

360   SPOT PAYMENT
Payment in cash by way of an
immediate settlement.

f   Paiement du comptant
d   Barzahlung

361   SPOT PURCHASE
The purchase of shares or currency
immediately available, as distinct
to forward or future transactions.

f   Achat du disponible
d   Sofortkauf

362   STAG
A person who applies for a number
of shares in a new issue, with the
intention of selling quickly to
make a profit.

f   Spéculateur de titres

d   Konzertzeichner;
     Aktienspekulant

363   STOCK CONVERSION
The process of exchanging one
type of share for another type.
The term usually applies to the
exchange of bonds or debenture
certificates for ordinary or
preferred shares. (See:
Securities, convertible 329)

f   Conversion d'actions
d   Aktienkonversion

364   STOCK DIVIDEND
Dividend paid out of accumulated
profit by way of additional
shares. (See: Capitalization of
reserves 902)

f   Dividende d'action
d   Aktiendividende

365   STOCK EXCHANGE
       INTRODUCTION
The introduction of one or more
classes of the securities of a
company on to the Stock
Exchange.

f   Introduction de bourse
d   Börseneinführung

366   STOCK TURN
The average rate at which stock
is turned over in a year,
calculated by dividing sales by
stock price.

f   Changement des actions
d   Aktienumsatz

367   STOCK, AUTHORIZED;
       SHARES, AUTHORIZED
The maximum amount of all
classes of shares or stocks that
can be issued by a corporation,
as prescribed in the Charter of
Incorporation, and as approved
by the company law authorities.

f   Actions autorisées
d   Autorisierte Aktien

368 STOCK, INSCRIBED;
    INSCRIBED SHARES
    Shares for which in lieu of
    certificates, a register is maint-
    ained wherein the names of
    holders are inscribed.

f   Actions nominatives;
    Titres nominatifs
d   Namensaktien

369 STOCK, SPOT PRICE OF;
    STOCK, CASH PRICE OF
    The price quoted for the immediate
    sale and delivery of stock, shares
    and other commercial papers.

f   Prix du comptant des actions
d   Barkurs von Aktien;
    Geldkurs von Aktien

370 STOCK, WATERED;
    WATERED SHARES
    Shares of a company issued to
    insiders for a nominal consider-
    ation.

f   Capital-actions dilués
d   Verwässertes Aktienkapital

371 STRADDLE
    A contractual right conferred on
    a holder to buy or sell specified
    amounts of shares at stated
    prices over a stipulated period
    of time.

f   Opération à cheval
d   Gegentransaktion;
    Stellagegeschäft;
    Stellgeschäft

372 SWITCHING
    The process of changing from one
    form of investment to another
    according to circumstances; for
    example, relative yield rates.
    Switching generally helps to even
    out prices and makes a contribut-
    ion to the smooth functioning of
    the gilt-edged market.

f   Transaction de "switch"

d   Switchgeschäft;
    Effektenengagementumstellung

373 SWITCHING ANOMALY
    Switching between securities of
    comparable maturity to profit
    from some fleeting anomaly in
    their prices. The purpose is
    always a profit on trading
    without any change in the broad
    pattern of an investor's port-
    folio. Large stakes are needed
    to show a profit on the fine
    margins available.

f   Anomalie de "switch"
d   Anomalieswitchgeschäfte;
    Anomalieumstellung im
    Effektenengagement

374 SWITCHING COUPON
    Transfer of investment to take
    advantage of immediate
    possibilities of profit.

f   Coupon de "switch"
d   Switchkupon;
    Switchabschnitt

375 SWITCHING POLICY
    Transfer of investment to take
    advantage of future possibilities
    in relation to an investor's
    requirements; it may involve the
    redistribution of a portfolio.

f   Politique de "switch"
d   Switchpolitik

376 TENOR
    The period of time stated on a
    bill of exchange before payment
    is due.

f   Echéance;
    Terme d'échéance
d   Laufzeit

377 USANCE
    A time fixed by custom for the
    payment of a bill of exchange.

f   Usance
d   Usance

378 USURY
The charging of an exhorbitant
rate of interest on a loan.

f Usure
d Wucher

379 VALUE, NOMINAL;
VALUE, PAR;
VALUE, ISSUE
The value of a share at the time
it is issued.

f Valeur nominale
d Nennwert;
Nominalwert

380 WARRANT
Right to buy a stock at a specific
price. Generally, warrants run for
longer periods of time than the
ordinary subscription rights,
occasionally given existing stockholders, when a corporation wishes
to raise new capital. Some issues
of warrants are perpetual.

f Certificat
d Ermächtigung

381 WASH SALES
A situation where transactions in
shares are camouflaged amongst
the same or related persons.

f Ventes diluées
d Börsenmanöver;
Scheinverkäufe

PART TWO
DEVELOPMENT BANKING

IV.
DEVELOPMENT INSTITUTIONS AND AGENCIES
INSTITUTIONS ET AGENCES DE DEVELOPPEMENT
ENTWICKLUNGSINSTITUTIONEN UND EINRICHTUNGEN

382   AGENCY, COORDINATING

Institutional arrangements evolved within a development bank, a development agency or a government-promoted organization, with the basic aim of contributing to the project identification task by bringing together men with new ideas or technical knowledge about a product or process, with men with capital to invest.

f   Agence de coordination
d   Koordinationsstelle

383   AGRO-BUSINESS ESTABLISHMENT

Individuals or corporate entities involved in the supply, production or distribution of agricultural inputs or in the storage, processing or marketing of agricultural products; some development banks are designed specially to assist and develop such enterprises.

f   Etablissement agro-industriel
d   Agro-industrielles Unternehmen

384   APEX INSTITUTION

A mother institution set up to coordinate the working of individual institutions which have identical objectives and operational spheres; other functions include supplementing capital requirements, providing guidelines of operation, technical expertise and training facilities to the individual members of the group. Normally, apex institutions are to be found amongst development banks and cooperatives of various types and kinds.

f   Maison-mère
d   Mutterhaus;
    Muttergesellschaft

385   BANK;
      BANKING INSTITUTION

A comprehensive term for an institution carrying on certain kinds of financial business.

f   Banque;
    Etablissement bancaire;
    Maison de banque
d   Bank;
    Bankanstalt;
    Bankinstitut;
    Bankhaus

386   BANK OF ISSUE;
      ISSUING BANK

Any bank that is authorized to issue paper money in the form of bank notes; normally this is the prerogative of the Central Bank of the country.

f   Banque d'émission;
    Banque de circulation
d   Emissionsbank;
    Ausgabebank

387   BANK, CENTRAL

A bank occupying a central position in the banking system

49

of a country in the sense that it functions as banker to the government and to other banks, and is the manager of the currency unit and credit policy.

f   Banque centrale
d   Zentralbank

388   BANK, COMMERCIAL
A financial institution that accepts deposits of various types and maturities, operates checking accounts, makes short-term loans and generally maintains the greater part of its resources in liquid or near-liquid forms. Commercial banks, in most countries, and of most types, are distinguished from other financial institutions by the type of facilities offered, namely, allowing customers the use of cheques, providing overdraft facilities, discounting bills of exchange, etc.

f   Banque commerciale;
    Banque de commerce
d   Handelsbank;
    Commerzbank

389   BANK, COOPERATIVE
A bank catering to the requirements of a particular social or economic sector of the population, set up and operating on the principles of cooperation. These banks mobilize basically the savings of their members - though deposits may be accepted from the non-member public - and provide for the credit requirements of only its members.

f   Banque coopérative
d   Genossenschaftsbank

390   BANK, CORRESPONDENT
A relationship between banks in different localities or countries whereby mutually advantageous

business is carried on, e.g. exchanging information, lending and borrowing funds, clearing of cheques, making collections for one another.

f   Banque de correspondance
d   Korrespondenzbank

391   BANK, DEVELOPMENT
An institution promoted or assisted by the Government mainly to provide development finance to one or more sectors or sub-sectors of the economy. The institution distinguishes itself by a judicious balance as between commercial norms of operation, as adopted by any private financial institution, and developmental obligations; it emphasizes the "project approach" - meaning the viability of the project to be financed - against the "collateral approach"; apart from provision of long-term loans, equity-capital, guarantee and underwriting functions, a development bank normally is also expected to upgrade the managerial and the other operational prerequisites of the assisted projects. Its insurance against default is the integrity, competence and resourcefulness of the management, the commercial and technical viability of the project, above all the speed of implementation and efficiency of operation of the assisted projects. Its relationship with its clients is of a continuing nature and of being a "partner" in the project than that of a mere "financier". (See: Investment policy 525)

f   Banque de développement
d   Entwicklungsbank

392 BANK, AFRICAN
DEVELOPMENT;
ADB
A regional development finance
institution set up for promoting
the development of agriculture,
industry, health, education and
infra-structure facilities of the
countries in the African continent.

f Banque Africaine de Développement
d Afrikanische Entwicklungsbank

393 BANK, AGRICULTURAL
DEVELOPMENT
A development bank specializing
in the provision of development
finance of various types and
duration to the agricultural sector.
(See: Bank, development 391)

f Banque de développement agraire
d Agrarentwicklungsbank

394 BANK, ASIAN DEVELOPMENT;
ADB
A regional development finance
institution initiated through the
efforts of ECAFE member countries
for promoting the industrial,
agricultural, educational development of developing regional
member countries. Membership
comprises of 37 countries throughout the world; 23 from the regional
area.

f Banque Asiatique de Développement
d Asiatische Entwicklungsbank

395 BANK, INDUSTRIAL
DEVELOPMENT;
INDUSTRIAL CREDIT AND
INVESTMENT CORPORATION
A development bank specializing in
the provision of development
finance to the industrial sector.
(See: Bank, development 391)

f Banque de développement
industriel
d Industrieentwicklungsbank

396 BANK, INTER-AMERICAN
DEVELOPMENT
A regional development
finance institution sponsored
mainly through the initiative of
the USA for promoting the
economic development of its
22 Latin American member
countries. The membership of
this Bank is restricted to the
nations that belong to the
Organization of American
States.

f Banque Inter-américaine de
Développement
d Interamerikanische Entwicklungsbank

397 BANK, EXPORT-IMPORT
A national institution, usually
sponsored and/or supported
by the government, with the
objective of promoting external
trade, mainly exports, through
provision of financial
assistance.

f Banque d'exportation-
importation
d Export-Importbank

398 BANK, INVESTMENT
A financial institution
specializing in the buying and
selling of shares and securities.

f Banque de placement
d Investitionsbank;
Anlagebank

399 BANK, LAND MORTGAGE
A financial institution set up by
the Government, or mainly
through Government initiative,
to assist farmers in the
acquisition of agricultural land,
or improving existing agricultural holdings, through
appropriate credit facilities.

f Banque foncière;
d Bodenkreditbank;

Hypothekenbank

400   BANK, MANAGING
Financing institution which takes
up the leadership, on behalf of
other similar institutions, in
matters of project appraisal for
a joint loan, coordination of other
activities in a participation loan,
initiation of new industrial
projects and to solicit participation of other banks in financing
such projects. Originally, the
managing institution was associated with the function of organizing
the floatation in the market of new
issues on behalf of enterprises.

f   Banque gestionnaire;
     Banque directoriale
d   Geschäftsführende Bank;
     Geschäftsleitende Bank

401   BANK, MERCHANT
The type of institution which
combines the functions of a
managing bank with those of investment banking.

f   Banque de placement et de
     direction
d   Investitions-und geschäftsleitende
     Bank

402   BANK, MUTUAL SAVINGS
A banking institution which is
owned and operated wholly for
the benefit of its depositors,
mostly individuals. It is directed
by a self-perpetuating board of
directors.

f   Caisse d'épargne mutuel
d   Wechselseitige Sparkasse

403   BANK, POST OFFICE SAVINGS
A department within Post Offices
to facilitate the collection of
savings, to provide the safest
possible custody of savings, and
to encourage savings by paying
interest on the money deposited.

Such arrangements are to be
found particularly in rural areas
where commercial banking has,
for one reason or another, not
yet ventured.

f   Caisse d'épargne de la poste
d   Postsparkasse

404   BANK, PRIVATE
Financial institution, usually
small partnerships, undertaking commercial banking
operations. These are contrasted
to joint-stock commercial
banks.

f   Banque privée
d   Privatbank

405   BANK, SAVINGS
An institution which marshals
the savings of small investors
and channels them in appropriate
investment outlets.

f   Caisse d'épargne
d   Sparkasse;
     Sparbank

406   BANK, STATE
A banking institution chartered
by the State and undertaking
normal commercial banking
operations on behalf of the
Government and Government-
sponsored agencies in addition
to providing such facilities for
the public. The State Bank
normally has larger social-
and developmental responsibilities than joint stock commercial
banks.

f   Banque d'Etat;
     Banque nationale
d   Staatsbank;
     Nationalbank

**407   BANK, TRADING;
        BANK, TRADE**
Name for Australian (and
early British) commercial

banks, which specialize in financing internal and external trading
activities.

f   Banque commerciale;
    Banque de commerce
d   Handelsbank;
    Commerzbank

408   BANKING FACILITIES
      Existence of institutions to accept
      deposits of various types and
      maturities, to extend credits of
      various types and maturities and
      to perform various services, such
      as opening of letters of credit,
      discounting of bills, etc., to
      channelize savings and to promote
      the normal working and the growth
      of industry, commerce and trade
      in an economy.

f   Facilités de banque
d   Bankmöglichkeiten

409   BANKING SYNDICATE
      A group of banks associated
      together to underwrite and sell a
      new issue of securities.

f   Syndicat de banque;
    Syndicat de banquiers
d   Banksyndikat;
    Bankkonsortium

410   BANKING, BRANCH
      A banking system with a smaller
      number of banks each with a
      large number of branch offices.
      The main advantage of branch
      banking lies in the greater stabil-
      ity of such banks compared with
      unit banks.

f   Banque à succursales
d   Filialbankbetrieb;
    Filialbankwesen

411   BANKING, GROUP
      An arrangement whereby two or
      more separately incorporated
      banks are brought under the control
      of a holding company.

f   Consort de banques
d   Bankengruppe;
    Bankenkonsortium

412   BANKING, UNIT
      A system in which a bank is
      not permitted to open branches,
      as in many States of the
      United States. Unit banks tend
      to be weaker in a crisis than
      branch banks.

f   Banque à unité
d   Einheitsbankbetrieb

413   BOURSE
      A popular term used for stock
      exchanges of Paris, Zurich,
      Frankfurt, Milan and Amsterdam.

f   Bourse
d   Börse

414   BROKER, SHARE
      Professional dealer in shares
      registered at stock exchange,
      acting as agent on behalf of the
      public for share transactions.

f   Agent de banque
d   Bankmakler

415   BROKER, BILL
      A small firm engaged in discount
      business on the money market.

f   Courtier d'escompte;
    Escompteur
d   Wechselmakler;
    Diskontmakler

416   BROKER, FLOOR
      Registered agent of a stock
      exchange engaged in transacting
      business on behalf of another
      member.

f   Agent de bourse
d   Makler im Börsensaal;
    Makler im Parkett

417   BROKER, FOREIGN
      EXCHANGE

A broker who deals in foreign
currencies, acting as an intermediary between banks.

f   Courtier de bourse;
    Agent de change
d   Börsenmakler;
    Wechselagent;
    Kursmakler

418   BROKER, PLACING
      A broker who approaches other
      brokers to cover portions of a
      risk accepted by him on behalf
      of a client.

f   Agent de placement
d   Investitionsmakler

419   BROKER, SPECIALIST;
      JOBBER;
      JOBBER, STOCK
      A broker who specializes in
      particular types of securities
      and shares, mainly buying from
      and selling to other members of
      the exchange. He is essentially
      "wholesaler" and has no direct
      dealings with the public.

f   Marchand de titres
d   Börsenhändler;
    Effektenhändler

420   BUILDING SOCIETY
      Institution which accepts deposits
      and then uses its funds to lend
      on mortgage to people who wish
      to buy their own houses.

f   Société coopérative de
    construction
d   Baugenossenschaft

421   CHAMBER OF COMMERCE
      Association of industrialists,
      business trading and banking
      community organized on local,
      national or international levels,
      designed to provide a forum or
      collective representation on
      problems, dissemination of
      information amongst constituents

and to facilitate flow of information of mutual benefits for
members.

f   Chambre de commerce
d   Handelskammer

422   COMPANY;
      CORPORATION
      An association of individuals or
      a group for the specific
      purpose of carrying on a
      business of any type.

f   Compagnie;
    Société;
    Société commerciale
d   Gesellschaft;
    Handelsgesellschaft

423   COMPANY, ASSOCIATED;
      COMPANY, AFFILIATED
      Situation where two or more
      companies have interlinking
      ownership, directorship or
      interests.

f   Société affiliée;
    Société associée;
    Société filiale
d   Tochtergesellschaft;
    Zweiggesellschaft

424   COMPANY, CLOSED-END
      INVESTMENT
      Investment company that has a
      fixed capital structure and
      where shareholding and member-
      ship is restricted amongst a
      close group of persons or
      institutions. (See: Company,
      open-end investment 435)

f   Maison de placement fermé
d   Investierungsgesellschaft mit
    geschlossenem Anlagefonds

425   COMPANY, COMMERCIAL
      CREDIT;
      COMPANY, SALES FINANCE
      A firm engaged in the business
      of buying installment contracts
      and accounts receivables from

other businesses.

f   Maison de crédit commercial
d   Handelskreditgesellschaft

426   COMPANY, CONSUMER
         FINANCE;
         COMPANY, PERSONAL
         FINANCE;
         COMPANY, SMALL-LOAN
         A financial institution which
         specializes in small and personal
         loans.

f   Société de petit crédit
d   Kleinkreditverein

427   COMPANY, FACTORING
         An institution specializing in the
         collection of trade debts on behalf
         of other enterprises, thereby
         enabling these enterprises to
         obtain insurance against bad
         debts. The procedure is for the
         factoring company to buy up
         its clients' invoices.

f   Société de "factoring";
       Agence de recouvrement de créances
d   Faktorei;
       Debitorenverkauf

428   COMPANY, FINANCE;
         FINANCE HOUSE
         An institution primarily concerned
         with the financing of hire
         purchase transactions.

f   Compagnie de finance;
       Société financière
d   Finanzierungsgesellschaft

429   COMPANY, HOLDING
         A corporation that owns the
         majority of stock or securities
         of one or more other corporations
         for purposes of control, rather
         than of investment.

f   Société holding;
       Société de contrôle;
       Trust de valeurs
d   Holdinggesellschaft;
       Dachgesellschaft

430   COMPANY, INVESTMENT;
         INVESTMENT TRUST
         An organization that combines
         the funds of many persons and
         invests them in a wide
         selection of securities.

f   Société de placement;
       Société de portefeuille
d   Investierungsgesellschaft

431   COMPANY, JOINT STOCK
         A form of organization where
         the capital is divided into
         shares of small denomination
         to enable investors to
         participate in small or large
         numbers of shares, and the
         profit earned, distributed in
         proportion to the number of
         shares held; also has other
         features associated with a
         "Limited Liability Company".
         (See 432)

f   Société par actions;
       Société anonyme
d   Aktiengesellschaft

432   COMPANY, LIMITED
         COMPANY, LIMITED
         LIABILITY

         A type of organization wherein
         a shareholder is not held
         personally liable for a company's
         liabilities beyond the fully-paid-up
         value of the shares held by him.
         The evolution of this form of
         organization has been instru-
         mental in enlisting wider public
         participation in newly
         promoted enterprises and to
         that extent helped mobilize
         private savings to be channelled
         to private industrial develop-
         ment.

f   Société à responsabilité limitée
d   Gesellschaft mit beschränkter
       Haftung;
       Ges.m.b.H.

433 COMPANY, PUBLIC LIMITED
A limited company enjoying the
following status and privileges:
a minimum number of prescribed
members, with no maximum
membership limitations, can
invite the general public to subscribe to its shares, and whose
shares can be transferred without
any restrictions. A form of
organization generally prevalent
in countries under British tradition
and influence.

f   Société publique à responsabilité
    limitée
d   Öffentlichliche Gesellschaft mit
    beschränkter Haftung

434 COMPANY, MULTINATIONAL
An enterprise that operates in
more than one country.

f   Société multinationale
d   Multinationale Gesellschaft

435 COMPANY, OPEN-END
    INVESTMENT;
    MUTUAL FUND
An investment company that has
a flexible capital structure;
because it continuously sells
shares in mutual funds and
because of continuous redemption
of outstanding shares, its capital
structure is almost constantly
changing.

f   Société anonyme avec un fonds
    d'investissements ouvert
d   Kapitalanlagegesellschaft mit in
    der Höhe unbegrenztem
    Investmentfonds

436 COMPANY, SMALL BUSINESS
    INVESTMENT
A corporation whose purpose is
to provide long-term loans and
equity capital to small scale
enterprises.

f   Société financière pour la petite
    industrie

d   Kleingewerbefinanzierungs-
    gesellschaft

437 COOPERATIVE, AGRI-
    CULTURAL CREDIT
Institutional arrangement
fostered through governmental
or Central Banking institutions
to channel developmental
credit to the unorganized
agricultural sectors of the
economy.

f   Coopérative agricole de crédit
d   Landwirtschaftliche Kredit-
    genossenschaft

438 CORPORATION, AGRI-
    CULTURAL MORTGAGE
An institution established with
the basic objective to grant, for
the purchase of land, long-term
loans on first mortgage; it has
also the function to help
farmers to make additions and
improvements.

f   Société hypothécaire agricole
d   Landwirtschaftliche Hypotheken-
    gesellschaft

439 CORPORATION, INDUSTRIAL
    AND COMMERCIAL FINANCE
An institution drawing funds
mainly from government,
commercial banks, insurance
companies and other financial
concerns, to engage in medium
and long-term financing of
industry.

f   Société financière de l'industrie
    et commerce
d   Industrie- und Handelsfinan-
    zierungsgesellschaft

440 CORPORATION, PRIVATE
Enterprise floated and controlled
by an exclusive group, or a
small number of persons.

f   Corporation du droit civil
d   Körperschaft des bürgerlichen

Rechtes;
Juristische Person des Privatrechtes

441 CORPORATION, PUBLIC
Enterprise promoted and controlled
by government, semi-government
or other public authorities and
agencies.

f Corporation du droit public
d Körperschaft des öffentlichen
Rechtes;
Öffentlich-rechtliche Körperschaft

442 ENTERPRISE, PRIVATE
An organized manufacturing,
trading or service activity,
promoted and managed by private
individuals.

f Entreprise privée
d Privates Unternehmen

443 ENTERPRISE, PUBLIC
An organized manufacturing,
trading or service activity
promoted and managed by the
government in the course of
promoting public good.

f Entreprise publique
d Öffentliches Unternehmen

444 FINANCIAL INSTITUTIONS;
FINANCIAL INTERMEDIARIES
Intermediaries collecting from
savers their excess funds and
directing them to investors who
have a need of these funds to meet
some economic purpose.

f Sociétés financières
d Finanzierungsgesellschaften;
Finanzierungsinstitute

445 GUARANTEE SOCIETIES
Private agencies engaged in providing credit guarantee or
insurance cover to financing
institutions catering unorganized
sectors such as small industry,
housing, farming. The guarantee
provided by these agencies
enables entities in these unorganized sectors to avail themselves of institutional finance
for productive purposes, and
substitutes or supplements
their collateral for borrowings.

f Sociétés de garantie
d Garantiegesellschaften

446 HOUSE, ACCEPTING
A financial institution whose
endorsement in a bill of exchange is recognized as a
guarantee of the borrowers'
or purchasers' creditworthiness;
such houses are also known to
engage in ordinary banking
business, as investment advisors,
merchant bankers and issuing
houses. (See: Credit, acceptance
775)

f Banque d'acceptation
d Akzeptbank

447 HOUSE, CLEARING;
HOUSE, BANKERS' CLEARING
A voluntary association of banks
in a city or country joined
together to facilitate their
daily exchange of checks, drafts,
and notes. (See: Clearing 256)

f Chambre de compensation des
banquiers
d Bankenabrechnungsstelle;
Bankclearingstelle

448 HOUSE, CONFIRMING
Agencies through which overseas
buyers undertake import transactions; among the functions
included are arrangements to
pay for the manufacture of goods
to be exported; attendance to
documentation and shipment
requirements.

f Banque de confirmation
d Bestätigungsbank

449 HOUSE, DISCOUNT;
DISCOUNT BANK
A financial institution specializing
in discounting of bills of exchange.

f Maison d'escompte;
   Banque d'escompte
d Diskontobank

450 HOUSE, EXPORT COMMISSION
A firm which acts as agent for
manufacturers whose operations
individually are not large enough
to warrant their having export
departments of their own.

f Maison de commission des
   exportations
d Exportvermittlungsbank

451 HOUSE, HIRE PURCHASE
FINANCE
An institution specializing in the
provision of loans for the purchase
of certain types of goods on the
condition that repayments of the
loan with interest are done on
regular installments over a stated
period of time. (See: Credit, hire
purchase 480)

f Maison financière de vente à
   tempérament
d Ratenzahlungsfinanzierungsbank

452 INSTITUTIONAL INVESTORS
Corporate and other forms of
organizations, such as insurance
companies, provident funds, unit
trusts, mutual funds, savings
associations - that hold public
savings seeking opportunities of
investment outlets of various
maturities for these funds.

f Investisseurs institutionnels
d Institutionelle Investoren;
   Institutionelle Kapitalanleger

453 INTERNATIONAL BANK FOR
RECONSTRUCTION AND
DEVELOPMENT;
IBRD;

WORLD BANK
Bank set up under the Bretton
Woods Agreement in 1945 with
the main objective of helping
finance the rebuilding of war-
devastated areas and helping
in the advancement of less-
developed countries. Besides
lending funds, the Bank provides
technical advice to governments,
or other borrowers on a wide
range of development problems.

f Banque Mondiale
d Weltbank

454 INTERNATIONAL
DEVELOPMENT ASSOCIATION
IDA
An affiliate of the World Bank, it
was formed in 1960 to help
developing nations by extending
financial aid on easy interest
terms, and long amortization
periods, for agriculture and
farm development programs,
and infra-structure development
schemes, such as transportation
power generation and supply,
irrigation projects, industrial
estates, water supply, education
and special training programs.

f Association de Développement
   International
d Internationale Entwicklungs-
   vereinigung

455 INTERNATIONAL FINANCE
CORPORATION;
IFC
Established in 1956, as an
affiliate of the World Bank, to
help finance productive private
undertakings by investing in
them. Unlike the World Bank
and the IDA, IFC investment is
done without any guarantee
from the governments concerned

f Corporation Financière
   Internationale

d   Internationale Finanzierungs-
    gesellschaft

456   INVESTMENT CENTER
      An institution providing economic
      and commercial intelligence about
      investment opportunities in a coun-
      try, particularly to entrepreneurs
      outside the country and trying to
      foster joint ventures. The role of
      the Center is normally liaising
      or advisory.

f   Centre d'information des
    investissements
d   Anlage-Informationszentrum

457   SAVINGS AND LOAN
      ASSOCIATION
      A cooperative savings organization
      through which savers can accumul-
      ate funds to purchase houses, and
      borrowers can obtain house-mort-
      gage credits.

f   Coopérative d'épargne et de prêt
d   Spar- und Anleihegenossenschaft

458   SYNDICATE
      Group of financial institutions or
      investment firms formed to under-
      write and sell a new issue of
      securities.

f   Syndicat;
    Association
d   Syndikat;
    Konsortium

459   THRIFT INSTITUTION
      Institutions organized to promote
      savings amongst individuals of
      fixed income and small means.

f   Association d'épargne;
d   Sparverein

460   TRADE ORGANIZATION
      Association of units or interests
      representing individual industries,
      trade, commerce designed to pro-
      mote the common interests of
      constituents. Examples are

association of engineering
industry, automobile industry,
textile industry, or association
of dealers in textiles, electric
goods, etc.

f   Organisation de l'industrie
d   Handelsorganisation

461   TRUST;
      TRUST COMPANY
      A body or entity appointed to
      safeguard and administer, ac-
      cording to specified rules and
      regulations, a fund of money
      or property, for the benefit of
      an individual, or number of
      individuals or an organization.

f   Société fiduciaire
d   Treuhandgesellschaft

462   TRUST, CLOSED-END
      An investment company, or unit
      trust whose ownership and
      investments are restricted
      amongst a close group of
      interests.

f   Société fiduciaire fermée
d   Treuhandgesellschaft mit
    geschlossenem Anlagefonds

463   TRUST, FIXED
      A type of unit trust whose trust
      deed specifies a portfolio of
      securities for the investment
      of trust monies.

f   Société fiduciaire avec un fixe
    programme d'investissements
d   Anlagegesellschaft mit fest-
    stehendem Investitionsprogramm

464   TRUST, UNIT
      An investment company that is
      organized under a trust indent-
      ure or a similar instrument,
      managed by a board of trustees,
      issuing only redeemable
      securities which represent an
      individual interest in a unit of
      specified securities.

f   Fonds d'investissements
d   Investmentfonds;
    Anlagefonds

465   UNDERWRITER
    A financial institution or other
    professional agency which offers
    to cover or bear a portion of risk
    in new issue of shares by an
    issuing house. (See: Underwriting
    573)

f   Membre d'un syndicat de garantie

d   Emissionsfirma;
    Mitglied eines Emissionssyndik

466   UNDERWRITER, SUB-
    Small underwriters, normally
    individuals or firms who accept
    smaller proportion of risks for
    a new issue from main under-
    writers.

f   Sous-membre d'un syndicat de
    garantie
d   Unter-Emissionsfirma

V.

OBJECTIVES, POLICIES AND ACTIVITIES
OBJECTIFS, POLITIQUES ET ACTIVITES
ZIELSETZUNG, POLITIK UND TÄTIGKEITEN

467 ADVANCES, SELF-LIQUIDATING
Bank advances to customers for the
purpose of tiding over a temporary
shortage of funds only; e.g. "seed-
time to harvest" in agricultural
financing, or short-term working
capital to industrial enterprises.

f   Crédit de liquidation de soi-même
d   Kurzfristiger Warenkredit;
Sich automatisch abdeckende
Vorschüsse

468 AGENCY MARKETING
The undertaking of responsibility,
by a development bank or a
financing institution, to act as a
marketing agency on behalf of an
enterprise, for the latter's new
issues of shares and debentures;
this dealing has no underwriting
commitment or obligation.

f   "Agency marketing"
d   Vertriebsagentur

469 BANKING
The business of accepting deposits
and extending credits. Some
development banks, particularly
in countries where commercial
banking has not developed, undertake these functions, partly as a
means for augmenting their
operational resources and partly
as a service to industry, commerce
and trade and the general economy.

f   Opération de banque
d   Bankwesen;

Bankgeschäft;
Bankfach

470 CAPITAL MARKET
PROMOTION
An important function expected
of a development bank, performed normally by underwriting
of equity and debenture issues
of new companies, stipulating
enlistment of such offerings in
the stock exchange, or as pre-
condition of assistance, by
farming out sub-underwriting
rights to others and by
generally disseminating information on corporate industrial
sector and capital market
institutions.

f   Promotion du marché de capital
d   Kapitalmarktförderung

471 CATALYTIC FUNCTION
An attribute associated with the
working of a development bank,
related particularly to the high
degree of professional expertise it is supposed to bring to
bear on projects passing through
the sieve of its evaluation, and
hence the confidence and the
financial participation it can
enlist from institutional and
individual (local and foreign)
investors in these projects,
without the development banks
themselves having to take up a
substantial financial commitment

61

in individual projects.

f   Fonction catalytique
d   Katalytische Funktion

472   COUNSELLING PROGRAMME
A facility provided under extension service programme consisting of formulation of pre-investment studies, project identification and formulation facilities, in-plant diagnostic services, among others. (See: Extension facilities 802)

f   Programme de conseil;
Programme de consultation
d   Beratungsprogramm

473   COUNTER GUARANTEE
The process of risk-sharing whereby a development bank seeks to provide guarantee to an original guarantor on a transaction involving loans or supplies of plant and equipment.

f   Contre-garantie
d   Gegen-Garantie

474   CREDIT INSURANCE SERVICES
Facilities made available for protecting development banks against risks involved in extending financial assistance; suppliers or purchasers also seek to protect respective risks till final settlement of bills or receipt of goods by means of adequate insurance coverage.

f   Services d'assurance-crédit
d   Kreditversicherungsdienste

475   CREDIT SUBSTITUTES, PROVISION OF
Generally connotes provision of assistance in kind, such as built-up factory premises, machinery and equipment, developed sites for locating industries; in regard to farming sector, provision of improved seeds, agricultural implements and fertilizers, insecticides and pesticides.

f   Prestation de succédané de crédit;
Prestation de substitution de crédit
d   Bereitstellung von Kreditsubstituten

476   CREDIT, COMMERCIAL
Provision of credit on commercial terms; some development banks, particularly sponsored through private institutions, operate on these norms mainly in regard to interest rates and repayment period.

f   Crédit commercial
d   Handelskredit;
Warenkredit

477   CREDIT, CONSUMER
A method of financing consumer durables, either by way of mortgage, installment credit, or hire purchase.

f   Crédit de consommation
d   Konsumentenkredit

478   CREDIT, DEFERRED
The process of financing durable and non-durable articles and equipment normally, and fixed assets particularly, by suppliers whereby the articles, equipment and fixed assets are received in advance, but payment thereof is deferred for a number of years. Some development banks provide guarantee facilities in these transactions. (See: Credit, suppliers' 485)

f   Crédit différé
d   Kreditaufschub

479 CREDIT, DOCUMENTARY
The process of paying for supplies procured from foreign countries; involves opening of letters of credit favoring foreign suppliers, and drawing up of documentary bills by the importer in favor of the supplier.

f   Crédit documentaire;
    Accréditif documentaire;
    Crédit sur titres
d   Kredit gegen Sicherheit;
    Dokumentenkredit

480 CREDIT, HIRE PURCHASE
Financing arrangements to "buy now and pay in installments". A method normally made use of by suppliers of consumer durables and of plant and equipment as a sales promotion device; normally has stringent features by way of relatively higher costs. Some development banks also have such programs. The title to the fixed assets, articles and equipment remain the property of the financier, till full payment is made.

f   Crédit de vente à tempérament
d   Ratenkaufkredit;
    Kredit zur Finanzierung von Abzahlungsgeschäften

481 CREDIT, INSTALLMENT
A method of financing consumer durables, or industrial machinery and equipment, whereby the purchaser - against a proportion of down payment - acquires the assets and the title to the property at the outset. Some development banks engage in these operations.

f   Crédit de paiement partiel;
    Crédit de versements échelonnés
d   Teilzahlungskredit

482 CREDIT, MORTGAGE;
    CREDIT ON MORTGAGE

Extension of credit against a collateral of assets created from the loan amount; normally associated with housing finance, including factory building. The ownership rests with the purchaser, right from the day of acquisition.

f   Crédit hypothécaire
d   Hypothekarkredit

483 CREDIT, ROLLOVER;
    CREDIT, REVOLVING
A method of replenishing working funds by reviving old credits. Also used as a method to re-fund maturing bonds with new ones. (See: Funding 915; Funding operation 916)

f   Accréditif automatiquement renouvelable;
    Crédit par acceptation renouvelable
d   Kredit gegen automatisch verlängerbaren Kreditbrief;
    Kredit gegen Prolongationsakzept

484 CREDIT, SUPERVISED
Extension of loan assistance for productive purposes such as farming, small industry, wherein the development bank regulates withdrawals from the loan amount against specific acquisition of assets or services and provides assistance in the proper utilization of the funds.

f   Crédit contrôlé
d   Überwachter Kredit

485 CREDIT, SUPPLIERS'
Facilities offered by manufacturers and overseas suppliers of plant and machinery to their purchasers, of paying the cost of these over a number of years. Generally, this facility is offered to enterprises in

developing countries by manufacturers from developed countries as an inducement to buy plant and equipment and is generally associated with more stringent terms.

f Crédit d'approvisionnement
d Ausstattungskredit;
  Maschinenkredit

486 CREDIT, WORKING CAPITAL;
    CREDIT, TRADING CAPITAL
    Provision of working funds, particularly a portion or full amount of the permanent element as a part of project financing.

f Crédit de roulemement
d Betriebskapitalkredit

487 DEVELOPMENTAL
    ACTIVITIES;
    PROMOTIONAL ACTIVITIES
    Functions allied primarily to the development of projects for financing and also to the sectors served by the development bank; includes such activities as project identification, promotion of capital market, technical and managerial counselling, economic, commercial and technical intelligence service, policies oriented towards upgrading of organizational, financial and technical practices of assisted enterprises.

f Activités de promotion;
  Activités de développement
d Entwicklungsfördernde Aktivitäten

488 DISBURSEMENT
    The process of allowing withdrawals (or making payments) from loan amounts already sanctioned and committed against pre-determined schedules in the implementation of the project.

f Déboursement;
  Avance

d Auszahlung;
  Ausgabe;
  Verauslagung

489 DIVERSIFICATION OF RISK
    The objective of development banks, investors and enterprises respectively, seeking to invest in different classes of shares, in different types of business and/or to produce several products.

f Diversification de risque
d Risikostreuung

490 ECONOMIC EFFICIENCY,
    PROMOTION OF
    The efficiency with which scarce resources are used and organized to achieve stipulated economic ends; one of the important functions of development banks performed through their project evaluation and post-finance supervisory activities.

f Promotion de l'efficacité
  économique
d Förderung der wirtschaftlichen
  Leistungsfähigkeit

491 ENTREPRENEUR DEVELOP-
    MENT
    The process of involving in industrial development new promotores who are capable of bearing risks, exploiting opportunities as they present themselves within a time horizon, with abilities to do things which have not been done before.

f Développement des entrepreneurs
d Entwicklung des Unternehmer-
  tums;
  Unternehmerentwicklung

492 EQUITY INVESTMENT
    Subscribing to equity shares, not necessarily of new

floatations, as a means of
profitable deployment of investment funds.

f   Investissement au capital
    originaire
d   Investierung in Grundkapital

493   EQUITY PARTICIPATION
    Development bank subscription
    to the equity shares of newly
    floated enterprises, as a
    measure to enlist larger public
    or institutional participation in
    the stocks of the new enterprise.

f   Participation au capital
    originaire
d   Beteiligung am Grundkapital

494   EQUITY SALES
    The process of selling from out
    of development bank's portfolio,
    as a means to activate the capital
    market and feed capital market
    demand for such scrips; also
    resorted to as a method for
    revolving a development banks'
    own resources.

f   Ventes du capital originaire
d   Verkäufe von Grundkapital

495   EXPORT FINANCE ASSISTANCE
    One of the functions of some
    development banks; provision of
    financial assistance particularly
    geared to export oriented
    industries and export promoting
    activities.

f   Assistance au financement
    d'exportation
d   Exportfinanzierungsunterstützung

496   FINANCING, ACCOUNTS
      RECEIVABLE
    A type of business financing in
    which firms either sell their
    accounts receivable (factoring)
    or pledge them as collateral for
    loans (discounting).

f   Financement de dettes actives;
    Financement de créances
d   Finanzierung von Aussen-
    ständen

497   FINANCING, AGRICULTURAL
    Financing of agricultural
    development projects; some
    development banks are designed
    primarily to promote the
    modernization and development
    of agriculture.

f   Financement du secteur
    agricole
d   Agrarfinanzierung;
    Finanzierung des Agrarsektors

498   FINANCE, BALANCING;
      SUPPLEMENTAL CREDIT
    Additional loan financing
    provided by a development
    bank on a project already
    financed by it to meet unfore-
    seen cost escalation; also
    denotes financing of gaps left
    after participations by major
    financing institutions.

f   Crédit supplémentaire
d   Zusatzkredit

499   FINANCING, BALANCING
      EQUIPMENT
    Small loans, particularly in
    foreign currency, provided by
    development banks, to finance
    the importation of pieces of
    equipment, which are found to
    be crucial for the efficient
    operation of an enterprise. Such
    financing in small volumes
    are not generally encouraged
    by development banks since
    these are not regarded as pro-
    ject-financing.

f   Financement des machines
d   Maschinenteilfinanzierung

500   FINANCING, CONCESSIONAL;
      SOFT LOAN

Arrangements whereby an
international or national financing
agency extends assistance on
terms and conditions more lenient
than applicable to its conventional
programmes of assistance.

f   Financement de concession;
     Prêt à taux de faveur
d   Vorzugsfinanzierung;
     Weiche Anleihe

501   FINANCING, CONSORTIA
       A situation where one national or
       international agency enlists, under
       its aegis, the participation of one
       or more other national and/or
       international agency, or agencies,
       for financing a project.

f   Financement de consortium
d   Konsortiumfinanzierung

502   FINANCING, CONVENTIONAL
       Extending financial and related
       services with normal terms and
       conditions as determined on the
       basis of commercial norms.

f   Financement conventionnel
d   Konventionelle Finanzierung

503   FINANCING, DEVELOPMENT
       Constitutes the primary function
       of a development bank; consists of
       providing a variety of financial
       and related assistance with a view
       to promote development, bearing
       the risk of the capacity of the
       financed project to generate funds
       for repayment, as against the
       traditional concept of lending
       against collateral.

f   Financement de développement
d   Entwicklungsfinanzierung

504   FINANCING, JOINT
       A situation where two or more
       national and/or international
       agencies combine to finance a
       project in agreed proportions
       and terms.

f   Financement commun;
     Financement en participation
d   Gemeinsame Finanzierung

505   FINANCING, LONG-TERM
       Extending financial assistance
       to projects with maturities
       beyond six to seven years.

f   Financement à long terme
d   Langfristige Finanzierung

506   FINANCING, MEDIUM-TERM
       Extending project loans with a
       period of maturity ranging over
       one year and normally under
       five to six years.

f   Financement à moyen terme
d   Mittelfristige Finanzierung

507   FINANCING, PARALLEL
       A situation where several
       national and/or international
       agencies finance parts of a
       project, the decision to
       finance being taken independent-
       ly.

f   Financement parallèle
d   Parallelfinanzierung

508   FINANCING, PUBLIC
         UTILITY
       Extending financial assistance
       to enterprises catering essential
       services or producing
       commodities of importance
       to public life or the economy.
       Such financing normally is
       motivated not primarily by
       commercial norms but by de-
       velopmental obligations.

f   Financement des entreprises
     de service public
d   Finanzierung von gemein-
     nützigen Unternehmen

509   FINANCING, SHORT-TERM
       Extending loans of a working
       capital nature with maturities
       under one year at the first

instance.

f   Financement à court terme
d   Kurzfristige Finanzierung

510   FINANCING, SUBSIDIZED
Arrangements whereby a development bank extends assistance, at
the instance of national governments or other developmental
agencies, at rates of interest
lower and repayment periods
longer than those applicable to
its conventional financing, the
difference in interest rates
often being made good by the
initiating agency concerned.

f   Financement subventionné
d   Subventionierte Finanzierung

511   FREE LIMIT
The discretionary power accorded
by a lending agency to a development bank to process and approve
individual sub-loans out of a given
line of credit, below certain
amounts, without prior approval
of the lending agency. Normally,
these limits are relaxed from
time to time depending upon the
maturity of the development bank
in regard to its professional
competence and decision-making
process.

f   Limite libre
d   Freigrenze

512   IDENTIFICATION OF PROJECTS
The process of determining the
prospect for the project in terms
of an overall development plan,
of market and of overall viability.

f   Identification des projets
d   Projektidentifizierung

513   IMPORT SUBSTITUTION
Process of substituting an imported
product by indigenous production
through the project; an important
objective expected of development

banks by giving preference in
the selection of projects for
financing.

f   Substitution des importations
d   Importsubstitution;
Importersatz

514   INTEREST RATE
In the context of development
banks, the interest rate bears
a relationship to their own costs,
average or marginal, of borrowings and the prevailing market
rate. Besides, the rates charged
may also differ amongst sectors
or industries assisted, or
amongst clients; the latter
particularly for closely-held
companies as a means of sharing
in the increased profits resulting
from proffered assistance.

f   Taux d'intérêt
d   Zinssatz

515   INTEREST RATE CEILING
The maximum rate that can be
charged to any clients by a
development bank; may be self-
imposed, or regulated by
monetary or financial authorities.

f   Plafond de taux d'intérêt
d   Höchstgrenze des Zinssatzes

516   INTEREST RATE,
EFFECTIVE
The actual cost of money to a
borrower; includes, in addition
to stated rate of interest,
incidental expenses in obtaining
the loan, as also interest
earnings foregone, if any, for
collaterals offered.

f   Taux d'intérêt effectif
d   Effektiver Zinssatz

517   INTEREST RATE, FOREIGN
CURRENCY
The rate of interest charged by

a development bank on its foreign
currency loans; often these rates
reflect the scarcity value of
foreign currency, and hence, bear
a relatively higher charge.
Instances of subsidization by way
of a lower rate relative to local
currency loans are also observed.

f   Taux d'intérêt de devises
d   Devisenzinssatz

518   INTEREST RATE, PENALTY
A higher rate of interest enjoined
on borrowers for failure to meet
repayment obligations in stipulated
intervals.

f   Taux d'intérêt pénal;
     Taux d'intérêt de pénalité
d   Strafzinssatz

519   INTEREST RATE, SUBSIDIZED;
       INTEREST RATE,
       CONCESSIONAL
Making available long-term funds
to development banks at nominal
rates of interest, or rates of
interest much below the prevailing market rate.

f   Taux d'intérêt subventionné
d   Subventionierung des Zinssatzes

520   INTEREST SPREAD
The difference between the average
rate of interest paid by a development
bank for long-term borrowings
and the average rate of interest
charged to its clients.

f   Echelonnement de taux d'intérêt
d   Zinssatzspanne

521   INTEREST SPREAD,
       NEGATIVE
A situation when the average rate
of interest paid for long-term
borrowings exceeds the average
rate of interest recovered.

f   Echelonnement négatif de taux
     d'intérêt

d   Negative Zinssatzspanne

522   INVESTMENT
Normally refers to direct
subscriptions to stocks, shares
and other instruments; also for
obligations arising out of
underwriting commitments.

f   Placement;
     Investissement
d   Investierung;
     Anlage

523   INVESTMENT BANKING
The marketing of new corporate
shares; the institution acts
as the middleman between the
issuer of securities and the
investing public, facilitating
the flow of available savings
into investment.

f   Banque de placement
d   Bankgeschäft in Anlagewerten;
     Investitionsgeschäft

524   INVESTMENT PLAN
The expectation of a business
firm for investment in new
plants and equipment.

f   Plan d'investissement
d   Investitionsplan

525   INVESTMENT POLICY
Guidelines enjoined on development banks, either through
specific provision in their
Charter of Incorporation, or as
specially adopted policy
resolutions, in matters
connected with volume of total
assistance, or types of assistance in one enterprise, or in
one industry, or in enterprises
promoted by one group. The
obligation to revolve its funds
and to be able to provide assistance to as many number of new
enterprises as possible, the
need to feed the capital market

with a regular supply of new
scrips, the need for holding on
to its newly acquired investment
portfolio, to enable such new enterprises to acquire stability, are
also some of the factors governing
the investment policy of a development bank. (See: Bank, development 391; Investment strategy 526)

f Politique de placement
d Investitionspolitik

526 INVESTMENT STRATEGY
The policy adopted by a development bank to maximize its income
from operations, on the one hand,
and to regulate and help the assisted
enterprises and the capital market
on the other; e.g. investment in new
shares or debentures is risky
besides locking up funds for a long
time. On the other hand, this is
necessary to help new enterprises
come up; likewise, when assisted
enterprises enter profitable
commercial operations, the need
to revolve funds and to feed the
capital market enjoins development banks to sell from their
portfolio. The investment strategy
strikes a mean between these and
other similar situations.

f Stratégie de placement
d Investitionsstrategie

527 INVESTMENT, TOKEN
A part of the catalytic role of
development banks wherein their
major contribution consists in
enlisting the participation of
other institutional or individual
investors in a project, on the
basis of their nominal financial
participation, but more important-
ly, on the basis of the confidence
inspired by the fact that the
project investigated is testified
as being viable, by the development bank.

f Investissement symbolique;
Placement symbolique
d Symbolinvestierung;
Symbolische Investierung

528 LENDING OPERATIONS
Activities concerned with
extending various types of
loan assistance.

f Opérations de prêt
d Darlehensgeschäfte

529 LENDING, COMMERCIAL
Loans under commercial terms,
normally for large industrial
projects.

f Prêt commercial
d Handelsdarlehen

530 LENDING, INDIGENOUS
Organizational mechanism
evolved by some development
banks for providing loans for
industries promoted by the
indigenous population, as
opposed to enterprises promoted
by expatriate population.

f Prêt indigène;
Prêt pour les indigènes
d Darlehen für Einheimische

531 LENDING, RURAL
Organizational mechanism
evolved by some development
banks which provides industrial
and agricultural loans in rural
areas.

f Prêt rural
d Ländliche Darlehen

532 LIMIT FOR EQUITY
INVESTMENT
Stipulations prescribing
limitations on the volume of
assistance proffered as investment in equities; such
limitations are imposed in
regard to total equity investments that can be extended at

a point of time, or the volume of equity investment in one enterprise; the former being measured as a proportion of the equity plus quasi-equity of the development bank, and the latter as proportion of the equity of the assisted enterprise.

f   Limite de placement
d   Grenze für Grundkapitalinvestierung;
Limitierung der Grundkapitalinvestierung

533   LOAN PROGRAMME, SMALL
Activities concerned with extending loans to small enterprises or loans in small volumes.

f   Programme de petit crédit
d   Klein-Anleiheprogramm

534   LOAN, BRIDGING
Financial assistance rendered by a development bank to a project to fill the gap left uncovered by other financing agencies; normally forms a part of the catalytic role of the development bank.

f   Financement pour combler une lacune
d   Überbrückungsfinanzierung

535   LOAN, CALL;
CALLABLE LOAN
A commercial bank loan payable on demand.

f   Crédit remboursable sur demande
d   Sichtkredit

536   LOAN, CONVERSION
Loans which carry the right to be renewed as loans with new terms, or to be converted at a future date into other forms of investments. Development banks attach such concessional terms and rights on borrowers depending on the situation of cash flow and profitability rates of the borrower.

f   Emprunt de conversion
d   Umschuldungsanleihe;
Konversionsanleihe

537   LOAN, DEBENTURE;
LOAN ON DEBENTURES
Loans floated by corporations or development banks themselves in the capital market, normally without the backing of collateral; such debentures are negotiable instruments.

f   Emprunt-obligations;
Emprunt d'obligations
d   Obligationenanleihe

538   LOAN, FACTORY TYPE
Specialized financing schemes evolved by some term financing institutions including development banks, particularly in regard to working capital requirements of small enterprises, whereby clean loans are provided, subject to the raw materials so purchased being legally regarded as the property of the financing institution, with the borrower given the use of the raw materials for day-to-day operations.

f   Financement du capital de roulement
d   Rohmaterialkredit

539   LOAN, FOREIGN CURRENCY
Sub-loans made to local enterprises by development banks on the lines of credits obtained by them from international agencies.

f   Crédit en devises;
Prêt en devises
d   Darlehen in Devisen;
Devisenanleihe

540   LOAN, HARD
Loans with conventional terms and conditions, such as maximum

rate of interest, minimum repayment period, absence of grace period, tied to particular sources for procurement. (See: Financing, conventional 502)

f   Prêt de dures conditions
d   Harte Anleihe

541   LOAN, HARD CURRENCY
A foreign currency loan repayable in a hard currency, usually U.S. dollars. (See: Loan, soft currency 545)

f   Prêt en devise forte;
     Crédit en monnaie forte
d   Anleihe in harter Währung

542   LOAN, LOCAL CURRENCY
Loan operations of development banks or financial institutions in the currency of the country, as oppposed to foreign currency loans from external sources. (See: Loan, foreign currency 539)

f   Prêt en monnaie locale
d   Anleihe in Inlandswährung;
     Anleihe in lokaler Währung

543   LOAN, PERSONAL
A loan made by a bank to a private individual to cover personal expenditure of a specified kind - an alternative to hire purchase.

f   Prêt personnel
d   Personalkredit

544   LOAN, SECURED
Loans normally of long term duration which are secured by specific assets of the borrower.

f   Prêt garanti;
     Crédit nanti
d   Gedeckte Anleihe

545   LOAN, SOFT CURRENCY
A foreign loan repayable in the receiving country's own currency.

(See: Loan, hard currency 541)

f   Prêt en monnaie faible
d   Anleihe in weicher Währung

546   LOAN, SUB-
Individual loans extended by development banks from a credit line obtained by it from an international lending agency or from the Government.

f   Sous-prêt
d   Unteranleihe;
     Subanleihe

547   LOAN, TIED
Loans, normally in foreign currency, that can be utilized for purchase of equipment and services only in the country from which the original line of credit or assistance was obtained by the development bank or the Government.

f   Prêt lié;
     Prêt à clause restrictive
d   Gebundene Anleihe;
     Gebundener Kredit

548   LOAN, UNSECURED;
       LOAN, CLEAN
A loan made without security or other legal claim upon specific property to back the debt.

f   Prêt non-garanti;
     Crédit en blanc
d   Ungedeckte Anleihe

549   MANAGED FUNDS
Resources provided by the government or other official agencies to a development bank for being sub-lent to given sectors or industries, either on the basis of an agency commission, or on stated nominal interest mark-up.

f   Fonds administrés
d   Verwaltete Geldmittel

550 OVERDRAFT
One of the methods adopted by
commercial banks for lending,
the borrower being given
permission to draw cheques for
an agreed sum - the amount of
the overdraft - for a specific
period of time in excess of the
amount standing to his credit,
interest being calculated on a
daily basis on that part of the
amount which is drawn.

f Découvert
d Kontenüberziehung

551 PERFORMANCE GUARANTEE
An activity involving extension
of guarantee in favor of a supplier
of plant and equipment or that of
a process, against risks involved
in their performance as claimed by
the supplier; normally this con-
stitutes an important device for
the induction of technology, processes and techniques of production, hitherto untried in the
country.

f Garantie d'exécution;
Garantie d'accomplissement
d Ausführungsgarantie;
Leistungsgarantie

552 POLICY STATEMENT
Basic guidelines governing the
capitalization, organization,
management and operational
criteria, stipulated in unambigu-
ous terms, either in the Incorporation Charter of the
development bank, or as special
resolutions passed by its Board
of Directors, from time to time.
These guidelines include proportion of borrowed funds to equity
of a development bank itself, total
volume and permissible volume of
term loans to an assisted enterprise, volume and variety of
investments in one group or in
one company, extent of collateral
and assets coverage, extent of
promoters' contribution, type
of representation in the
management of assisted firms,
among others.

f Formule politique;
Prise de position politique
d Erklärung über die einzuschlagende Politik

553 POST-FINANCE SUPER-
VISION
Essentially an extension of the
project evaluation function of
a development bank, seeking to
ensure that the various con-
figuration of circumstanses
assumed for the project at the
appraisal stage, in fact are made
available in its construction and
implementation stages. Measures
taken by development banks include keeping a close watch on
the project through periodic
returns, field visits, and provision of facilities, either on
their own or through other
agencies, to facilitate the
timely construction and efficient
operation of the project.

f Contrôle d'après financement
d Nachfinanzierungskontrolle

554 PRE-INVESTMENT SERVICES
Activities undertaken by
development banks, on their
own or in cooperation with
development agencies, to
identify industrial investment
opportunities and to disseminate
such information to prospective
investors. Preparation of a
variety of economic, market
and technical studies such as
industry prospect sheets,
market studies, model schemes,
feasibility studies and/or
crystalizing specific ideas of
prospective entrepreneurs in
the form of bankable projects,

are some of the activities in
these respects.

f   Services de pré-financement
d   Vor-Investierungsdienste

555   PROCEDURES, TENDER
Procedures laid down by a
development bank in regard to
procurement of plant, equipment
and other services, required for
the assisted project.

f   Procédure d'approvisionnement
d   Beschaffungsverfahren

556   PROCUREMENT POLICY
The procedure set forth by a
development bank on its borrower,
or by an international financing
company on a development bank,
in regard to the manner and
sources for obtaining supplies
under the proceeds of the loan;
basically such procedures are
meant to vouchsafe the quality
of plant and equipment, the competitiveness of prices, the suitability of the process and the associated facilities required for the
given project. It is normal for
international development banks
to prescribe different procurement procedures (international
bidding, canvassing, shopping)
depending on the volume of the
sub-loan on the one hand and the
competence and the level of
expertise of the development bank
to evaluate and safeguard these
factors, on the other.

f   Politique d'approvisionnement;
Politique d'acquisition
d   Maschinen- und Materialbeschaff-
ungspolitik

557   PROGRAMME-BASED
ASSISTANCE
Financial assistance provided by
international or regional development financing institutions to
national development agencies
or financing institutions intended for financing a package
of related projects under a
programme of development.
Examples are regional development programmes, development
of individual industries, farm
improvement and irrigation
development programmes.

f   Assistance à titre d'un programme
d   Programmfinanzierung

558   PROJECT-BASED
ASSISTANCE
Financial assistance provided
by national development banks
or regional and international
finance agencies, that is based
on an evaluation of the project
as to its operational viability,
financial requirements, and
volume and variety of assistance
required. A related assumption
is that the security for the
repayment of the assistance
granted is the inherent viability
of the project as contrasted to
the collateral approach of a
term-financing institution.

f   Assistance à titre d'un projet
spécifique
d   Projektfinanzierung

559   PROJECT FORMULATION
The process of assessing the
necessary resources, schedul-
ing of inputs and outputs, time
preference, discount rates,
managerial and manpower
requirements in order to
develop a "project idea" into
a bankable or fundable project
report.

f   Elaboration d'un projet;
Formulation d'un projet
d   Projektformulierung

560 PROJECT LINE
The procedure adopted by an international financing agency to channel funds through a development bank for financing specific projects as against a general credit line which a development bank can utilize for financing a number of projects from a variety of industries. (See: Programme-based assistance 557; Project-based assistance 558)

f Ligne de projet
d Projektlinie

561 RATE, BORROWING
The rate of interest to be paid by the development bank for its own borrowed funds.

f Taux de crédit;
Taux d'emprunts
d Borgzinssatz

562 RATE, COMMERCIAL LOAN
The rate of interest charged by an international finance agency or a development bank under conventional operational procedures as against concessional operational procedures.

f Taux de crédit commercial
d Zinssatz für Handelsanleihen

563 RATE, LENDING
The normal rate of interest plus associated charges levied by a development bank on borrowers.

f Taux de prêt
d Leihzinssatz

564 RATIO, CONCENTRATION
The percentage of total assistance provided by a development bank to a given industry, a given number of borrowers, or a given region.

f Taux de concentration
d Konzentrationsintensität;
Konzentrationsgrad

565 REFINANCING;
REDISCOUNTING
A method adopted by a national central financing agency, such as the Central Bank, or an apex development bank, to replenish the funds of a financial intermediary or a development bank – against the latter's fund commitments generally, or in specified categories of industries.

f Refinancement
d Refinanzierung

566 RESOURCE MOBILIZATION
An important objective of a development bank, expected to be attained by highlighting investment opportunities in the economy through various measures of project identification and other promotional activities, as also by promoting the productive use of the capital so mobilized through its project evaluation disciplines and post-finance assistance. Other ways of resource mobilization pursued by a development bank consist of promotion of new- or activation of dormant capital markets, introduction of new investment papers, increasing underwriting activities, among others. Development banks, because of their knowledge of local conditions and expertise, serve as an important channel for external private and institutional capital into the country.

f Mobilisation des ressources
d Kapitalmobilisierung

567 RISK SPREAD
The process whereby a development bank or an investment company seeks to diversify its investments amongst a wide

range of industries.

f   Diversification de risque
d   Risikostreuung

568   RISK, CALCULATED
Exposure to uncertainties in extending financial assistance of various types, the extent of which is reckoned beforehand by development banks through the process of project appraisal.

f   Risque calculé
d   Berechnetes Risiko;
     Kalkuliertes Risiko

569   RISK, CREDIT
Assessments made by the development bank of a borrower or a project as to whether and to what extent the latter is worth and dependable for extending the assistance sought.

f   Risque de crédit
d   Kreditrisiko

570   RISK, FOREIGN EXCHANGE
The uncertainties associated with official changes in the par value of a local currency vis-a-vis the foreign-currency sub-loans extended by development banks. A development bank usually protects itself against this risk in a variety of ways, but eventually by passing on this risk to the sub-borrowers. Other ways include securing guarantees of the Government or the Central Bank; and securing commercial insurance coverage, among others.

f   Risque de devises
d   Devisenrisiko

571   SUPERVISION OF PROJECTS
The process of controlling the procurement, disbursements,

accountability and construction phase of individual projects through progress reports and plant visits.

f   Surveillance de projets;
     Contrôle de projets
d   Überwachung von Projekten

572   TECHNICAL ADVISORY
SERVICES
An important function in extension service facilities, comprising advice on sources, prices and selection of machinery and equipment provided by development banks or development agencies. (See: Extension facilities 802)

f   Services consultatifs techniques
d   Technische Beratungsdienste

573   UNDERWRITING
An important function of development banks consisting in providing guarantees to take over a stated proportion of newly floated shares or debentures offered to the public. The development bank's readiness to purchase such newly floated papers serves as an essential inducement for other institutions or industrial investors to come forth to buy such papers. (See: Underwriter 465)

f   Garantie d'émission
d   Emissionsgarantie

574   WITHDRAWAL PROCEDURES
The methods prescribed by a development bank for drawing down amounts of money from a loan committed for a project.

f   Procédure de retrait de fonds
d   Kapitalabhebungsverfahren

VI.
PROJECT EVALUATION ASPECTS AND TECHNIQUES
ASPECTS ET TECHNIQUES D'EVALUATION DE PROJET
GESICHTSPUNKTE UND TECHNIKEN DER PROJEKTBEGUTACHTUNG

575   ANALYSIS, COST BENEFIT
Economic calculation to arrive
at a single indicator of the
worth of a project; derived by
comparing all items of costs
against the value of all benefits
to be derived from the project.

f   Analyse coût-bénéfice
d   Kosten-Ertragsanalyse;
Kosten-Gewinnanalyse

576   ANALYSIS, CREDIT
Collection and examination of
data concerning the extent and
volume of financial accommodation
that can be granted to an enterprise; term used normally by
commercial bankers in assessing
overdraft facilities for clients.

f   Analyse de crédit
d   Kreditanalyse

577   ANALYSIS, CROSS-SECTION
The process of collecting, collat-
ing and deriving conclusions from
economic, commercial and
financial data for different groups
of firms, agencies, sectors or
countries at the same or different
points of time.

f   Analyse de secteurs croisés
d   Kreuzsektorenanalyse

578   ANALYSIS, DEMAND
The study of the consumers'
demand for goods and services.

f   Analyse de demande

d   Nachfrageanalyse

579   ANALYSIS, INVESTMENT-
EFFECTIVENESS
A process of economic evaluation
of the costs and benefits of a
given project taking into
account the totality of cost –
direct, indirect – and output or
benefits both not normally
reflected in money value.

f   Analyse d'efficacité d'un
investissement
d   Investitionsertragsanalyse

580   ANALYSIS, PROBABILITY
An extension of the sensitivity
test; which allows for variations
in costs and benefits value,
based on the probabilities that
different values will be realized.
A probability of distribution for
the rate of return can be
generated through simulation
techniques. This test offers a
better picture of risk involved
in a project than a single value
calculation. (See: Sensitivity
test 742)

f   Analyse de probabilité
d   Wahrscheinlichkeitsanalyse

581   ANALYSIS, RATIO
Yardsticks to measure
performance, profitability,
capital structure, liquidity
position, etc. as well as the
overall situation of an enterprise

by relating various accounting items.

f   Analyse de taux
d   Bilanzanalyse

582   APPRAISAL, COLLATERAL
Assessment of the worth of the assets offered as security, in terms of their liquidation value, against financial assistance considered.

f   Evaluation de garantie
d   Deckungsbewertung;
Sicherheitsbewertung

583   APPRAISAL, CREDIT
WORTHINESS
Assessment of the borrower in terms of the risk involved in extending the financial assistance.

f   Evaluation de bon état de crédit
d   Bewertung der Kreditwürdigkeit

584   APPRAISAL, ECONOMIC
The study of the economic implications of a project, as a first step in assessing its acceptability.

f   Evaluation économique
d   Ökonomische Bewertung;
Wirtschaftliche Bewertung

585   APPRAISAL, FINANCIAL
Assessment of a project in regard to requirements of capital, determination of the capital structure including proportion of owners' capital to borrowed capital, fixed and working capital, ideal structure of means of financing, determination of the cash-flow and profitability of the project, with the overall view of assessing its financial viability.

f   Evaluation financière
d   Finanzielle Bewertung;
Finanzbewertung

586   APPRAISAL, MANAGEMENT
An assessment of entrepreneural resourcefulness of the project promoter including his managerial competence and those of key personnel likely to be brought in by him against the assessed needs of the project for implementing and operating it. This aspect is considered to be the most challenging exercise in project evaluation.

f   Evaluation de la gestion
d   Bewertung der Geschäftsleitung

587   APPRAISAL, MARKET
An assessment of the volume, extent and expected unit realization in the context of competing producers, both indigenous and overseas. Additionally, it also consists of visualizing the appropriate selling arrangements and other marketing requirements to be evolved by the enterprise.

f   Evaluation du marché
d   Marktbewertung

588   APPRAISAL, TECHNICAL
An assessment of the engineering aspects of a project including process, plant capacity, suitability of plant and equipment, plant facilities and essential input requirements, such as power, water, materials, technical skill with the overall view of ascertaining the technical viability of a project.

f   Evaluation technique
d   Technische Bewertung

589   AREA SURVEYS
Study undertaken by a development bank or development agency by itself or in collaboration with other institutions, to identify potential new avenues

of industrial development in
particular areas or regions, to
spot specific projects, to develop
these projects and to interest new
entrepreneurs - local or overseas - in these projects, to
take up the establishment of these
projects on their own in various
centres in the country.

f   Etudes de la région
d   Gebietsstudien;
    Gebietserhebung;
    Gebietsuntersuchungen

590   BANKABILITY OF A PROJECT
      A measure of the viability of a
      project as revealed by docu-
      mentation and project details, to
      elicit the confidence of a develop-
      ment bank or a financial insti-
      tution for financial support.

f   Banquabilité d'un projet
d   Bankfähigkeit eines Projektes

591   BANKER'S REFERENCE
      A process of ascertaining the past
      financial stability of a prospective
      borrower on the basis of records
      of his dealings with his commercial
      bank and other trade channels.

f   Référence de banquier
d   Bankreferenz

592   BENEFITS, DIRECT,
      PRIMARY
      Generally the term denotes a
      measure of the visible and
      immediate benefits accruing from
      the project. Such benefits are
      evidenced from the additional
      units of output, such as kW of
      power generated, or facilities
      created, such as additional
      mileage of roads laid, acres
      of land brought into irrigation,
      etc.

f   Bénéfices directs et primaires
d   Direkt-primäre Nutzen

593   BENEFITS, INDIRECT,
      SECONDARY
      A measure of the additional
      social and economic satisfaction
      expected to be fulfilled by
      goods and services generated
      through the project.

f   Bénéfices indirects et
    secondaires
d   Indirekt-sekundäre Nutzen

594   BENEFITS, INDUCED
      Benefits likely to accrue from
      the project to dependent enter-
      prises or to individuals not
      directly employed by the pro-
      ject, by way of sub-contracting
      or tertiary employment
      opportunities.

f   Bénéfices induits
d   Zusätzlich herbeigeführte
    Nutzen

595   BENEFITS, NATIONAL
      A measure of the utility of a
      project to the community as a
      whole by way of augmenting
      supplies of goods and services,
      promoting import substitution
      and hence, savings in foreign
      exchange or export promotion
      and thus increasing foreign
      exchange earnings, or in-
      creasing employment avenues.

f   Bénéfices nationaux
d   Nationale Nutzen

596   BENEFITS, NET
      The excess of cash receipts
      over cash expenses for any
      year; the term is not the
      equivalent of profits since the
      latter includes depreciation and
      some other items which normal
      accounting procedures do not
      recognize as "profits".

f   Bénéfices nets
d   Nettonutzen

597 BENEFITS, STEMMING
A concept used in national accounting; consists of net value added as a result of subsequent handling, processing, marketing of the product or services generated by the main project.

f Bénéfices de procédé additionnel; Bénéfices d'opération de finissage
d Nutzen durch Weiterverarbeitung von Produkten; Nutzen durch Veredlungsverfahren

598 BEST PROFIT EQUILIBRIUM
The point at which a firm's marginal cost of production equals its marginal revenues.

f Equilibre de profit optimum
d Bestes Profitgleichgewicht

599 BREAKEVEN POINT
That level of production at which total cost equals gross income; in other words, that rate of plant utilization when neither a loss is incurred nor profit made.

f Point à jeu égal; Point "breakeven"
d Nutzschwelle

600 CAPACITY, EXCESS
A situation where the output potential exceeds the demand potential in the market; may be brought about, either by falling demand, or unfulfilled expectations of market demand which production potential has created.

f Excédent de capacité
d Uberkapazität

601 CAPACITY, MAXIMUM; CAPACITY, INSTALLED
Production or output potential of a unit with its existing set of machinery and equipment, assuming that other operative conditions are assured (availability of raw materials, demand for its products, etc.) and that the unit functions uninterrupted throught the year.

f Capacité maximum; Capacité montée
d Maximalkapazität; Installierte Kapazität; Höchstkapazität

602 CAPITAL RECOVERY FACTOR; C.R.F. ·
Represents the annual cost of depreciation and interest accruing to a volume of investment; obtained by multiplying the investment to be recovered by the given coefficient. (See: Present worth factor 672)

f · Facteur de la récupération du capital
d Kapitalrückgewinnungsfaktor

603 CAPITAL, COST OF
The aggregate of costs incurred in the total capitalization of a development bank or an enterprise, i.e. expected dividend rate on equity, the cost of issuing equity capital, interest on borrowed funds and the costs associated with such borrowings.

f Coût de capital
d Kapitalkosten

604 CAPITAL, FIXED
Comprises assets of a firm which are of a fairly durable character. such as the premises, fixtures and fittings, or the factory buildings and equipment.

f Capital fixe; Capitaux fixes; Capital mobilisé
d Anlagekapital; Anlagevermögen

605 CAPITAL, INSTITUTIONAL
The volume of participation,

in the capitalization of a project, by institutional investors or term lending agencies, including the development bank, as opposed to the capital brought in by the owner.

f   Capital institutionnel
d   Institutionelles Kapital

606   CAPITAL, OPTIONAL
Difference between the amounts of capital costs of two truly alternative projects.

f   Capital d'option
d   Optionskapital

607   CASH-FLOW
The stream of funds flowing into and out of an enterprise during a period of time; generally on the inflow side it comprises net earnings including depreciation and other chargeable allowances, and withdrawals from committed borrowings; and on the outflow side, statutory obligations (taxes), dividends, interest and payment of principal.

f   Ressources et applications des fonds
d   Kassenzu- und Abfluss; Cash-flow

608   CASH-FLOW FORECAST
A tabulation of the plans of the enterprise in terms of the effect of these plans on the cash resources.

f   Prévision de ressources et applications des fonds
d   Cash-flow Planung; Planung des Kassenzu- und Abflusses

609   CASH-FLOW, DISCOUNTED; DCF
Process of ascertaining the present investment worth of a project in terms of future earning

values. The basic underlying concept consists in the fact that money has an earning power over time. (See: Yield method 750; Present value method 671)

f   Ressources et applications des fonds escomptées
d   Diskontiertes Cash-flow

610   CHECKLIST
A standard list of points for eliciting information on a project, or a promoter of a project, as a basis for evaluation

f   Liste de contrôle
d   Kontrolliste

611   CIF
Abbreviation for "cost, insurance and freight"; denotes responsibility of the supplier to meet the shipping and related cost up to on board including freight and insurance.

f   CIF; Coût, assurance et fret
d   CIF; Kosten, Versicherung und Fracht

612   COLLATERAL; SECURITY
Additional assets offered as backing for the financial assistance sought.

f   Garantie
d   Sicherheit; Pfand

613   COMPANY PROMOTER
A person who undertakes to form a new company and who carries out all the preliminary work in connection with its establishment as a going concern.

f   Créateur de société; Fondateur de société
d   Gesellschaftsgründer

614 CONSTRUCTION SCHEDULE
A chronological presentation of
the various phases involved in the
implementation of a project.

f Plan de construction
d Bau-Arbeitsplan;
Konstruktions-Arbeitsplan

615 CONTINGENCIES:
CONTINGENT EXPENSES
Provision for unforeseen
expenditures in a project.

f Dépenses imprévues
d Unvorhergesehene Ausgaben

616 COST EFFECTIVENESS
A generalized variant of cost
benefit analysis emphasizing the
process of maximizing effectiveness of a given volume of
investment; usually related to
analysis of public sector
programmes.

f Efficacité de coût
d Kosteneffizienz

617 COST ESTIMATES
A statement of costs to be incurred on a project, itemized in
terms of individual sections of
plants and equipment, facilities
and services, shown on the basis
of best available evidences and
fair assumptions.

f Etat estimatif;
Devis appréciatif
d Kostenanschlag;
Kostenvoranschlag

618 COST PRICE
The cost incurred in acquiring
the asset, normally considered
while providing insurance
coverage.

f Prix coûtant
d Kostenpreis;
Selbstkostenpreis

619 COST OF CAPITAL,
OPPORTUNITY
The opportunity of profits
sacrificed in a possible alternative use.

f Coût alternatif de capital
d Alternative Kapitalkosten

620 COST OF INVESTMENT,
OPPORTUNITY
The cost of opportunities
foregone, or sacrifices gone
through by the society, of fore-
going current consumption or
attainment of other social
objectives, by opting for one
type of investment rather than
the other.

f Coût alternatif d'investissements
d Alternative Investitionskosten

621 COST OF PRODUCTION
A statement of expenses
itemized as to individual
elements entering into the
manufacture of a product, or a
combination of products; an
important exercise undertaken
in the appraisal of a project for
determination of its viability
and competitiveness.

f Coût de la production
d Produktionskosten;
Herstellungskosten

622 COST, EXTERNAL
Disabilities suffered by an
enterprise by virtue of non-
existence of essential overhead
or supporting facilities; reflected in reduced turnover or
increased expenses.

f Coût externe
d Externe Kosten

623 COST, FACTOR
The cost incurred on account
of employing factors of

production valued at the market price.

f   Coût de facteur
d   Faktorkosten

624   COST, INDIRECT FOREIGN
      EXCHANGE
      Cost of spares, components and
      other related imported sub-
      equipment forming a part of a
      composite plant or machinery
      assembled indigenously.

f   Coût indirect des devises
d   Indirekte Devisenkosten

625   COST, OPPORTUNITY,
      COST, ALTERNATIVE
      The value of the productive
      resources used in producing one
      product instead of another. The
      real cost to society of pro-
      ducing one good is the value of
      the other products that have been
      foregone.

f   Coût alternatif
d   Alternative Kosten

626   COST, PRIVATE OPPORTUNITY
      The value of the opportunities
      foregone by a private individual
      in terms of his own subjective
      valuation of benefits.

f   Coût alternatif privé
d   Private Alternativkosten

627   COST, SOCIAL
      Generally consists of costs of
      investment sacrifices and dis-
      advantages suffered by the society
      for the promotion of the project,
      such as investment in overhead
      facilities, pollution effects,
      traffic congestion.

f   Coût social
d   Soziale Kosten

628   COST, SOCIAL OPPORTUNITY
      The value of the sacrifice made

by the society for the promotion
of a project in terms of the
society's objectives.

f   Coût alternatif social
d   Soziale Alternativkosten

629   COST, TRANSFER
      Cost that must be offered to
      attract a supply of a factor of
      production away from alternative
      avenues of employment. This
      sum of money is the necessary
      supply price of that factor in
      its new employment.

f   Coût de cession
d   Übertragungskosten

630   CREDIT STATUS;
      CREDIT STANDARD
      An assessment of the past
      credit record of the borrower,
      as assessed normally by
      reference to the borrower's past
      volume and status of borrowing
      and relationship respectively
      with the latter's bankers and
      others, like suppliers, with
      whom the borrower had credit
      dealings. (See: Banker's
      reference 591)

f   Etat de crédit
d   Kreditstand;
      Kreditfähigkeit

631   CREDITWORTHINESS
      The ability of an enterprise to
      repay its debt obligations; forms
      an important aspect in project
      evaluation; covers examination
      of such aspects as earning
      capacity, past financial perform-
      ance and standing in the banking
      and commercial community.

f   Crédibilité;
      Digne de crédit
d   Kreditwürdigkeit

632   CUT-OFF POINT
      Rate of return offered by the

last project that will be carried out which is just above, or equal to, the cost of raising the funds needed for that project. Cut-off point is established by the marginal cost of capital in an economy. (See: Project, cut-off 694)

f   Point "cut-off"
d   "Cut-off" Punkt

633   DEBT SERVICE COVERAGE
Number of times total net cash accruals cover outstanding debt repayments; derived by dividing the annual cash generated by annual amortization and interest payment on long term debts.

f   Couverture de service de dettes
d   Deckung des Schuldendienstes

634   DEMAND, AGGREGATE;
DEMAND, EFFECTIVE
The total effective volume of sales anticipated for a product at a given price.

f   Demande effective;
Demande agrégée
d   Tatsächliche Nachfrage;
Effektive Nachfrage

635   DEMAND, DERIVED
The demand for a commodity not required for its own sake, but for its contribution to the manufacture of another commodity.

f   Demande dérivée
d   Abgeleitete Nachfrage

636   EARNEST MONEY
The proportion of cost of machinery supplied on installment credit basis by specialized development finance institutions paid as down payment by purchasers of machinery. (See: Margin money 664)

f   Dépôt de garantie
d   Angeld;

Aufgeld;
Handgeld

637   ECONOMIC INDICATORS
Data or series of data compiled for important activities, in an economy and sectors of an economy, designed to reflect variations in the state of industry, trade, commerce, finance, etc. These form important appraisal aids as also basis for management decisions and hence, serve to reduce enterpreneural risks. These include market research series, price indices, production indices, income and expenditure series, import and export statistics.

f   Indicateurs économiques
d   Wirtschaftliche Indikatoren

638   ELASTICITY OF DEMAND
The response of demand to a change in the price of a commodity.

f   Elasticité de demande
d   Nachfrageelastizität

639   ELASTICITY OF
EVALUATION
A term used in connection with the assessment of the capacity for promotion of a project.

f   Elasticité d'évaluation
d   Beurteilungselastizität

640   ELASTICITY OF
SUBSTITUTION
A measure of the ease with which a variable factor of production can be utilized for others.

f   Elasticité de substitution
d   Substitutionselastizität

641   ELASTICITY OF SUPPLY
The response of supply to a

change in the price of a
commodity.

f   Elasticité d'offre
d   Angebotselastizität

642   ELASTICITY, INCOME
The response of the demand for
a product to changes in the real
income of the consumers.

f   Elasticité de revenus
d   Einkommenselastizität

643   ENTREPRENEUR
The key person behind the promotion of a project to be
distinguished from the manager
of a project and its main
financier; basically it refers to
a person or persons actively
engaged in organizing and promoting a new project.

f   Entrepreneur
d   Unternehmer

644   EXPENSES, PRELIMINARY;
EXPENSES, PRE-OPERATIVE;
EXPENSES, PRE-FORMATION
Cost items incurred before a
project enters the stage of
commercial production, such as
promotion expenses, administration and other overhead
expenses during the construction
period, training expenses, payment for interest on borrowings,
floatation, issuing and other
charges and commissions related
to raising of capital.

f   Dépenses préliminaires;
Dépenses préparatoires;
Dépenses préalables
d   · Vorbereitende Ausgaben;
Einstweilige Ausgaben

645   EXPENSES, PROJECT
DEVELOPMENT
The initial outlays expected or
incurred by a project promoter,
on items such as preparation of

feasibility reports, tie-up with
foreign collaborators, locating
plant-suppliers and so on, which
are allowed to be capitalized as
part of total project cost.

f   Dépenses de développement de
projet
d   Ausgaben der Projektentwicklung

646   FEASIBILITY STUDY
A report containing a detailed
examination of the inputs,
economic, technical, financial,
commercial and organizational
requirements of a project to
determine its viability in
principle.

f   Etude de praticabilité;
Etude sur les possibilités de
réalisation
d   Durchführbarkeitsuntersuchung;
Feasibilitystudie

647   FEASIBILITY STUDY,
ECONOMIC
Study examining whether the
demands for goods and services
created by the project or
programme can be met by the
available resources.

f   Etude de praticabilité
économique
d   Wirtschaftliche Durchführbarkeitsstudie;
Ökonomische Feasibilitystudie

648   FEASIBILITY STUDY,
FINANCIAL
Evaluation of capitalization
alternatives, determination of
financing requirements, both
equity and debt, analysis of
future profitability and rates of
return on invested capital;
determination of cash flows,
analysis of production and
operating costs.

f   Etude de praticabilité
financière

d Finanzielle Durchführbarkeitsstudie;
Finanz-Feasibilitystudie

649 FEASIBILITY STUDY,
MANAGERIAL
Study examining whether - with
the available skill and know-how
of the managerial personnel -
the work of construction and
operation of the project can be
performed as outlined.

f Etude de praticabilité gestionnaire;
Etude de praticabilité directoriale
d Management Feasibilitystudie

650 FEASIBILITY STUDY,
TECHNICAL
Study examining whether the
technical processes described
or implied in the project report
are within the range of the
available scientific and engineering know-how.

f Etude de praticabilité technique
d Technische Durchführbarkeitsstudie;
Technische Feasibilitystudie

651 FINANCIAL CAPACITY
The capacity of raising necessary
funds through borrowings from
financing institutions; related
normally to volume of net worth
of the borrowing enterprise; in
the case of development banks,
net worth plus quasi-equity; i.e.
long-term subordinated borrowings.

f Capacité financière
d Finanzkapazität

652 FINANCIAL PROJECTIONS
Financial analysis for project
studies, investment analysis and
working capital determination.

f Projections financières
d Finanzprojektionen

653 FOREIGN EXCHANGE
EARNINGS;
FOREIGN EXCHANGE
SAVINGS
A criterion to measure the
worth of a project in terms of
its potential to earn/save
foreign exchange.

f Recettes en devises
d Deviseneinnahmen

654 FOREIGN EXCHANGE
EFFECT
Foreign currency value of a
new product (process), minus the
foreign exchange value of some
of its imports which will come
from the country's foreign trade.

f Effet de devises
d Deviseneffekt;
Devisenauswirkung

655 GESTATION PERIOD
The period of time that elapses
between the beginning of an investment project and the time
when the project operates on a
profit-yielding basis.

f Période de gestation
d Gestationsperiode

656 GUARANTEE CHARGES
The commission charged by a
development bank or any
guaranteeing agency for the
contingent liability incurred as
a result of a guarantee undertaking.

f Prix de garantie;
Taxe de garantie
d Garantiegebühr

657 GUARANTEE COVER
The collateral accepted for
providing guarantee services,
or the cushion provided within
the guaranteeing institution
against the contingent
obligation.

f   Couverture de garantie
d   Garantiedeckung

658   INSUFFICIENCY GAP
       A measure of the volume of
       demand that cannot be met by
       existing production facilities.

f   Lacune d'insufficance
d   Unzulänglichkeitslücke

659   INVESTMENT ALLOCATION
       CRITERIA
       The criteria adopted by develop-
       ment banks for allocating
       available funds amongst different
       sectors, such as industry, infra-
       structure, public utility, agri-
       culture, housing, transport;
       again, among these, to individual
       enterprises and among the
       different units, the type of assist-
       ance, whether underwriting, loan
       operations, guarantee, direct
       investment in equities, etc.

f   Critères d'allocation des
     investissements
d   Investitionszuteilungskriterien

660   JOINT VENTURE
       An association of an overseas and
       local entrepreneur to carry out
       a specific project. It differs from
       a partnership in so far as it is
       limited to the success or failure
       of the specific project for which
       it was formed.

f   Entreprise en participation
d   Beteiligungsgeschäft;
     Gemeinschaftsgründung

661   LIFE, ECONOMIC
       Normally refers to the number of
       years a fixed asset, or a comple-
       ment of project assets, is expected
       to function satisfactorily and
       productively, with normal mainten-
       ance.

f   Vie économique
d   Wirtschaftliche Lebensdauer

662   LIFE, USEFUL
       The "life" of capital assets
       assumed for the purpose of
       making economic appraisals,
       or for making depreciation
       provision. This "life" is esti-
       mated as the average life for
       the classes of assets considered
       and has regard to physical life
       and obsolescence.

f   Vie utile
d   Nützliche Lebensdauer

663   LOAN SERVICING
       Ability of an enterprise to
       generate adequate cash to meet
       the loan repayment obligations
       over a period of time; an im-
       portant consideration in the
       project's viability.

f   Services de prêt
d   Schuldendienst

664   MARGIN MONEY
       Denotes the amount deposited
       by a trader in a stock exchange
       with his broker for transactions
       in the market; also
       denotes the down-payment
       required of clients availing
       themselves of machinery and
       equipment on installment credit
       or hire purchase lease. (See:
       Earnest money 636)

f   Arrhes
d   Angeld

665   MARKET SHARE
       The proportion of total volume
       expected to be sold in a market
       for a product.

f   Part de marché
d   Marktanteil

666   MODEL SCHEMES
       An important pre-finance
       promotional activity of a de-
       velopment bank particularly
       concerning promotion of small

enterprises, comprising formulation of minifeasibility reports concerning individual industry-lines, specifying basic details as to capacity, plant and equipment requirements, specifications of these and the sources of their supply; other input requirements, total financial requirements and the possible sites of locations for such plants.

f Plans de modèle
d Modellpläne;
   Musterpläne

667 OUTPUT, GROSS
     Value of commodities turned out, or services rendered, by a unit over a period of time valued at selling prices.

f Production brute;
   Production totale
d Brutto-Produktion;
   Brutto-Output

668 OUTPUT, NET
     The value of the contribution made by the enterprise itself, computed by deducting from the gross output the incoming supplies. Therefore, it is the value added by a firm. (See: Value added 746)

f Production nette
d Nettoproduktion;
   Nettooutput

669 PAY-BACK;
     PAY-OFF;
     PAY-OUT PERIOD;
     RECOUPMENT PERIOD
     A method of assessing capital investments by determining how quickly a company can get its money back from a capital investment. The Pay-Back Method is one of the traditional techniques employed for measuring investment worth.

f Période de récupération

d Rückzahlungsperiode

670 PRESENT VALUE;
     PRESENT WORTH
     The sum of the annual benefits of an investment discounted by the opportunity cost of capital. The capital sum which, if invested at the time of commissioning of a plant, would together with interest earned, suffice to pay the annual capital charges on the plant as they occur year by year. (See: Present worth factor 672)

f Valeur actuelle
d Gegenwartswert;
   Barwert;
   Zeitwert

671 PRESENT VALUE METHOD
     A variant of the discounted cash-flow technique, wherein the streams of cash-flows are determined by a stipulated rate of discount.

f Méthode de valeur actuelle
d Methode des Gegenwartswertes

672 PRESENT WORTH FACTOR;
     P.W.F.
     The reciprocal value of the "capital recovery factor". (See: Capital recovery factor 602)

f Facteur de valeur actuelle
d Gegenwartswertfaktor

673 PRICE, ACCOUNTING
     An approximation of shadow prices, quantified by informed judgments, or by short-run analyses. (See: Price, shadow 680)

f Prix de compte
d Rechnungspreis

674 PRICE, ANTICIPATED
     The market price expected to be prevalent for the product or

services to be turned out by the project after implementation; in many instances the price assumed determines the profitability and hence, the viability of a new project.

f   Prix prévu
d   Erwarteter Preis

675   PRICE, COMPETITIVE
A measure representing the viability of a project in reference to its ability to bring out the product or products into the market at a level of price which while providing a reasonable margin of profit, will also be on level with, if not lower to, those charged by competitors.

f   Prix compétitif
d   Wettbewerbspreis

676   PRICE, DEMAND
The price consumers are willing to pay for the marginal unit of a commodity.

f   Prix de demande
d   Nachfragepreis

677   PRICE, FACTOR
The prices of the factors of production, e.g. the prices of labor, capital, land; derived indirectly from their productivity in producing ultimate consumables.

f   Prix de facteur
d   Faktorpreis

678   PRICE, IMPUTED
Price derived on the basis of ruling market practices, for commodities or services actually made use of, but not paid for, since these commodities or services belong to the owner; e.g. an owner-occupied residential building, the services of an owner-manager.

f   Prix imputé
d   Unterstellter Preis

679   PRICE, MARKET
The actual prices at which goods or services are bought or sold.

f   Prix de marché
d   Marktpreis

680   PRICE, SHADOW
A set of "connected values" employed in cost-benefit analysis to rectify over- or undervaluation involved in prevailing market prices normally for exchange rate, interest rate, wage rate. (See: Price, accounting 673)

f   Prix fictif
d   Schattenpreis

681   PRICE, SOCIAL DEMAND
The society's willingness to pay for the marginal unit of a commodity, which may be different from the demand price reflected in the free market.

f   Prix de demande sociale
d   Sozialer Nachfragepreis

682   PRICE, WORLD MARKET;
      PRICE, INTERNATIONAL
Prices in terms of a convertible foreign currency, at which the country can buy and sell commodities in the international market. A developing country, whose demand or supply conditions do not affect the world market, can take international market quotations for the purposes of determining its trade and production policies.

f   Prix de marché mondial;
    Prix international
d   Weltmarktpreis;
    Internationaler Preis

683   PRODUCTIVITY OF CAPITAL
Output per unit of capital input.
The ratio of the physical productive capacity (output) to the
current real value of the stock of
capital facilities and equipment.

f   Productivité de capital
d   Produktivität des Kapitales;
Kapitalproduktivität

684   PRODUCTS, JOINT
Two or more commodities produced by a single process, or from
a single raw material, in such a
manner that it is impossible or
uneconomic to produce one good
without the other.

f   Produits conjoints;
Produits commune
d   Gemeinschaftsprodukte

685   PROFIT EXPECTATION
The rate of return anticipated by
investors.

f   Expectation de profit
d   Profiterwartung

686   PROFIT SHARING
The process of imposing
contingent interest on borrowers,
particularly proprietary, partnership or other closely-held corporations; normally forms a certain
percentage rate over the normal
interest rates charged, to be
applicable, should the profit of
the assisted enterprise exceed
a stated percentage.

f   Participation au profit
d   Profitbeteiligung

687   PROFITABILITY
Rate of return on investments;
criterion by which an investor
judges the worth of an investment
project.

f   Rentabilité
d   Rentabilität

688   PROFITABILITY,
COMMERCIAL
The net returns on a project
calculated on the basis of the
given market prices.

f   Rentabilité commerciale
d   Handelsrentabilität

689   PROJECT
A self-contained investment
proposition, brought up to a
development bank for financing,
or initiated by the development
bank for inducing investment
by others; may include expansion
and diversification of existing
facilities, or promotion of new
ones.

f   Projet
d   Projekt

690   PROJECT COST
Total capital involvement to
implement a specific project
including developmental- and
current expenditures from the
project design stage until start
of commercial operations.

f   Coût d'un projet
d   Projektkosten

691   PROJECT EVALUATION;
PROJECT APPRAISAL
A comprehensive assessment
of the various aspects of a
project such as economic,
technical, managerial, market,
financial and locational, to
determine the viability of the
project as a commercial proposition.

f   Evaluation d'un projet
d   Projektbewertung

692   PROJECT LOCATION
Determination to locate the
plant site of a new project
taking into consideration the
financial and marketing impli-

cations as well as the availability
of overhead and infra-structure
facilities.

f Situation d'un projet;
   Emplacement d'un projet
d Projektlokalisierung

693 PROJECT SELECTION
     Screening methods adopted by a
     development bank to take up for
     examination the suitability of the
     projects or financing propositions
     brought to it for assistance.

f Sélection d'un projet
d Projektauswahl

694 PROJECT, CUT-OFF
     A project for which the cost of
     capital is equal to the profits it
     is expected to generate. (See:
     Cut-off point 632)

f Projet "cut-off"
d "Cut-off" Projekt

695 PROJECT, SELF-LIQUIDATING
     Project whose economic and
     financial return over a period of
     time pays off the cost incurred
     in setting it up.

f Projet de liquidation de soi-même
d Selbst-liquidierendes Projekt

696 PROJECT, SHADOW
     A project which is unrealistically
     conceived as to technical and
     financial viability; the result
     often is bankruptcy in the case of
     private sector projects and drain
     on resources by continuous
     subsidization, in the case of public
     sector projects.

f Projet fictif
d Schattenprojekt

697 PROJECT, "TIME SLICE"
     Project that usually forms a
     continuous development of a
     unity.

f Project continuel
d Kontinuierliches Projekt

698 RATE, CAPACITY
     UTILIZATION;
     RATE, OPERATING
     The ratio of physical output to
     physical capacity; a key factor
     in evaluating the short-run
     business outlook; specially
     with regard to investment in
     facilities for expansion.

f Taux d'utilisation de la capacité;
   Taux d'exploitation
d Kapazitätsbenützungsrate;
   Betriebsintensität

699 RATE OF RETURN
     A method of calculating the
     expected profitability of an item
     of capital investment based on
     the relationship of its expected
     profit to its capital cost.

f Taux de rendement
d Ertragsrate

700 RATE OF RETURN ON
     INVESTED CAPITAL
     The ratio of profits to capital
     or assets.

f Taux de rendement de capital
   investi
d Ertragsrate des Investitionskapitales

701 RATE OF RETURN,
     DISCOUNTED
     The process whereby future
     values of a project are reduced,
     through a discounting factor,
     to their present worth.

f Taux de rendement escompté
d Diskontierte Ertragsrate

702 RATE OF RETURN, FAIR
     Profitability conforming to
     normal expectations of in-
     vestors.

f   Taux de rendement juste;
Taux de rendement équitable
d   Angemessene Ertragsrate

703   RATE OF RETURN, INTERNAL
A model depicting an idealized
growth rate or earning power of
an initial investment put out at
compound interest rate. This is
a key factor in selecting alternative investment projects, based
on the pay-off period and the
volume of net benefits.

f   Taux de rendement interne;
Taux de rendement marginal
d   Interne Ertragsrate;
Interner Zinssatz

704   RATE OF RETURN, SOCIAL
Measures the real rate of return
to the economy of a given investment for a project.

f   Taux de rendement social
d   Soziale Ertragsrate

705   RATIO, ACID TEST;
RATIO, QUICK;
RATIO, LIQUIDY
Ratio of an enterprise's current
liquid assets (cash or near cash),
trade receivables (readily
marketable securities), to its
current liabilities. This ratio
provides a better check on a
firm's current operations than
the current ratio, which includes
inventories that may not prove
to be liquid enough to meet current
debts. It is basically a measure
of the ability of an enterprise to
meet its short-term obligations.
(See: Ratio, current 709)

f   Taux de liquidité
d   Liquiditätsrate

706   RATIO, AVERAGE CAPITAL-
OUTPUT
Relates the existing total stock of
capital to the total output.

f   Taux moyen de rendement de
capital
d   Durchschnittliche Kapitalertragsrate

707   RATIO, BENEFIT COST
Value of the aggregate benefits
of a project expressed as the
ratio, or percentage, of the
value of aggregate costs. It
gives a measure of the profitability of the project and may be
expressed in a variety of ways,
such as: (i) the ratio of the
present value of all benefits to
the present value of all costs;
(ii) the ratio of the present
value of the future net recurring
benefits to the present value of
all investment costs; (iii) the
ratio of the annual benefits to
the direct and imputed value of
annual costs.

f   Taux de coûts-bénéfices
d   Kosten-Nutzenverhältnis

708   RATIO, CAPITAL-OUTPUT
A measure of the relationship
between a given investment and
the output associated with it.
The more productive the capital
is the lower the ratio will be, and
vice versa.

f   Taux de rendement de capital
d   Kapitalertragsrate

709   RATIO, CURRENT;
RATIO, BANKER'S;
RATIO, CURRENT POSITION
A measure of the relationship
between current assets and
current liabilities; normally
represents the liquidity position
and the working capital
situation. (See: Ratio, acid test
705)

f   Taux courant
d   Laufendes Flüssigkeitsverhältnis;
Laufendes Liquiditätsverhältnis

710   RATIO, CUT-OFF
The minimum level of profitability (as expressed by the
benefit-cost ratio) that any project should show in order to
qualify for acceptance.

f   Taux de "cut-off"
d   "Cut-off" Punkt

711   RATIO, DEBT-EQUITY
A measure representing the
relationship between volumes of
long-term borrowed funds and
owners' unimpaired capital and
reserves.

f   Taux de dette-propriété
d   Verhältnis von langfristigen
Schuldverpflichtungen zu
Eigenkapital

712   RATIO, DEBT-SERVICE
A measure representing a
country's annual debt servicing
capacity in relation to the
country's exports proceeds and
other foreign exchange earnings.
As related to an enterprise the
term refers to the relationship
between its debt amortization
and related annual obligations
and its annual income. (See:
Debt service coverage 633)

f   Taux de service des dettes
d   Schuldendienstverhältnis

713   RATIO, DEBT-TO-NET-
WORTH
Relation of the total liabilities
of a firm to its net worth.

f   Taux de dette-capital actif
d   Verhältnis von Schuldverpflichtungen zu Aktivvermögen

714   RATIO, DEPRECIATION-
RESERVE
The ratio of the total depreciation
reserve for a specific class of
fixed assets to the original cost
of the total capital assets still

in use.

f   Taux de réserve d'amortissement
d   Verhältnis der Amortisations-
reserven zu Originalkosten des
Kapitalanlagevermögens

715   RATIO, DERIVED
Used to express the mutual
relationship that exists among
capital, labor and output; it
seeks to assess the relative
contribution or efficiency of the
various inputs that combine in
production (capital-output,
capital-labor, capital-invest-
ment per worker, labor-output
ratio).

f   Taux dérivé
d   Abgeleitete Verhältniszahl

716   RATIO, DYNAMIC
A yardstick of judging operating
efficiency by indicating the
annual turnovers of various
kinds of assets (including turnover ratios of trade receivables,
inventories, fixed assets,
operating capital) in relation to
sales.

f   Taux dynamique
d   Dynamische Verhältniszahl

717   RATIO, FIXED ASSET
COVERAGE
Shows the number of times the
value of the fixed assets covers
the amount of the loan.

f   Taux de couverture de l'actif
fixe
d   Deckungsverhältnis des Kapitalanlagevermögens

718   RATIO, INVESTMENT
COVERAGE
A measure representing the
relationship between net
income and interest charges
payable. This is a statutorily

enjoined norm on institutional
borrowers, like insurance
companies, in the U.S.A. International finance agencies,
seeking to replenish their
resources through international
capital markets have also found
it necessary to maintain a
respectable level of net income
to interest obligations to obtain
a fair market rating.

f   Taux de couverture de l'investissement
d   Investitionsdeckungsverhältnis

719   RATIO, LOAN SAFETY
A yardstick to determine the
degree of financial risk inherent
in a project. A company should
be financed in such a way that
it can confidently be expected to
survive business reverses. The
ratios defined in this context
are the current ratio, quick ratio,
debt/equity ratio, portfolio ratio,
fixed asset coverage ratio, and
debt coverage ratio.

f   Taux de sécurité de prêt
d   Lohn-Sicherheitsverhältnis

720   RATIO, MARGINAL
CAPITAL-OUTPUT;
RATIO, INCREMENTAL
CAPITAL-OUTPUT
Relates the addition to the stock
of capital (assuming other factors
can be increased as required) to
the addition to the total output.

f   Taux de rendement marginal de
capital
d   Marginale Kapitalertragsrate

721   RATIO, OPERATING COST
A measure of operating costs
expressed as a percentage of
value of net sales.

f   Taux de coûts d'exploitation
d   Betriebskoeffizient

722   RATIO, PAY-OUT
A measure of dividends paid to
net earnings.

f   Taux de paiement des dividendes
d   Auszahlungsverhältnis;
Dividendenzahlungsverhältnis

723   RATIO, PORTFOLIO;
RATIO, DEBT
CAPITALIZATION
This ratio is essentially the
same as the debt/equity ratio.
Debt is defined as borrowings
maturing over one year, and
capitalization is defined as the
total amount of long-term money,
long-term borrowings and owner's
capital that is invested in the
project. Thus, capitalization
is term debt plus equity. (See:
Ratio, debt-equity, 711)

f   Taux de portefeuille
d   Portfolioverhältnis

724   RATIO, PRODUCT-CAPITAL
The ratio between capital and
value added. It measures the
profitability of a project in a
social sense.

f   Taux de productivité de capital
d   Produktivitätsintensität des
Kapitales

725   RATIO, PROFITABILITY
Measure for assessing the
profit earning potential of an
enterprise; used as a loan/safety
device. Some of the important
among these ratios include
return on sales, return on
equity, return on capital employed, return on assets.

f   Taux de profitabilité
d   Rentabilitätsrate;
Profitrate

726   RATIO, SOLVENCY
Tests to analyze the future
solvency of an enterprise by

means of the following ratios:
current ratio, profitability ratio,
inventory turnover, portfolio ratio.

f   Taux de solvabilité
d   Solvenzverhältnis;
Zahlungsfähigkeitsverhältnis

727   RATIO, STATIC
A yardstick for judging the soundness and stability of capital
composition from the structure of
the respective assets and
liabilities based on a comparison
between balance sheet items
(includes liquid ratio, current
ratio, fixed ratio, and debt
ratio).

f   Taux statique
d   Statisches Verhältnis

728   RETURN, ECONOMIC;
RETURN, SOCIAL
The gross profit, or the net
benefits accruing to an economy
from a given investment or
economic activity.

f   Rendement économique;
Rendement social
d   Ökonomischer Ertrag;
Sozialer Ertrag

729   RETURN ON ASSETS
A measure representing the
relationship between net profits
to net worth.

f   Rendement de l'actif
d   Anlagevermögensertrag

730   RETURN ON CAPITAL
A measure of relationship of
profit earned by an enterprise
in relation to total capital
employed.

f   Rémunération du capital
d   Kapitalertrag

731   RETURN ON EQUITY
A measure representing net

profit after taxation to paid-in
capital plus reserves.

f   Rendement de la propriété
d   Eigenkapitalertrag

732   RETURN ON INVESTMENT
A measure representing operating profit in relation to total
capitalization; or, operating
profit in relation to equity and
fixed debt; or, net profit and
interest in relation to total
capitalization.

f   Rendement de l'investissement
d   Investitionsertrag

733   RETURN ON SALES
A measure representing total
sales, net or gross, in relation
to capitalization, net worth, or
capital employed.

f   Rendement de ventes
d   Verkaufsertrag

734   RISK, BUSINESS;
RISK, COMMERCIAL
The uncertainties inherent in
the physical operation of the
firm; it arises mainly from the
inability to ensure absolutely
stable sales, costs and profits.

f   Risque d'entreprise;
Risque de commerce
d   Geschäftsrisiko;
Handelsrisiko

735   RISK, ECONOMIC
Uncertainties affecting the
operation of an enterprise
arising out of the positive policy
hindrances of the government
or disincentives within the
framework of the economy.

f   Risque économique
d   Wirtschaftsrisiko

736   RISK, FINANCIAL;
RISK, LENDING

Elements of uncertainties attendant
on investments or loans, including
the repayment risk.

f   Risque financier
d   Finanzielles Risiko;
    Finanzrisiko

737   RISK, POLITICAL
Elements of uncertainties involving
exchange and repatriation facilities, which can be only ensured by
a government commitment and investment in the project.

f   Risque politique
d   Politisches Risiko

738   SALES MIX PROBLEM
Optimum sales allocation, based
on varying costs and market
problems.

f   Problème de vente-mixte
d   Verkaufs-mix Problem

739   SALES POTENTIAL
The maximum possible sales
volume for an enterprise, a
product, or an area during a
stated period.

f   Potential de vente
d   Verkaufspotential

740   SECURITY ARRANGEMENT
The types (assets including land,
building, machinery, personal
or bank guarantee) and the nature
(an english or equitable mortgage, floating charge, pari-passu
charge, second mortgage) of
collateral offered against loans,
or other types of assistance to
be obtained from a development
bank. These are aspects of policy
specified in the policy statement
of a development bank.

f   Arrangement de sécurité;
    Arrangement de couverture
d   Sicherheitsvorkehrungen;
    Deckungsvorkehrungen

741   SECURITY MARGIN
The extent to which the value
of securities measures up to
the volume of borrowings.

f   Marge de sécurité
d   Sicherheitsgrenze

742   SENSITIVITY TEST
Process of imputing alternative
values to key variables to see
how the rate of return, or
other results will be affected.
This test offers a better
estimation of risk involved in a
project than a single value
calculation. (See: Analysis, probability 580)

f   Examen de sensitivité
d   Empfindlichkeitstest

743   SOURCES, EXTERNAL
Funds for financing projects
provided by the capital market,
banks and sources outside of
project promoters.

f   Sources externes
d   Externe Mittel

744   SOURCES, INTERNAL
Funds for financing projects
generated within the enterprises
themselves, such as undistributed
profits, depreciation (or other
reserves) and obsolescence reserve, and the compensation
for depletion of natural resources.

f   Sources internes
d   Interne Mittel

745   SUPPLY, AGGREGATE
The total volume of a particular
product that could be sold at
a given price.

f   Offre agrégé
d   Aggregiertes Angebot

746   VALUE ADDED
Indicates that part of the value

of a product which is created
in the factory and is arrived at
after deducting from the gross
ex-factory value of the product,
the value of fuels and materials
used, work done for the factory by
other concerns and depreciation
of fixed assets. (See: Output, net
668)

f   Valeur ajoutée
d   Mehrwert

747   VIABILITY, FINANCIAL
The ability of the project to with-
stand unexpected adversity during
construction and operating phases.

f   Viabilité financière
d   Finanzielle Durchführbarkeit

748   VIABILITY, OVERALL
The consistency of a project in
regard to the totality of
circumstances - such as technical,
financial, market - assumed during
its construction and operational
phase.

f   Viabilité générale
d   Allgemeine Durchführbarkeit;
Generelle Realisierbarkeit

749   VIABILITY, TECHNICAL
The soundness of the technical
components of a project such as
the appropriateness of the proces
suitability of the plant and equipment, including capacity potential
internal balance amongst various
sections and segments, adequacy
of plant engineering and civil
work facilities - all related in a
manner to be in balance with the
rest of the project components.

f   Viabilité technique
d   Technische Durchführbarkeit

750   YIELD METHOD
Method based upon the assumption
that the best investment is that
from which the proceeds would
yield the highest rate of
compound interest in equating
the present value of the investment with future proceeds.
(See: Present value method 671;
Cash-flow, discounted 609)

f   Méthode de rendement
d   Ertragsmethode

VII.
PRE- AND POST- FINANCING ASPECTS
ASPECTS D'AVANT- ET D'APRES-FINANCEMENT
GESICHTSPUNKTE DER VOR- UND NACHFINANZIERUNG

751 ACCEPTANCE, BANK;
ACCEPTANCE, BANKERS'
A document - draft, bill of exchange - which has been "accepted"
by a bank or similar financing
institution engaged in providing
acceptance credit. (See: Credit,
acceptance 775)

f Effet de banque;
Billet de banque
d Bankwechsel;
Bankakzept

752 ACCEPTANCE, TRADE
Bill of exchange drawn by the
seller of goods at the time of the
sale and accepted by the purchaser.

f Billet de commerce
d Warenakzept;
Kundenakzept

753 ALLOTMENT OF SHARES
The process of allocating specified numbers of newly issued
shares or debentures amongst
applicants in proportion to the
volume applied for by each. (See:
Letter of allotment 823)

f Répartition d'actions
d Aktienzuteilung

754 AMALGAMATION
Methods incorporating reorganization processes such as: (i)
complete amalgamation or absorption, where there is full in-
tegration within the existing

legal framework; assets are
taken over, the company assumes
all liability; and (ii) pooling
arrangements where the
companies continue to operate
as separate entities, but pool
their activities and share the
profits in an agreed proportion.

f Fusion;
Fusionnement
d Vereinigung;
Fusion;
Verschmelzung

755 ANNUAL RETURN
A statutory obligation on all
incorporated and limited
liability enterprises requiring
submission of factual statements to regulating authorities
in regard to capital and shares,
names and background of directors, indebtedness of the
company, and its last audited
balance sheet. Also denotes the
various types of information to
be submitted to development
banks by assisted enterprises,
as a part of post-finance supervisory obligation.

f Rapport annuel
d Jahresbericht

756 ARTICLES OF ASSOCIATION;
ARTICLES OF IN-
CORPORATION;
ARTICLES OF PARTNERSHIP
The rules for the management

and regulation of the internal arrangement of a joint-stock company. These include details of share capital, qualification of directors, arrangements for meetings, etc. (See: Memorandum of association 833)

f   Contrat de société;
     Statuts sociaux;
     Contrat d'association;
     Acte d'association
d   Gesellschaftsvertrag;
     Gesellschaftssatzungen;
     Statuten

757   ASSIGNMENT
       The legal process of making over of property from one person or institution to another. An important legal pre-condition to be fulfilled by the borrower before availing himself of credit sactioned by a development bank or financial institution; consists in fulfilling documentation requirements to make over assets and other properties provided as collateral for the loan to the development bank or financing institution.

f   Acte de cession;
     Acte de transfert
d   Abtretungsurkunde;
     Übertragungsurkunde

758   ASSOCIATION CLAUSE
       An important provision in the Memorandum of Association of a limited company providing for the names of initial promoters of the company, the number of shares each is prepared to take up and the background of the members.

f   Article de société;
     Clause de société
d   Gesellschaftsklausel

759   BANKRUPTCY

A condition, legally declared by a court of law, of insolvency of individuals, partnerships, or corporations. (See: Solvency 1246)

f   Faillite;
     Banqueroute
d   Konkurs;
     Konkursverfahren

760   BIDDING, INTERNATIONAL;
       BIDDING, COMPETITIVE
       Procurement of plant, machinery and equipment on a competitive price basis from international sources of supplies for projects financed; normally a pre-condition stipulated by international development agencies or development banks to ensure price and quality competitiveness for procurements.

f   Enchères internationales;
     Surenchères compétitives
d   Internationales Anbotemachen;
     Wettbewerb-Bieten

761   BILL OF EXCHANGE;
       BILL, COMMERCIAL
       An order for making payment, particularly for purchases from overseas, addressed by the drawer to a second party, with instructions to pay a third party a stated amount of money at a stated date.

f   Lettre de change;
     Effet commercial;
     Traite
d   Warenwechsel;
     Handelswechsel;
     Tratte

762   BILL OF EXCHANGE, SIGHT
       A bill of exchange payable immediately upon acceptance.

f   Lettre de change à vue;
     Traite payable à presentation

d   Sichtwechsel;
    Sichttratte

763   BILL OF EXCHANGE, TERM
      A bill of exchange with a maturity
      of normally up to 90 days after
      acceptance by the drawee.

f   Lettre de change à terme
d   Fristwechsel;
    Fristtratte

764   BILL OF LADING
      A document providing a description
      of goods received for shipment,
      terms on which these are to be
      çarried and, regarded as the title
      for goods received for shipment.

f   Certificat de prise de charge;
    Connaissement
d   Seefrachtbrief;
    Schiffsfrachtbrief;
    Konnossement

765   CERTIFICATE OF
      INCORPORATION
      A document issued by company
      law authorities after the
      ¿ompany has fulfilled and
      complied with all statutory re-
      quirements for registration.

f   Acte constitutif;
    Contrat de société
d   Gründungsvertrag

766   CHARGE, FIXED
      The process through which a
      lender obtains a security on
      specified assets of the borrower.
      (See: Charge, floating 767)

f   Charge fixe
d   Feste Belastung;
    Fundierte Belastung;
    Fixe Belastung

767   CHARGE, FLOATING
      The process through which a
      lender obtains a global security
      over all the fixed and movable
      assets of the borrower. (See:

Charge, fixed 766)

f   Charge flottante
d   Schwebende Belastung;
    Nichtfundierte Belastung

768   COMPANY
      REORGANIZATION;
      COMPANY
      RECONSTRUCTION
      The reorganization of an
      assisted company, brought
      about by a development bank as
      a post-finance supervisory
      function. The reorganization
      may be in regard to capitaliza-
      tion of the firm, or for one or
      more of the following reasons:
      (i) for the purpose of effecting
      a redistribution of the capital
      among the different share
      holders or classes of share-
      holders; (ii) to enable a bonus
      issue of shares to be made;
      (iii) to increase the capital of
      the company; or, (iv) to give
      effect to amalgamation with
      another firm. Other aspects of
      reorganization may include
      change of management and top
      functionaries.

f   Réorganisation d'une entreprise
d   Umorganisation eines Unter-
    nehmens

769   COMPANY, CLIENT
      An enterprise which has ongoing
      financial obligations with the
      development bank or financing
      institution.

f   Entreprise de client
d   Kundenunternehmung

770   COST OVERRUNS
      Increases in the costs of a
      project over those estimated
      and provided for at the project
      planning phase, or at the time
      a decision on financing the
      project was taken.

f   Excédent de coût
d   Kostenüberzug

771   COST OF PURCHASE
A principal method of evaluating
inventories; a device particularly
employed to understate the value
of inventories at a time when the
current market prices are increasing, or vice-versa; also
used as an element of standard
costing in the above circumstances.

f   Coût d'acquisition
d   Einkaufskosten;
     Anschaffungskosten

772   COST-PLUS CONTRACT
A contract under which the
contractor provides all the
necessary material, equipment
and labor at actual cost, plus an
agreed amount for his services.

f   Coût et contrat
d   Kosten und Vertrag

773   COVER
A measure representing annual
earnings in relation to volume of
annual long-term loan repayment
obligations; used as a collateral
concept; also used in the sense
of buying a security that previously has been sold short in the
stock exchange.

f   Couverture;
     Garantie;
     Nantissement
d   Deckung

774   CRASH PROGRAMME
A programme aiming at the
shortest possible completion for
a project.

f   Programme de "crash"
d   Rekordprogramm

775   CREDIT, ACCEPTANCE
The process whereby an accepting house, after ascertaining the

credit worthiness of the overseas importer, opens a credit
account on his behalf, thus en-
abling the financing of the indigenous exporter by means of
a bill of exchange on the
accepting house.

f   Crédit par acceptation
d   Wechselkredit;
     Akzeptkredit

776   CUM BONUS
A method of quoting shares in
the stock exchange whereby the
current purchaser is entitled
to a bonus issue which is
contemplated, or already
announced.

f   Avec prime
d   Inklusive Bonus;
     Inklusive Prämie

777   CUM DIVIDEND
Represents a situation where
price quoted for a share in the
stock exchange entitles the
purchaser to the dividend which
is due for payment.

f   Avec dividende;
     Coupon attaché
d   Einschliesslich Dividende;
     Inklusive Dividende

778   CUM INTEREST
Debentures or bonds whose
quotations include the interest
accrued for the current period.

f   Avec intérêt
d   Einschliesslich Zinsen;
     Inklusive Zinsen

779   CUM RIGHTS;
       RIGHTS ON
A method of quoting shares in
a stock exchange whereby the
current purchaser is entitled
to a rights issue by the company
which is contemplated, or
already announced.

f   Avec droit
d   Inklusive Bezugsrechte

780   CUMULATIVE VOTING
A privilege associated with
holders of certain types of
shares whereby they may concen-
trate the entire voting strength on
one candidate, or distribute these
votes among many candidates.

f   Faculté de réunir sur un seul
candidat plusieurs voix
d   Stimmenhäufung

781   DEED OF ARRANGEMENT
An agreement made by a debtor
with his creditors in order to
avoid bankruptcy.

f   Contrat d'arrangement;
Concordat
d   Vergleichsurkunde;
Vergleichsvertrag

782   DIVERSITY FACTOR
The probability of a number of
pieces of equipment being in
use simultaneously; a technique
of plant utilization and production
control.

f   Facteur de diversité
d   Diversitätsfaktor

783   DIVIDEND LIMITATION
A condition imposed by lenders
on enterprises to ensure adequate
liquidity for meeting prior commitments and claims; sometimes such
a limitation is also imposed by
governments for restraining
inflationary conditions in the
economy.

f   Limitation de dividende
d   Dividendenbegrenzung

784   DIVIDEND MANDATE
An order to a company by a
shareholder to pay all dividends
to a third party, usually a banker.

f   Ordonnance de paiement de
dividendes
d   Dividendenverfügung

785   DIVIDEND WARRANT
The documentary instrument
through which dividend is
actually paid to shareholders,
consisting of three parts: a
tax voucher, a dividend counter-
foil giving details of the payment, and a cheque.

f   Coupon de dividende
d   Gewinnanteilschein;
Dividendenauszahlungsschein

786   DIVIDEND, CUMULATIVE;
DIVIDEND,
ACCUMULATIVE
A situation where an enterprise
accumulates its fixed dividend
payment obligations on specific
types of shares such as cumulative preference shares, by not
being able to pay when such
dividends have accrued and due
for payment.

f   Dividende cumulatif
d   Kumulative Dividende;
Kumulativer Gewinnanteil

787   DIVIDEND,
GOVERNMENT-GUARANTEED
Situation when the Government
has to induce institutional
participation in the equity
capital of a development bank
by assuring minimum guaranteed
dividends, normally paid by the
government, particularly in the
initial years of operation of a
development bank.

f   Dividende garanti par le
Gouvernement
d   Von der Regierung garantierte
Dividende

788   DIVIDEND, GROSS
A dividend before it has been
taxed.

f   Dividende brut
d   Bruttodividende;
     Bruttogewinnanteil

789 DIVIDEND, INTERIM
     The distribution of profits made
     on account of those earned in a
     trading period, i.e. before the
     final dividend.

f   Acompte de dividende;
     Acompte sur dividende
d   Abschlagsdividende;
     Vorläufige Dividende

790 DIVIDEND, NON-CUMULATIVE
     A dividend not paid when due to
     shareholders, which does not
     become a liability of the company
     and need not be paid at a future
     date. (See: Dividend, cumulative
     786; Preference shares,
     cumulative 348)

f   Dividende non-cumulatif
d   Nichtkumulative Dividende

791 DIVIDEND, OPTIONAL
     A dividend which is payable in
     cash or securities, according to
     the wishes of the holder.

f   Dividende d'option
d   Optionsdividende

792 DIVIDEND, ORDINARY
     The dividend paid to the holder
     of ordinary shares.

f   Dividende ordinaire
d   Ordentliche Dividende;
     Gewöhnliche Dividende

793 DIVIDEND, TAX-FREE
     A privilege granted by the govern-
     ment to induce private investment
     into preferred sectors of the
     economy or industry line; earnings
     from such investment (dividend),
     is free from taxes.

f   Dividende net d'impôts
d   Steuerfreie Dividende;
     Steuerfrei gezahlte Dividende

794 DOCUMENTATION
     The contractual basis of future
     relationship between the
     development bank and the client
     legally defined in various
     documents such as Heads of
     Agreement, Letter of Accept-
     ance, Mortgage deed.

f   Documentation
d   Dokumentation.

795 DRAWBACK FACILITIES
     An arrangement whereby duties
     or tax impositions to be paid
     at the first instance, are
     permitted to be claimed for
     reimbursement as a concession
     or inducement for promoting
     investment or development of
     priority sectors or activities.

f   Facilités de ristourne;
     Facilités de remboursement
d   Zollrückvergütungsmöglichkeite

796 DUMPING
     The sale of goods at less than
     true average cost.

f   "Dumping"
d   Ausfuhr von Waren zu
     Schleuderpreisen;
     "Dumping";
     Schleuderausfuhr

797 EX-BONUS
     A method of quoting shares in
     the stock exchange whereby the
     current purchaser is not
     entitled to a bonus issue which
     is contemplated, or already
     announced.

f   Ex-dividende extraordinaire
d   Ausschliesslich Extradividende;
     Exklusive Superdividende;
     Ohne Dividendenbonus

798 EX-CAPITALIZATION
     Description of share when
     buyer is not entitled to the
     "capitalization issue" attached

to the share. (See: Bonus issue 900)

f   Ex-émission de capitalisation
d   Ausschliesslich Kapitalisierungsemission

799   EX-COUPON
Without the coupon just paid.

f   Sans coupon
d   Ausschliesslich Gewinnanteilschein;
Ohne Kupon

800   EX-DIVIDEND;
Xd
Represents a situation where price quoted for a share in the stock exchange does not entitle the purchaser to an ensuing dividend. (See: Cum dividend 777)

f   Ex-dividende;
Sans dividende
d   Ausschliesslich Dividende;
Exklusive Dividende

801   EX-RIGHT;
Xr
A method of quoting shares in a stock exchange, whereby the current purchaser is not entitled to a rights issue by the company which is contemplated or announced to be issued.

f   Ex-droit
d   Ex-Bezugsrecht;
Ohne Bezugsrecht

802   EXTENSION FACILITIES
The provision of technical know-how designed to utilize modern techniques and technology in industry through a network of centers and agencies; usually complementary to provision of development finance, the assumption being that finance is only one among the factors required for development and a package of technical, managerial, organizational and other facilities, along with finance, would bring about the best results.

f   Facilités d'extension
d   Erweitertes technisches Programm

803   FORECLOSURE
A legal proceeding through which the lending institution or the development bank takes title to the property which has been mortgaged to it because the borrower has failed to fulfill obligations.

f   Exécution sur les biens immeubles
d   Zwangsvollstreckung aus einer Hypothek

804   GLUT
A situation wherein the supply of a commodity is greatly in excess of the demand, leading in consequence, to a considerable fall in price.

f   Encombrement du marché;
Pléthore du marché
d   Uberschwemmung des Marktes

805   GOING CONCERN
An enterprise that is in profitable working condition.

f   Affaire roulante;
Affaire qui marche
d   Gutgehendes Geschäft

806   GOODWILL
The commercial benefits arising from a firm's reputation or business connections. (See: Account, goodwill 861)

f   Fonds de commerce d'une maison;
Achalandage;
Clientèle

d   Ideeller Wert einer Handelsfirm;
    Geschäftswert;
    Kundschaft

807   GRACE PERIOD
      The interval between the first
      installment of loan withdrawals
      and the commencement of repay-
      ment obligations, either of
      principal, or principal plus inter-
      est accruals.

f   Délai de graçe
d   Stundung

808   GUARANTOR
      An individual or institution that
      undertakes to repay a given loan
      in the event of the borrower failing
      to fulfill the repayment obligations.
      In order to minimize borrowing
      costs involved in registration,
      court and stamp fees or for other
      considerations, as in the case of
      chattel or legal mortgage, develop-
      ment banks normally encourage
      these forms of collateral when
      other conditions are considered
      appropriate.

f   Garant;
    Donneur de caution
d   Bürge;
    Garant;
    Gewährsmann

809   INDENT
      A term used in foreign trade or
      orders from abroad, particularly
      when such orders are placed with
      agents or exporters.

f   Ordre d'achat;
    Commande de marchandises;
d   Kaufauftrag;
    Warenbestellung

810   INDENT, CLOSED
      A form of indent wherein the
      foreign buyer specifies the
      manufacturer from whom the
      goods are to be purchased.

f   Ordre fermé
d   Geschlossener Auftrag

811   INDENT, OPEN
      A form of indent wherein the
      agent receiving the order can
      obtain the goods from whomso-
      ever he pleases.

f   Ordre ouvert
d   Offener Auftrag

812   INFORMATION SYSTEM
      A rationalized arrangement for
      the provision of basic data and
      intelligence on the operations of
      an enterprise to enable follow-up
      control and to serve as basis
      for decision-making by develop-
      ment bank management.

f   Système d'information
d   Informationssystem

813   INSOLVENCY
      The condition of a firm or
      enterprise when liabilities
      exceed assets; the usual outcome
      is bankruptcy.

f   Insolvabilité
d   Zahlungsunfähigkeit

814   INSOLVENCY, TECHNICAL
      Circumstances where a firm
      cannot meet its current debts
      as they come due.

f   Insolvabilité technique
d   Technische Zahlungsunfähigkeit

815   INSURANCE COVERAGE
      The responsibility to ensure
      that the assets created out of
      the assistance, as also assets
      offered as collateral against
      a development bank's assistance,
      is adequately insured. It also
      involves the valuation of assets
      to be insured, e.g. on the basis
      of invoice value, replacement
      value, book value among others.

f   Couverture d'assurance
d   Versicherungsdeckung

816   INTER-PROJECT
      COORDINATION
The mechanism to coordinate the
implementation and the management of related but independent
projects, or projects sponsored
by holding companies, or industrial houses, or government
agencies.

f   Coordination entre projets
d   Inter-Projektkoordinierung

817   INTEREST, CONTROLLING;
      CONTROLLING SHARE
      OWNERSHIP
A predominant interest in the
management of an assisted
enterprise by virtue of owning
a majority of equity. Development
banks are normally forbidden -
as a matter of operational
policy - to obtain such a controlling interest in an assisted
firm.

f   Intérêt décisif
d   Ausschlaggebende Interessen;
     Kontrollierender Aktienbesitz

818   INVENTORY
Part of an enterprise's working
assets, consisting of raw
materials to be used in the
manufacture of a product, goods
in process of manufacture, and
finished goods ready for delivery
to customers.

f   Inventaire
d   Bestandliste

819   INVENTORY TURNOVER;
      STOCK TURNOVER
The volume of inventory to be
carried by an enterprise during
the production-cycle period in a
year.

f   Rotation de l'inventaire;
     Rotation du stock
d   Inventarumsatz;
     Lagerumsatz

820   ISSUE, OVERSUBSCRIBED
An issue of shares in the stock
market for which applications
to buy are in excess of shares
available.

f   Sous-émission
d   Unteremission

821   ISSUE, PUBLIC
A method of issuing shares to
raise new capital. Investors
are invited through the news-
papers and other modes of
publicity to apply for stated
amounts of the shares at fixed
prices. (See: Offer for sale
841; Placing 313)

f   Emission publique
d   Öffentliche Emission

822   ISSUE, UNDERSUBSCRIBED
An issue for which applications
to buy have fallen short of the
shares offered.

f   Emission excessive
d   Überemission

823   LETTER OF ALLOTMENT
A communication formulated
on a legally prescribed basis,
intimating those who have
applied for shares in a new
issue, of the actual number of
shares alloted to each applicant;
also applicable in the case of
"rights" issue to existing
shareholders. (See: Allotment
of shares 753)

f   Lettre de répartition;
     Avis de répartition
d   Zuteilungsschein;
     Zuteilungsbenachrichtigung

824   LETTER OF CREDIT;
      BILL OF CREDIT
      A document authorizing a bank
      to pay the bearer a specified sum
      of money; it provides a useful
      means of settlement for a foreign
      trade transaction, the purchaser
      establishing a credit in favor of
      his creditor at a bank.

f   Lettre de crédit
d   Kreditbrief

825   LETTER OF REGRET
      A letter conveying regret sent to
      an applicant who has applied for
      financial assistance in any form.
      The reasons for the inability of
      the development bank to concede
      to the request for assistance is
      also generally specified. Also
      applicable in case of applicants
      for new share issues, not alloted
      any shares.

f   Lettre négative
d   Ablehnungsbrief;
    Ablehnungsschreiben

826   LETTER OF RENUNCIATION
      Method by which a shareholder
      assigns part or all of his rights
      to subscribe to a rights issue to
      someone else.

f   Lettre de renonciation
d   Verzichtsbrief;
    Verzichtsschreiben

827   LIMITING FACTOR
      A factor in the activities of an
      undertaking or an enterprise which
      at a particular point in time,
      or over a period, tends to limit
      the volume of output.

f   Facteur limitant
d   Beschränkender Faktor;
    Limitierender Faktor

828   LIQUIDATION;
      WINDING-UP
      The process of terminating a

company, usually because of its
insolvency. The assets are turned
into cash for settling outstanding
debts and for apportioning the
balance, if any, amongst the
owners.

f   Liquidation
d   Auflösung;
    Liquidation;
    Abrechnung

829   LOAN CONTRACT
      Document legally prescribed
      and enforcible, governing terms,
      conditions and obligations of the
      creditor and the debtor in regard
      to the particular transaction.

f   Contrat de prêt
d   Anleihevertrag

830   MARK-UP
      The percentage of profit added
      to the cost price of goods by
      manufacturers in order to
      determine the selling price.

f   Marge de profit
d   Handelsspanne;
    Preisaufschlag

831   MARKET, SELLERS'
      A condition in the market when
      the level of demand for a
      product outpaces that of
      supplies, and hence, the market
      situation favors sellers.

f   Marché de vendeur
d   Verkäufermarkt

832   MATURITY OF A LOAN
      The date on which a loan comes
      due and must be repaid in full
      by the borrower.

f   Echéance d'un prêt
d   Fälligkeit einer Anleihe

833   MEMORANDUM OF
      ASSOCIATION
      One of the documents that has

to be drawn up when a new company is formed; it gives the title of the company, particulars of the types of business to be undertaken, the amount of its authorized capital, particulars of the shares into which capital is to be divided and a statement that its liability is limited. (See: Articles of association 75b)

f   Acte constitutif d'une société;
     Contrat d'association;
     Acte de société
d   Vertrag über die Errichtung einer
     Gesellschaft;
     Gesellschaftsvertrag

834   MERGER;
      ABSORPTION
The acquisition of one corporation by another, in which one loses its corporate existence. Development banks normally encourage, if not initiate, such mergers when confronted with delinquent clients who do not display prospects of recovery on their own ability.

f   Unification
d   Zusammenschluss;
     Verschmelzung

835   MODERNIZATION
The process of upgrading existing know-how in regard to management, production techniques and technologies, and organizational methods, to higher and modern levels.

f   Modernisation
d   Modernisierung

836   MONITORING SYSTEM
An important part of postfinance supervisory functions of a development bank, comprising a reporting and trouble-shooting system which would anticipate and identify problem projects, pin-point likely problem areas of individual

assisted projects, diagnose and render required assistance in the solution of identified problems.

f   Système de citation
d   Mahnsystem

837   MORTGAGE INSTRUMENT
A legal deed entered into by the debtor surrendering stated rights to the creditor for stated periods, or subject to stated pre-conditions being fulfilled, for value or consideration received.

f   Instrument hypothécaire
d   Hypothekendokument

838   OBJECTS CLAUSE
The clause in the Memorandum of Association of a company which indicates the field and scope of activity to be engaged in by the company.

f   Clause de l'objectif de l'entre-
     prise
d   Klausel der Zielsetzung einer
     Gesellschaft

839   OBSOLESCENCE
The loss in value of physical assets due to technological changes rather than due to physical deterioration. The depreciation allowance legally permissible sometimes provides against this element.

f   Désuétude
d   Überalterung

840   OFF THE SHELF GOODS
Plant, machinery and equipment readily available for delivery against order.

f   Biens disponibles
d   Bereitstehende Güter

841   OFFER FOR SALE

107

The offer of new securities to the public, not on behalf of the company itself, but by one or more holders to whom they have already been issued. Normally the holder is an issuing house which has bought the new issue from the company concerned and is now offering them to the public at a slightly higher price, the difference covering the expenses of the offer.
(See: Placing 313; Issue, public 821)

f   Offre pour vente
d   Verkaufsangebot

842   OFFICIAL RECEIVER
An official appointed under relevant legal frame of a country, to take control of a bankrupt's properties until a trustee is appointed; he has also to take charge of the winding-up of a company that has failed.

f   Administrateur officiel de faillite;
     Syndic officiel de faillite
d   Behördlich bestellter Konkurs-verwalter;
     Zwangsverwalter

843   OPERATIONAL PROBLEM
Uncontrolled situation encountered by enterprises in the stage of their day-to-day operations, e.g. lack of raw materials, uncoordinated delivery of supplies, market fluctuations, sales difficulties, competitive factors, etc.

f   Problème opérationel
d   Operationelles Problem

844   PROCEDURE, INCORPORATION
The legal formulation required to be undertaken for the formation and incorporation of a corporation.

f   Procédure d'incorporation
d   Gründungsverfahren

845   PROCUREMENT, SOURCES OF
Countries wherefrom supplies of plant and machinery can be procured out of the proceeds of a loan.

f   Sources d'approvisionnement
d   Maschinen- und Material-beschaffungsquellen

846   PROFIT MARGIN
A measure of net profit arising from the operations of an enter-prise in a given period, calcul-ated as a percentage of sales, net worth or capital invested.

f   Marge de profit
d   Profitspanne

847   PROFIT MAXIMATION
Efforts to maximize the level of output which will yield the largest total profit.

f   Maximation de profit
d   Profitmaximierung

848   PROSPECTUS
A document issued by a company to raise capital by public subscription; the minimum contents of a prospectus are defined in the Companies Act.

f   Appel à la souscription publique
d   Öffentliche Zeichnungsein-ladung

849   PROXY
Written authority given by a stockholder to some others, giving the latter the right to vote at a stockholders' meeting.

f   Pouvoir-mandat;
     Délégation de pouvoirs;
     Procuration
d   Stellvertretung;
     Vertretungsmacht

850   REDEPLOYMENT

108

A rearrangement of factors of production in an enterprise to bring about efficiency increases and to promote productivity.

f   Réorganisation
d   Umgruppierung

851   REPORTING SYSTEM
An institutionalized arrangement of communication of performances of enterprises, or individual departments and divisions of an organization, to enable the management, or those in charge of departments and divisions, to control and regulate the operations of these individual entities within the framework of targets and plans already set out. In the context of development banks, a rationalized reporting system (as between the assisted enterprises and the development bank and within the supervisory divisions and the management of the development bank) does serve as an effective follow-up monitoring system.

f   Système de reportage
d   Berichterstattungssystem

852   RIGHTS LETTER
A document entitling a shareholder to subscribe to additional issues of all types of shares and debentures by the company in a stated proportion.

f   Lettre de répartition des nouvelles émissions
d   Bezugsrechtschreiben

853   RIGHTS, CONVERSION
Debentures giving the holder the right, within a specified period, to convert them into ordinary shares of the company on specified terms. (See: Debenture, convertible 263)

f   Droit de conversion

d   Umschuldungsrecht;
    Konversionsrecht

854   SALES PROMOTION
Efforts to increase sales, by creating or expanding demand for a product. Means of sales promotion; includes displays, free samples, temporary reductions in price, among others.

f   Promotion de vente
d   Verkaufsförderung

855   TENDER DOCUMENTS
Papers relating to offer of supplies for plant, equipment and machinery, to be made against the proceeds of a loan.

f   Documents de soumission
d   Lieferungsangebotdokumente;
    Submissionsoffertedokumente

856   TENDER SPECIFICATION
A descriptive account of the type, capacity, dimensions, processes, and the individual items of procurement offered for bidding.

f   Spécification de soumission;
    Précisions de soumission
d   Einzelheiten der Lieferungs-
    angebote;
    Spezifikation der Submissions-
    offerte

857   TRANSFER OF SHARES
The process of changing share ownership title from the original owner to the present owner in the register of the company.

f   Cession de titres
d   Übertragung von Wertpapieren

858   TRUSTEE, PUBLIC
An official appointed by the State to act as executor or trustee to anyone wishing to make use of his services.

f   Fiduciaire publique;
    Curateur publique
d   Öffentlicher Treuhänder

859   TURNOVER
    The number of times during a
    year the inventory of a firm is
    sold; the annual stock turnover
    can be computed by dividing
    annual sales by the average
    inventory.

f   Chiffre d'affaires
d   Umsatz

860   UNSECURED CREDITOR
    A creditor whose claim is on the
    general assets of the debtor as
    distinct from a secured creditor
    whose claim rests on a specified
    asset of the debtor.

f   Créditeur sans garantie
d   Ungesicherter Gläubiger;
    Ungedeckter Gläubiger

PART THREE
DEVELOPMENT BANK

VIII.
CAPITALIZATION
CAPITALISATION
KAPITALSTRUKTUR

861 ACCOUNT, GOODWILL
The capitalized value of
intangibles accompanying the
reputation of an enterprise or a
financing institution; such good
reputation normally ensures
continuity in the levels of the
operation of the unit in the event
of change of ownership. Goodwill
is capitalized as an intangible
asset when change of ownership
is contemplated.

f Compte de clientèle;
Compte de fonds de commerce
d Firmenwertkonto

862 APPLICATION MONEY
The initial amount of money
accompanying an application for
new issues of shares or debentures.

f Versement de souscription
d Zeichnungsbetrag

863 ASSET
A physical property or intangible
right, owned by an enterprise.

f Actif;
Valeur active;
Poste de l'actif
d Vermögenswert;
Aktivposten

864 ASSET APPRECIATION
An increase in the market value
of an asset (stocks, bonds, plant
and equipment, real estate) above
its value at some prior period.

f Plus-value d'actif
d Vermögenszuwachs

865 ASSETS OF A BANK
Comprise items which are:
readily liquid in nature, such as
coins, notes and balances at
the Central Bank; money at call
and short notice and bills
discounted; and less liquid items,
such as special deposits at the
Central Bank, investments, and
advances to customers.

f Valeurs actives d'une banque
d Aktivposten einer Bank

866 ASSETS, CURRENT;
ASSETS, FLOATING
Assets that can readily be
turned into cash, including cash
on hand, accounts receivable,
inventories and marketable
securities.

f Actif courant
d Laufende Aktivposten;
Umlaufsvermögen

867 ASSETS, EARNING
Assets that earn, e.g. interest-
earning securities possessed
by a development bank or an
enterprise.

f Actif d'exploitation;
Actif de capacité d'acquérir
d Ertragsfähige Vermögenswerte

113

868 ASSETS, FIXED;
ASSETS, NON-CURRENT;
FIXED CAPITAL
Assets of a relatively permanent
nature, with a life greater than
one year, such as land, buildings,
and machinery.

f Capital fixe;
Capitaux fixes;
Valeurs immobilisées
d Anlagekapital;
Anlagevermögen;
Feste Aktiven

869 ASSETS, FROZEN
Assets that are not readily
convertible into cash, or those
which can be sold only with great
loss in value; it is the opposite
of liquid assets.

f Avoirs bloqués;
Avoirs immobilisés
d Blockierte Vermögenswerte

870 ASSETS, INTANGIBLE
Consist of certain non-material
rights and benefits of a firm,
such as patents, copyrights,
trademarks, and goodwill.

f Valeurs immatérielles;
Valeurs intangibles
d Immaterielle Aktiva;
Unantastbare Vermögenswerte

871 ASSETS, LIQUID
Readily realizable current assets.

f Valeurs disponibles;
Actif disponible;
Disponibilités;
Actif liquide
d Verfügbare Mittel;
Flüssige Mittel;
Flüssige Anlagen

872 ASSETS, NET;
NET CAPITAL
The assets attributable to the
share capital after deducting external liabilities including the

future taxation reserve and the
nominal value of any debentures,
added to any premium payable
on them and any arrears of
interest.

f Actif net
d Reinvermögen;
Nettovermögen

873 ASSETS, NET EQUITY
The net assets minus the repayment value of the preference
capital including any arrears of
preference dividend.

f Actif intact
d Unbelastetes Anlagevermögen

874 ASSETS, QUICK;
ASSETS, READY
An accounting term referring
to current assets excluding inventories.

f Actif disponible
d Rasch umsetzbare Vermögenswerte

875 ASSETS, SLOW
Assets convertible into cash
at book value only after a long
time.

f Actif indisponible
d Langfristig umsetzbare
Vermögenswerte

876 ASSETS, SUNDRY
Assets, such as land held for
future use or long-term investment in securities, which do not
fall into the other classifi-
cations.

f Actif divers
d Sonstige Vermögenswerte;
Verschiedene Aktiva

877 ASSETS, TANGIBLE
All assets of "physical" nature
which are durable, including
plant, machinery, land, etc.

(See: Assets, intangible 870)

f   Valeurs tangibles;
    Valeurs matérielles
d   Greifbare Vermögenswerte

878   ASSETS, WASTING
    An irreplaceable asset, and one,
    the life of which cannot be
    prolonged, e.g. a mine.

f   Actif périssable
d   Unersetzbare Vermögenswerte

879   ASSETS COVERAGE, FIXED
    Indicates the degree of consoli-
    dation of an enterprise; derived
    by dividing equity by fixed
    assets.

f   Couverture des capitaux fixes
d   Anlagekapitaldeckung

880   BORROWING BASE;
    BORROWING CAPACITY
    Refers to the equity and
    quasi-equity components in the
    total capitalization of an enter-
    prise, which forms the basis
    for its present and future term-
    borrowing. (See: Leverage 919;
    Capital gearing 883)

f   Base de crédit;
    Capacité de crédit
d   Kreditbasis;
    Kreditkapazität

881   BORROWING POWER
    Authorization provided by the
    Charter of Incorporation to the
    Board of Directors, and/or to
    management in regard to the
    volume (related to owner's capital
    or equity), varieties and sources
    to augment the resources of the
    enterprise.

f   Pouvoir de crédit
d   Kreditfähigkeit

882   CALL;
    CALLABLE CAPITAL

When the shares of a development bank or a limited company
are not fully paid at the time
of issue the development bank
or company may call for payment of the amount outstanding
or a portion of it, when it
requires additional capital.
In regard to international
financing agencies, the
"callable" part of the subscribed
capital normally forms a
guaranty to the agency concerned
for its market borrowings.

f   Capital appelé
d   Zur Einzahlung aufgerufenes
    Kapital

883   CAPITAL GEARING
    Refers to the extent of borrow-
    ings related to the volume of
    equity of an enterprise.

f   Intensité de crédit
d   Kreditintensität

884   CAPITAL PARTICIPATION;
    CAPITAL SUBSCRIPTION
    Contribution towards the equity
    capital of a development bank
    or an enterprise, or contri-
    bution by the government towards
    the initial capitalization of a
    project of infrastructure
    nature.

f   Capital de participation
d   Kapitalbeteiligung

885   CAPITAL, AUTHORIZED;
    CAPITAL, REGISTERED
    The amount of capital a new
    development bank indicates to,
    and is authorized by, the
    company law authorities as its
    ultimate equity level.

f   Capital déclaré;
    Capital nominal;
    Fonds social
d   Grundkapital;

Gesellschaftskapital;
Nominalkapital

886   CAPITAL, AUXILIARY;
       CAPITAL, INSTRUMENTAL
All the machinery and equipment
used in production.

f   Capital auxiliaire
d   Hilfskapital

887   CAPITAL, DEBT;
       CAPITAL, LOAN
That part of a company's capital
represented by long term loans
and debentures.

f   Capital d'emprunt
d   Anleihekapital;
    Darlehenskapital

888   CAPITAL, EMPLOYED
The amount of total funds in use
in an enterprise; normally
computed as a balance of total
assets minus current liabilities.

f   Capital de roulement
d   Eingesetztes Kapital

889   CAPITAL, ISSUED
That part of the authorized capital
which is issued to the general
public.

f   Capital émis;
    Capital mis en circulation
d   In Umlauf gesetztes Kapital

890   CAPITAL, NOMINAL
The amount of share capital
fixed by a company's
memorandum of association.
(See: Capital, authorized 885)

f   Capital nominal;
    Capital social
d   Nominalkapital;
    Grundkapital

891   CAPITAL, OWNERS'
The volume of funds, in the total
capitalization of a project, brought
in by the promoters, in one
form or the other, such as equity
held by them, unsecured subordinated advances, among
others.

f   Capital de propriétaire
d   Eigenkapital

892   CAPITAL, PRODUCERS';
       CAPITAL, REAL
Fixed assets comprising plant,
equipment, facilities and raw
materials for use in production.

f   Capital de production;
    Capital réel
d   Produktionskapital

893   CAPITAL, RESERVE
That part of the issued and
subscribed capital which is not
called yet and which is not
included in the borrowing base.

f   Capital de réserve
d   Reservekapital

894   CAPITAL, SHARE;
       CAPITAL, STOCK
Represents the permanent
element of capital of a development bank or an enterprise
raised through shares and
stocks of various types.

f   Capital-actions;
    Capital originaire;
    Capital initial;
    Capital d'établissement
d   Aktienkapital;
    Stammkapital;
    Gesellschaftskapital;
    Grundkapital

895   CAPITAL, SUBSCRIBED;
       CAPITAL, PAID-IN;
       CAPITAL, PAID-UP
That part of the issued capital
which is actually called-up and
paid-in by subscribers.

f   Capital souscrit;

Capital versé;
Capital effectif;
Capital réel;
Mise de fonds
d   Gezeichnetes Kapital;
Eingezahltes Kapital

896   CAPITAL, UNCALLED
Issued and subscribed capital,
remaining uncalled. The uncalled
capital is regarded as reserve
capital. (See: Capital, reserve
893)

f   Capital non appelé
d   Noch nicht zur Einzahlung aufgerufenes Kapital

897   CAPITAL, UNIMPAIRED
Capital which is not subordinated
to any debts or liabilities.

f   Capital intact
d   Unbelastetes Kapital

898   CAPITAL, VENTURE;
CAPITAL, RISK
Capital that is subject to considerable risk, e.g. portfolio investments of development banks in
a new enterprise, or the equity
participation of the public in
enterprises.

f   Capital de risque
d   Risikokapital

899   CAPITALIZATION;
CAPITAL STRUCTURE
The initial combination of equity
capital, ordinary and preferred,
and borrowed funds.

f   Capitalisation
d   Kapitalstruktur;
Kapitalisierung

900   CAPITALIZATION ISSUE;
BONUS ISSUE;
SCRIP ISSUE
A free issue of securities to those
who are already shareholders,
with the object of bringing a

company's capital structure into
line with the true value of its
assets.

f   Emission de capitalisation
d   Kapitalisierungsemission

901   CAPITALIZATION RATIO
Proportion of each type of stock
and share issued by a company.

f   Taux de capitalisation
d   Kapitalisierungsverhältnis

902   CAPITALIZATION OF
RESERVES
The process of formally
allocating unimpaired reserves
amongst eligible shareholders
through issue of bonus shares.
(See: Stock dividend 364)

f   Capitalisation des réserves
d   Reservekapitalisierung

903   DEBT CEILING;
DEBT LIMIT
Placing a ceiling on the amount
of debt that may be outstanding
at any one time; the term refers
to debt limitations imposed by
lenders and authorized by
shareholders.

f   Limitation de dette
d   Schuldbegrenzung

904   DEBTS, FLOATING
Borrowings of short-term
duration.

f   Dette flottante
d   Unfundierte Schuld;
Schwebende Schuld

905   DEBTS, FUNDED
Long term debts incurred by
means of debentures or
securities as opposed to
short-term borrowings; and
whose amortization is provided
for.

f   Dette consolidée;

Dette fondée
d   Konsolidierte Schuld;
Fundierte Schuld

906   DEBTS, JUNIOR;
JUNIOR LOANS
Borrowings which rank last for
repayment in the event of
liquidation.

f   Dettes de dernière priorité
d   Schulden mit letzter Priorität

907   DEBTS, SENIOR;
SENIOR LOANS
Borrowings which rank first for
repayment in the event of
liquidation.

f   Dettes de première priorité
d   Schulden mit erster Priorität

908   EQUITIES;
ORDINARY SHARES
The ordinary shares of a limited
company; they carry the right
to the residual of a company's
assets after it has paid all its
creditors, and share in the
distribution of profits, if any,
after meeting all prior obligations
including dividend on preference
shares.

f   Actions ordinaires
d   Stammaktien

909   EQUITY;
EQUITY, SHAREHOLDERS'
A balance sheet concept; the
excess of a firm's assets over
its liabilities. Owners' capital
comprising paid-in share capital
and retained earnings.

f   Capital-actions
d   Grundkapital;
Stammkapital

910   EQUITY, NON-VOTING
Securities, the possession of which
does not entitle the holder to vote
at meetings of the shareholders.

f   Capital-actions sans droit de
vote
d   Grundkapital ohne Stimmrecht

911   EXPOSURE
The extent of risk, measured
in terms of volume of investment or loan portfolios, to
which the development bank
is exposed.

f   Exposition
d   Aussetzung

912   FLOATATION
The raising of new capital by
public subscription.

f   Emission d'obligations
d   Ausgabe von Obligationen

913   FUND, REVOLVING
A fund that is continually re-
plenished as it is used, either
through further appropriation
or by income generated by the
activity that it finances.

f   Fonds renouvelable
d   Sich stets erneuernder Fonds;
Revolvierender Fonds

914   FUND, SINKING
Specific provision made for
redeeming specific obligations.
A method of amortizing a debt
which will mature at a future
date.

f   Fonds d'amortissement
d   Amortisationsfonds;
Schuldentilgungsfonds;
Ablösungsfonds

915   FUNDING;
LOAN CONVERSION
The conversion of short-term
debts into long-term debts.

f   Conversion d'un emprunt
d   Umwandlung einer Anleihe;
Anleiheumwandlung

916 FUNDING OPERATION
The process of reducing the floating debt by replacing it through funded stocks and debentures for stipulated periods; the term also refers to the process of liquidating debt of long term duration carrying higher interests by new stocks and debentures bearing lower rates of interest, particularly at a time when interest rates tend to fall.

f   Opération de consolidation
d   Konsolidierungsoperation

917 HIGHLY GEARED COMPANY
A development bank or an enterprise where borrowed capital forms a disproportionately large component of total capital in relation to equity. Development banks are generally highly geared.

f   Entreprise à grande intensité de dettes
d   Unternehmen mit hoher Leih-kapitalquote

918 INVESTMENT, GROSS FIXED
The addition over the accounting year to the fixed assets of an enterprise without making allowance for depreciation.

f   Brut investissement fixe
d   Feste Bruttokapitalanlage

919 LEVERAGE
The ratio between the sum of term-borrowings and, preferred stocks in relation to common stock. A stock has a "high leverage" if the company has a large proportion of term-borrowings and preferred stock in relation to the amount of common stock. The leverage occurs when the return on total investment is greater than the interest on borrowed funds. (See: Highly geared company 917)

f   Intensité de dettes à long terme·
d   Leihkapitalquote;
    Leihkapitalintensität

920 LEVERAGE, REAL
The number of times the net worth a development bank or an enterprise is permitted to borrow; represents the borrowing limit authorized by lenders measured in terms of the equity base.

f   Limitation de crédit
d   Kreditlimitierung;
    Kreditbeschränkung

921 LIABILITY OF A COMPANY
The liabilities side of the balance sheet of an enterprise indicating what it owes to its shareholders, (subscribed share capital and free reserves) to lending institutions, (principal repayment and interest), and to sundry creditors.

f   Dettes d'une entreprise
d   Verbindlichkeiten eines Unter-nehmens

922 LIABILITY, CONTINGENT
Liability of technical nature which may become effective in future, subject to certain unlikely events, such as failure on the part of a guarantee.

f   Engagement éventuel
d   Bedingte Verbindlichkeit;
    Eventuell eintretende Verbind-lichkeit

923 LIABILITY, LIMITED
The restriction of the obligation of a shareholder in a corporation to the amount of capital he has invested in it.

f   Engagement limité
d   Beschränkte Verbindlichkeit;
    Beschränkte Schuld

924 LIABILITY, LONG-TERM
Liability maturing after a period
of one year, such as mortgages,
long-term notes, and bonds.

f Dette à long terme;
Passif non exigible
d Langfristige Verbindlichkeit;
Langfristige Schuld

925 LIABILITY, SECURED
Claims that have specific assets
pledged as security.

f Créance garantie;
Engagement garanti
d Gedeckte Verbindlichkeit;
Gesicherte Schuld

926 LIABILITY, SHORT-TERM;
LIABILITY, CURRENT
Liability to be discharged within
a year, e.g. payroll obligations,
accounts payable, taxes due,
accrued interest, short-term
notes.

f Dette à court terme;
Exigibilités;
Le passif exigible;
Passif courant
d Kurzfristige Verbindlichkeit;
Fällige Verbindlichkeit

927 LIABILITY, UNSECURED
Debts which depend on the general
resources of the firm for dis-
charging and not backed by specific
assets.

f Créance sans garantie;
Dette chirographaire
d Ungesicherte Verbindlichkeit;
Ungedeckte Schuld

928 LINE OF CREDIT;
CREDIT LINE
An arrangement by which an
international lender places loanable
funds at the disposal of a development bank for sub-lending and
hence, forms a significant part
of the operational resources of

several development banks.

f Ligne de crédit
d Kreditlinie;
Kreditrahmen

929 LOAN, SUBORDINATED
Loan, repayment of which ranks
lower to some other debt
obligations.

f Prêt inférieur;
Prêt subordonné
d Untergeordnete Anleihe

930 NET WORTH
The excess of assets over
liabilities as shown by the
balance sheet, i.e. the capital
owned by a business.

f Actif net
d Kapitalvermögen;
Reinvermögen;
Nettovermögen

931 OVER-CAPITALIZATION
Situation where an enterprise
operates with more capital of
all types than its real assets.

f Sur-capitalisation
d Überkapitalisierung

932 OVER-SUBSCRIPTION
A situation where requests from
subscribers for a new issue of
shares and other securities
exceeds the number offered.

f Dépassement de souscriptions
d Überzeichnung

933 PORTFOLIO
A list of investments of various
types.

f Portefeuille des effets
d Aktienbestand

934 PRIOR CHARGES
Securities or other sources of
funds including borrowings,
ranking before ordinary shares

for repayment and interest on dividend distribution, e.g. debentures and preference shares.

f Débit prioritaire
d Bevorrechtigte Kosten

935 RATIO, COMMON STOCK
The ratio of ordinary shares or stocks to the total of all shares or stocks and bonds by an enterprise.

f Taux des actions ordinaires
d Stammaktienintensität

936 REDEMPTION
A method for retiring bonded indebtedness; the other methods being refunding and conversion.

f Amortissement
d Tilgung

937 REDEMPTION DATE
The date on which the debentures will be redeemed.

f Date d'amortissement
d Tilgungsdatum

938 RESERVES
Amounts appropriated from net profits into specific funds as cushions.

f Réserves
d Reserven

939 RESERVES, CONTINGENCY;
CONTINGENT RESERVES
Special provisions made through annual appropriations for meeting unforeseen obligations.

f Réserves de prévoyance;
Réserves pour éventualités
d Notreserven;
Notrücklagen

940 RESERVES, DEPRECIATION
A valuation-reserve account used to record depreciation charges.

f Réserves d'amortissement
d Abschreibungsreserven

941 RESERVES, EXCESS
The difference between available reserves and reserves required statutorily, relevant for commercial banks and related financial institutions, operating under the banking legislation of the country concerned.

f Réserves extraordinaires
d Überschüssige Reserven

942 RESERVES, FREE
Reserves held in excess of legal requirements, or uncommitted reserves.

f Réserves libres
d Freie Reserven

943 RESERVES, LEGAL;
RESERVES, STATUTORY
The proportion of cash, or cash-like liquid assets to be held by development banks and other entities, prescribed by concerned law, enforced by the country's concerned authorities.

f Réserves légales
d Gesetzlicher Reservefonds;
Gesetzliche Reserven

944 RESERVES, MINIMUM LEGAL
The amount which legal reserve has to reach and is expressed as percentage of paid-up capital.

f Réserves légales minimales
d Gesetzliche Minimum-Reserven

945 TALON
A slip attached to dividend and interest coupons for the purpose of applying for further coupons when necessary.

f Talon
d Erneuerungsschein;
Talon

946 THIN CORPORATION
A corporation that owes a large
proportion of debt relative to its
equity capital.

f 'Corporation d'une faible
capitalisation
d Kapitalschwache Körperschaft

947 UNDER-CAPITALIZATION
Situation where an enterprise has
not enough capital; a likely cause
of failure if a firm is imprudent
enough to attempt operations
without sufficient capital and
reserves.

f Sous-capitalisation
d Unterkapitalisierung

948 VALUE, BOOK
The value of assets according to
the accounting records; normally
represents depreciated values in
regard to fixed assets, current
market prices in regard to
current assets.

f Valeur comptable
d Buchwert

949 VALUE, BREAK-UP
The value at current stock exchange prices of the stocks and
shares held; the value of an enterprise at the time of liquidation.

f Valeur de liquidation
d Abbruchswert;
Liquidationswert

950 VALUE, CAPITALIZED
The value of an asset or its
current earnings in relation to
the prevailing rate of interest;
derived by multiplying annual
earnings with the estimated
economic life of the asset.

f Valeur capitalisée
d Kapitalisierter Wert

951 VALUE, MARKET
The price of assets that could
be realized if offered for sale
on the free market.

f Valeur de marché
d Marktwert

IX.
ORGANIZATION, MANAGEMENT AND STAFF
ORGANISATION, ADMINISTRATION ET PERSONNEL
ORGANISATION, VERWALTUNG UND PERSONAL

952   ADVISER, ECONOMIC
A senior development bank
professional with achievement
and proficiency in the theory,
techniques and tools of economic
analysis, responsible for
structuring systems for the flow
of economic and commercial
intelligence, guiding analysis of
operational and environmental
data of relevance to the decision-
making processes of development
bank management, coordinating
economic aspects of project
appraisal and also on economic
studies of industries, market
studies, diagnostic studies of
assisted enterprises and such
other studies as are called for in
the operations of the development
bank.

f   Conseiller économique
d   Wirtschaftskonsulent

953   ADVISER, FINANCIAL;
INVESTMENT MANAGER
Head of division or department in
a development bank looking after
the portfolio investment and
capital market operations and
other short term investments of
the funds of the institution. Also
coordinates evaluation of the
financial aspects of project
appraisal.

f   Directeur de placement;
Directeur d'investissement
d   Investitionsleiter

954   ADVISER, TECHNICAL
A professional with the responsibilities of overseeing the
engineering aspects of project
appraisals in a development
bank.

f   Conseiller technique
d   Technischer Berater

955   AGENCY, AUTONOMOUS
A development banking institution with its own Articles of
Association and its responsibilities flowing therefrom;
hence, is independent, in regard
to its operation and decision-
making process, of external in-
fluences, although its ownership
may be in the hands of one or
more authorities or interests.

f   Agence autonome
d   Selbständige Niederlassung

956   APPRAISER;
VALUATOR
A professional valuator of
property.

f   Appréciateur;
Estimateur
d   Schätzer

957   AUDITOR
Traditionally applied to quali-
fied and recognized accounting
experts with the main job of
verifying the authenticity of
financial transactions and of

testifying to their correctness.
Under modern business management practices an auditor has
the added responsibility of
restructuring methods and
practices currently adopted.

f Expert comptable;
   Commissaire des comptes
d Buchsachverständiger;
   Rechnungsprüfer

958 AUDITOR, EXTERNAL
An auditor or auditing firm
statutorily to be employed by
an enterprise, with responsibilities to the shareholders for
undertaking audit functions of
the enterprise.

f Expert comptable externe
d Externer Buchprüfer

959 AUDITOR, INTERNAL
An auditor employed as a
member of the staff of the
institution with responsibilities
to the management of the
organization or enterprise.

f Expert comptable interne
d Interner Buchprüfer

960 BANK CHARTER;
     CHARTER OF INCORPORATION
The legal frame of a development
bank endowing it its status as
legal entity, defining its
objectives, powers and organizational set-up.

f Charte d'Incorporation
d Bankverfassung

961 BANKER, DEVELOPMENT
A professional incorporating the
diverse expertise involved in
development banking operations.

f Banquier de développement;
   Expert financier de développement
d Entwicklungsbankfachmann

962 BANKER, INVESTMENT
A professional specialized in
operations concerned with investment of public or corporate
funds in the capital market or
in other gilt-edged securities;
concept narrower than that of a
development banker.

f Banquier d'investissement;
   Banquier de placement
d Investitionsbankfachmann

963 BOARD OF DIRECTORS
A committee elected by the
shareholders of a national
development bank or a firm to
be responsible to the shareholders for the overall operation.
Sometimes full-time functional
directors are appointed, each
being responsible for some
particular department.

f Comité de directeurs
d Direktionsausschuss;
   Direktionskomitee

964 BY-LAWS OF THE CHARTER
Individual sections of a charter
of incorporation of a development bank laying down specific
duties, responsibilities,
obligations and rights and
privileges.

f Statut de la Charte
d Satzungen;
   Nebengesetze

965 CONSULTANT, INDUSTRIAL;
     CONSULTANT, TECHNICAL;
     CONSULTING ENGINEER
External expertise availed of
by development banks for
evaluating technical and
engineering aspects of a loan
proposal, or assigned to review
the operations of an assisted
project.

f Ingénieur conseil
d Beratender Ingenieur

966 CONSULTANT, MANAGE-
MENT
Outside expertise availed of by
development banks normally to
evaluate an assisted enterprise
in matters concerning managerial
aspects; also sometimes to
evaluate the managerial competence and other requirements
concerning a loan project.

f   Conseiller d'entreprise
d   Unternehmensberater

967 CONSULTATIVE GROUP
A body of persons representing
diverse fields of expertise
appointed by national or international development banks, to
whom specific aspects of loan
proposals are referred for
expert advice.

f   Groupe consultatif
d   Konsulentengruppe

968 CONSULTING FIRM
External expertise normally
made use of by development banks
to supplement their own project
evaluation and post-finance
follow-up expertise.

f   Maison de consultation
d   Konsulentenfirma

969 DECISION MAKING
The whole range of activities involved in establishing a
corporate policy or an effective
means of executing an existing
policy, including the collection
of facts needed to make judgment
on a specific proposal and the
analysis of alternative means of
achieving a desired goal.

f   Procédé de décision
d   Entscheidungsfällung

970 DECISION-MAKING PROCESS
Institutionalized arrangements
within a development bank to

arrive at judgments to base
decisions.

f   Processus de procédé de
    décision
d   Entscheidungsfällungsprozess

971 DEPARTMENT, ACCOUNTING
Organizational arrangements
within some development banks,
responsible for maintenance of
books of accounts, for making
and receiving payments and
housekeeping functions.

f   Comptabilité
d   Buchhaltungsabteilung

972 DEPARTMENT, CREDIT;
DEPARTMENT, LOAN
Organizational arrangements
within some development banks
for evaluating the credit rating
of a financing proposal, or an
intending borrower; functions
such as evaluating the commercial,
economic, financial and managerial aspects of a financing proposal are normally undertaken
by this department by itself
or under its supervision by other
appropriate divisions.

f   Département des crédits;
    Service des crédits
d   Kreditabteilung

973 DEPARTMENT, DIS-
BURSEMENT
Organizational arrangements
within a development bank for
finalizing, in cooperation with
the legal and loan departments,
the various legal and contractual pre-conditions concerning
a financing proposal and for
actual release of funds.

f   Département de déboursement
d   Auszahlungsabteilung

974 DEPARTMENT, END-USE;
DEPARTMENT, FOLLOW-UP

Organizational arrangements
within some development banks
for overseeing the performance
of assisted projects, during the
stage of implementation and
commercial operation; normally
a monitoring and troubleshooting
unit about likely problem areas
in individual projects.

f Département de "follow-up"
d Kontrollabteilung

975 DEPARTMENT, ENGINEERING;
DEPARTMENT, TECHNICAL
Organizational arrangement
within some development banks
for evaluating the technical
aspects of a project, particularly
analyzing the technical feasibility,
suitability of machinery, providing
technical advice regarding promotional activities and assisting
in follow-up functions.

f Département technique
d Technische Abteilung

976 DEPARTMENT, LEGAL
Organizational arrangements
within some development banks
for legal documentation and other
legal responsibilities associated
with its financing activities.

f Service du contentieux;
Bureau du contentieux
d Rechtsabteilung

977 DEPARTMENT, MARKET
RESEARCH
Organizational arrangements
evolved in some development
banks for identifying and promoting new projects, undertaking
market surveys, domestic and
export, and for undertaking
evaluation of the market and
marketing aspects of a project.

f Département de recherche du
marché
d Marktforschungsabteilung

978 DEPARTMENT, OPERATIONS
Organizational arrangements
within some development banks
for coordinating the various
project evaluation and follow-
up functions performed by
individual expert divisions, such
as economic, financial and
engineering divisions.

f Département d'opération;
Département opératoire
d Operationelle Abteilung

979 DEPARTMENT, PROJECTS
Organizational arrangements
evolved in some development
banks to pool their diverse
professional expertise for
evaluating projects and also for
performing other functions, such
as project identification,
preparation of feasibility studies
and undertaking diagnostic studies of assisted projects.

f Département de projet
d Projektabteilung

980 DEPARTMENT, SECURITIES
Organizational arrangements
within a development bank to
issue, transfer and maintain
records of the development
bank's own shares, safe custody
of collateral documents
received from borrowers and
in some instances, performing
share issue and other security
management functions on
behalf of clients.

f Département de titres
d Wertpapierabteilung

981 DEVELOPMENT
ADMINISTRATION
Organizational arrangements
evolved within the governmental
apparatus of the country to
implement and coordinate
developmental programmes;

also used for administrative activities geared towards, and with an emphasis on, developmental activities, as opposed to administration geared towards "law and order".

f   Administration du développement
d   Entwicklungsverwaltung

982   DEVELOPMENT BANK EXPERT
A professional with a development banking orientation and perspectives with the background of any one or, more expertise, such as financial, management, engineering, involved in the operation of a development banking institution.

f   Expert d'une banque de développement
d   Entwicklungsbankfachmann

983   ECONOMICS DIVISION
A department within a development bank for providing economic, statistical, commercial and capital market intelligence to the management; also in some cases, undertaking market research and industry profile studies, and providing economic and market evaluation for financial proposals.

f   Département économique
d   Wirtschaftsabteilung; Wirtschaftsforschungsabteilung

984   EXPORT INTELLIGENCE
A department or unit which computes and disseminates information appertaining exports to various entities.

f   Informations d'exportation
d   Exportnachrichten

985   FIELD STAFF
Personnel engaged at the grass root operations; investigators and extension staff in contact with client enterprises.

f   Personnel sur le terrain
d   Feldpersonal

986   FINANCIAL ANALYST
A professional trained in analyzing and interpreting financial and commercial data of an enterprise and experienced in arriving at judgments on crucial financial ratios applicable to enterprises in different industries.

f   Expert financier
d   Finanzfachmann

987   INVESTMENT COUNSELLOR
A person or firm engaged by a development bank, undertakes management of investments or assists clients in this regard.

f   Consultant d'investissements
d   Investitionsverwalter

988   LEGAL OFFICER; LEGAL COUNSEL
A professional with the training and background of the various laws governing the operations of corporate entities and responsible for the legal documentation aspects of the operations of a development bank.

f   Jurisconsulte d'une banque
d   Bankjurist

989   LINE RELATIONSHIP
Indicates the line of authority, e.g. in a workshop the works manager, foreman, chargehands, and workmen.

f   Relation hyrarchique des compétences
d   Kompetenzhyrarchie

990   LINE AND FUNCTIONAL ORGANIZATION
Denotes the functional relationship amongst functionaries as

e.g. between the sales manager and the chief buyer or purchasing officer. In practice the line and functional relationship are generally combined.

f   Organisation des compétences et des functions
d   Kompetenz- und Funktions-organisation

991   LINE AND STAFF ORGANIZATION
Denotes the organizational relationship existing amongst various echelons in an enterprise.

f   Organisation des compétences et du personnel
d   Kompetenz- und Personal-organisation

992   LOAN COMMITTEE
An institutionalized arrangement within a development bank to decide on individual applications for financial assistance; normally the highest executive authority, e.g. the Board of Directors delegate some of their authority to this body, or base their own decisions on an individual application on the recommendation of such a committee.

f   Comité des prêts
d   Anleihekomitee; Anleiheausschuss

993   MANAGEMENT INTERESTS
The presence of a development bank in the management of the assisted enterprise through a nominee in the board of directors or through other forms.

f   Intérêts gestionnaires
d   Interessen der Geschäftsführung; Managementinteressen

994   MANAGEMENT, COMMERCIAL
Expertise related to the organi-zation of commercial aspects including sales and marketing.

f   Gestion commerciale
d   Kaufmännisches Management

995   MANAGEMENT, CORPORATE
Expertise related to the organization of enterprises incorporated under the company law of individual countries as opposed to private, proprietory and partnership enterprises; involves knowledge of company and corporate law, registration and enlistment requirements.

f   Gestion d'une société
d   Management einer eingetragenen Gesellschaft

996   MANAGEMENT, MIDDLE
The second and third layer of executive or professional managerial personnel in a development bank or in an enterprise.

f   Administration moyenne; Gestion moyenne
d   Mittlere Geschäftsleitung

997   MANAGEMENT, MODERN
A form of organization and management where ownership and management are normally separated and where profession-alized management personnel are given power and authority to function independently within their respective province; forms a developmental objective of development banks.

f   Administration moderne
d   Moderne Geschäftsleitung

998   MANAGEMENT, OFFICE
The study and practice of organizing an office in the most efficient way.

f   Administration d'un office; Administration d'un bureau

d   Büroverwaltung;
Verwaltung einer Geschäftsstelle

999   MANAGEMENT,
TRADITION-ORIENTED
A form of organization and
management where both ownership and management rest in the
same hands and traditional
managerial methods are applied.

f   Administration traditionelle
d   Traditionelle Geschäftsleitung;
Altmodische Geschäftsleitung

1000   MANAGING BOARD;
EXECUTIVE COMMITTEE
A smaller committee elected
from amongst and/or nominated
by the board of directors of a
development bank to administer
the day-to-day management of the
institution on the basis of policies
and operational guidelines provided by the board.

f   Conseil d'administration;
Conseil de gérants
d   Vorstand;
Verwaltungsdirektorium

1001   MANAGING DIRECTOR
The executive head of a development bank or an enterprise,
normally a full-fledged member
of the board operating within the
policy framework and guidelines
provided by the board, responsible
and answerable to it for the
performance of the bank or enterprise.

f   Administrateur gérant;
Chef d'exploitation
d   Geschäftsleitender Direktor

1002   MANAGING ENGINEER;
CHIEF ENGINEER
A technical expert or an engineering firm, appointed by a client to
coordinate and oversee a project
at different stages of its concept-
ion and implementation. Some
development banks also have
staff chief engineers to
coordinate various technical
aspects of project appraisal,
follow-up and promotional
activities of the bank.

f   Directeur technique
d   Chefingenieur

1003   MARKET RESEARCHER
A professional working in a
development bank or an enterprise, responsible for evaluating
the market and the marketing
aspects of an assisted project
or an enterprise.

f   Investigateur du marché
d   Marktforscher

1004   MISSION, APPRAISAL
A team of experts deputed by a
development bank to undertake
on-the-spot investigation and
to evaluate a project as a basis
for arriving at financing
decisions.

f   Mission d'évaluation;
Délégation d'évaluation
d   Bewertungsmission

1005   MISSION, BANK
A team of experts deputed by
an international or regional
financing institution (World
Bank, African Development
Bank, Asian Development Bank,
Inter-American Development
Bank) to loanee countries with
the objective of on-the-spot
evaluation of projects, including
credit loans to development
banks, or reconnaissance or
fact-finding undertakings.

f   Mission de banque;
Délégation de banque
d   Bankmission

1006 MISSION, FACT-FINDING
A team of experts dispatched by
a development bank to objectively
identify and assess problem
areas and to recommend
appropriate means and methods
for their solutions.

f Mission de collection des faits
d Datenaufnahme-Mission;
Tatsachenaufnahme-Mission

1007 MISSION, PROJECT
PREPARATION
A team of experts deputed by a
development bank to evaluate, in
the field, potential projects and
to collect additional data for the
formulation of a specific project.

f Mission préparatoire de projet
d Projektvorbereitungsmission

1008 MISSION, RECONNAISSANCE
An advance team of experts to
identify general problem areas
for being studied in depth by a
subsequent mission.

f Mission de reconnaissance
d Vormission

1009 OPERATIONS OFFICER
A professional of a development
bank concerned with the coordination of various other professional
experts in regard to project
evaluation or project follow-up
operations.

f Fonctionnaire d'opération
d Betriebsstab

1010 ORGANIZATION CHART
A graphic representation of the
organizational line and staff with
their responsibilities and functions.

f Carte d'organisation;
Organisation schématique
d Organisationsplan

1011 OWNER-MANAGER;
SOLE PROPRIETOR;
ONE-MAN BUSINESS
A type of business unit where
one person is solely responsible
for providing the capital, for
bearing the risk of the enterprise and for the management
of the business.

f Patron-Manager
d Ein-Mann Geschäft;
Geschäftsinhaber-Manager

1012 OWNERSHIP, GOVERNMENT
A development bank whose
majority ownership rests in the
hands of the government.

f Propriété publique
d Staatseigentum;
Öffentliches Eigentum

1013 OWNERSHIP, MIXED
A development bank which is
owned by both governmental
and private interests; the
proportion of ownership interest
of each may vary.

f Propriété mixte
d Gemischtes Eigentumsrecht

1014 OWNERSHIP, PRIVATE
A development bank which
is exclusively owned by private
interests, but which may
incorporate various forms of
financial assistance (quasi-
equity, agency funds) from or
through the government.

f Propriété privée
d Privateigentum

1015 PROJECT DIRECTOR;
PROJECT MANAGER
A senior professional responsible for directing, coordinating
and guiding the work and the
staff of a project department
in a development bank.

f   Directeur de projet
d   Projektdirektor;
     Projektleiter

1016   PROJECT ECONOMIST
     A professional with the background
     and training in economics,
     responsible for analyzing the
     economic and market aspects of a
     project at the evaluation stage.

f   Economiste de projet
d   Projektnationalökonom

1017   PROJECT ENGINEER
     A professional with the training
     and background in engineering,
     responsible for evaluating the
     technical (plant and equipment,
     production facilities and capacity,
     process of production) aspect of
     a project at the evaluation stage.

f   Ingénieur de projet
d   Projektingenieur

1018   PROJECT EVALUATOR;
     PROJECT EVALUATION
     OFFICER
     A generalist professional working
     in a development bank with the
     background in economics or
     financial analysis or engineering
     and trained in most of these,
     mainly concerned with the
     evaluation of projects.

f   Evaluateur de projet
d   Projektbegutachter

1019   RURAL BANKING EXPERT
     A professional trained in the
     pre-requisites of identifying
     requirements of the rural economy
     and equipped with the basic
     knowledge for financing such
     requirements, e.g. financing
     farming and other agricultural
     and agro-based activities.

f   Expert de banque rurale
d   Agrarbankexperte

1020   STAFF TURNOVER
     The frequency with which the
     staff of a development bank
     are hired and replaced.

f   Mouvement de personnel
d   Personalumschlag

1021   STAFF, EXPATRIATE
     Development bank professionals
     of non-national origin
     employed with development
     financing institutions in
     developing countries obtained
     through secondment from over-
     seas sister institutions or
     international agencies.

f   Personnel étranger;
     Personnel expatrié
d   Ausländisches Expertenpersonal

1022   STAFF, FOLLOW-UP;
     STAFF, REVIEWING
     STAFF, SUPERVISORY
     Development bank professionals
     engaged in postfinance super-
     visory and follow-up activities.

f   Personnel de contrôle;
     Personnel de surveillance
d   Aufsichtspersonal;
     Kontrollpersonal;
     Follow-up Personal

1023   TASK FORCE
     A professional or a group of
     professionals specifically
     charged with the task of identi-
     fying and assisting in remedying
     problems; a sort of a trouble-
     shooting squad. Employed
     mostly in post-finance follow-up
     functions.

f   "Task force"
d   Sonderbelegschaft mit Spezial-
     aufgaben

1024   WORK PROCESS CHART
     A codification of individual
     responsibilities and processes
     involved in specific areas of

the operation of a development
bank in successive steps.

f Carte du procédé de travail
d Arbeitsprozessplan

X

PROFESSIONAL EXPERTISE AND TRAINING
EXPERTISE PROFESSIONNELLE ET FORMATION
BERUFLICHE FACHKENNTNIS UND AUSBILDUNG

1025 ANALYSIS, ACTIVITY
Determination of individual steps
in the chain of activities and
prescribing job specifications in
the context of work flow.

f   Analyse d'activité
d   Tätigkeitsanalyse;
      Beschäftigungsanalyse

1026 ANALYSIS, CRITICAL PATH;
ANALYSIS, NET WORK;
PROGRAMME EVALUATION
AND REVIEW TECHNIQUE;
PERT
A technique employed for efficient
implementation of projects;
determines the sequence of
activities in reference to the
total minimum time required for
their performance in synchronization with related tasks.

f   Chemin critique;
      Méthode du chemin critique;
      Technique d'évaluation et de
      contrôle de programmes;
      PERT
d   Kritischer Pfad;
      Analyse des kritischen Pfades;
      Netzplananalyse;
      Programmevaluierung und
      Kontrolle;
      PERT

1027 ANALYSIS, DISTRIBUTION
COST
Evaluation of existing distribution
organization, cost allocation by
product, alternative distribution

procedures and corresponding
costs and measurements of
effectiveness of distribution
activities.

f   Analyse de distribution de coût
d   Kostenverteilungsanalyse

1028 ANALYSIS, EFFICIENCY
An investigation into the
efficiency with which certain
precise objectives – such as
the expansion program of
firms – are to be reached; the
purpose is to reach the objectives
in the least expensive and/or
quickest way.

f   Analyse d'efficacité;
      Analyse de rendement
d   Analyse der Leistungsfähigkeit;
      Leistungsfähigkeitsanalyse

1029 ANALYSIS, INDUSTRY
POTENTIAL
A survey of a region or a
sub-region focused on highlighting the prospects for
development of new industry
lines.

f   Analyse du potentiel industriel
d   Analyse der industriellen
      Entwicklungsmöglichkeit

1030 ANALYSIS, INTER-INDUSTRY;
ANALYSIS, INPUT-OUTPUT
A systematic analysis of the
interrelationship between an
industry's or an economy's

output of goods and services and
the volume of related resources
by way of goods and services
needed to achieve the given volume
of production.

f Analyse intersectorielle
d Intersektorielle Analyse

1031 ANALYSIS, PRODUCT
PROFITABILITY
Determination of the individual
product contribution to
profitability as a basis for
marketing decisions, important
for enterprises with multi-product
ranges.

f Analyse de rentabilité par produit
d Produktrentabilitätsanalyse

1032 ANALYSIS, PRODUCTION
COST
A statement of the estimated
cost of production for each of
the major final products,
indicated separately and supported
by detailed calculations.

f Analyse de coût de production
d Produktionskostenanalyse

1033 APPLIED RESEARCH
Scientific investigation of social,
economic, technical or technological phenomena with a view
to subserve commercial or
operational policies, usually
with specific profit-making
objectives.

f Recherche appliquée
d Angewandte Forschung

1034 AREA SEMINAR
Training programmes organized to
suit the requirements of
professionals engaged in institutions with common objectives
and operating in geographic
areas with similar background.

f Séminaire régional
d Regionalseminar

1035 AUDIT, OPERATIONAL
The process of reviewing
individual operational aspects
of an enterprise to ascertain
its efficiency and to streamline
and rationalize the process to
increase productivity.

f Vérification opérationelle;
Contrôle d'exploitation
d Operationelle Prüfung

1036 AUTOMATION
A stage of industrial development beyond mechanization in
which processes are automatic-
ally adjusted to cope with
deviations or variations.

f Automation
d Automatisation

1037 BOOK-KEEPING;
ACCOUNTING
The systematic recording of
business accounts.

f Comptabilité
d Buchführung

1038 BUSINESS SCHOOL
An institution, normally a
department of a university,
specializing in studies concerne
with modern management
techniques, tools, practices
and problems.

f Ecole commerciale
d Wirtschaftschule;
Handelsakademie

1039 CAREER PLANNING
Synchronization of the process
of filling the existing and
anticipated expertise requirements of a development bank
with that of the development
of the individuals in regard to
their training and professional
expertise.

f Planification des carrières
professionnelles

d   Planung der Berufslaufbahnen

1040   CASE STUDY
A documentation of actual situation
in regard to any particular problem
or aspects sought to be discussed
in a training or seminar course,
developed on the basis of observed
situations, e.g. past-project profile
of development banks, in the
sequence of its maturity from
the stage of the receipt of the
proposal to the subsequent stages
of initial screening, evaluation,
documentation and post-financing
follow-up tasks, designed
primarily to focus on stages,
problems and techniques involved
in the process of a project.

f   Etude de cas
d   Fallstudie

1041   COMPREHENSIVE
PROFESSIONAL PERSONALITY
A development bank professional
trained in a particular expertise –
such as economics, financial analysis, marketing, business management, corporate law, oriented and
imbued with the "developmental"
and the "banking" prerequisites
of a full-fledged development
bank.

f   Expert compréhensif
d   Entwicklungbankfachmann mit
integrierten Wissensgebieten

1042   COMPUTER
An electronic calculating machine
capable of a mass of work at
great speed.

f   Opérateur
d   Computer

1043   CONSULTANCY,
PROFESSIONAL
Sources of external expertise
drawn upon by institutions in
their operational requirements.

f   Consultation professionnelle
d   Berufsmässige Beratung

1044   COST ACCOUNTING
METHODS
Techniques employed in
ascertaining the full cost of a
given product; these include
standard cost systems, variance
analysis, job costing, process
costs, cost reporting systems,
special cost studies and pricing
policy reviews.

f   Méthodes de la comptabilité
du prix de revient
d   Methoden der Kostenbuchhaltung

1045   COST CONTROL
The procedure by which the
management accountant
evaluates the actual cost of a
manufacturing operation with
a view to rationalizing cost
structure.

f   Contrôle de coût
d   Kostenkontrolle

1046   COST CONTROL TECHNIQUES
Expertise including establishment of profit control, direct
costing techniques and reporting systems, cost and expense
administration and statistical
methods and reports.

f   Techniques de contrôle des
coûts
d   Kostenkontrolltechniken

1047   COSTING
The technique and process of
ascertaining costs involved in
manufacturing, normally as a
basis for determining unit
cost of sales and as a technique
of operational control.

f   Etablissement du prix de
revient
d   Kostenberechnung;
Kostenpreisberechnung;

Kostenkalkulation;
Selbstkostenberechnung

1048 CYBERNETICS
The study of the use of automatic
feedback control devices for the
orderly performance of various
operational tasks.

f Cybernétiques
d Kybernetik

1049 DATA BANK;
DATA FILE
A center or source for compilation,
collation and dissemination of
economic, commercial, financial
and technical data of use to
development banks in their
operations.

f Centre d'informations techniques
d Datenbank

1050 DEFLATOR
A norm for weighting changes in
economic series of computation
for correcting seasonal or price
variations, or changes in money
values.

f Déflateur
d Deflator

1051 DELEGATION OF AUTHORITY
The authority conceded to
immediate juniors at various levels
for arriving at decisions and
implementing them.

f Délégation des compétences
d Kompetenzdelegation

1052 DEPTH INTERVIEW
A technique of investigation
employed by national development
bank professionals; focuses on
qualitative aspects of the respond-
ent to form the basis for arriving
at an integrated decision on the
promoter and the project.

f "Depth Interview"

d Tiefeninterview

1053 EXECUTIVE DEVELOPMENT
PROGRAMME
Permanent programme evolved
to develop appropriate managerial cadres in an organization.

f Programme du développement
des directeurs
d Programm zur Entwicklung von
leitendem Personal

1054 EXTERNAL TRAINING
ASSISTANCE
Facilities for assistance in
training made available by
agencies outside of the institution including overseas sources.

f Aide externe à la formation
d Ausländische Ausbildungshilfe

1055 EXTRA-MURAL COURSES
Evening classes for professiona
who wish to improve their
professional background.

f Courses externes
d Abendkurse für Erwachsene

1056 FINANCIAL COUNSELLING
Process of imparting advice
on matters concerning financial
operations.

f Consultation financière
d Finanzberatung

1057 FINANCIAL REPORTING
Method adopted to keep the
management informed about
the financial implications of the
operation of the enterprise; a
scientific decision-making tool
for management.

f Rapport financier
d Finanzberichterstattung

1058 FORECASTING
A technique of evaluating from
the known past and present

facts, the likely future levels of operation, e.g. turnover, cash-flows, expenses and profitability rates.

f   Prévision
d   Vorhersage

1059   FORECASTING, LONG-TERM
The prediction of the likely market demand for a good or service over a period, some years ahead.

f   Prévision à long terme
d   Langfristige Vorhersage

1060   FORECASTING, MULTI-
A forecast of the upper and lower limits that are expected for sales in a given period.

f   Multi-prévision
d   Rahmenvorhersage

1061   FORECASTING, SALES
The estimation of the future volumes of sales of a given product or company at different levels of prices.

f   Prévision de vente
d   Verkaufsvorhersage

1062   FORECASTING, SHORT-TERM
A projection of the likely market demand for a good or service which usually extends as much as six months ahead of the current period.

f   Prévision à court terme
d   Kurzfristige Vorhersage

1063   GENERALIST
A development bank professional who has academic proficiency in one particular discipline, but has acquired inter-disciplinary expertise to be capable of performing any functions involved in a development bank.

f   Généraliste
d   Experte mit allgemeinem Fach-wissen

1064   IN-PLANT COUNSELLING
The process of diagnosing particular aspects of the operation of an enterprise, e.g. engineering, production, finance, marketing, accounting; and restructuring these operations in the context of the operational situation appertaining the enterprise, both long-term and short-term.

f   Consultation sur le tas
d   Beratung auf der Arbeitsstelle

1065   IN-PLANT DIAGNOSTIC STUDIES
Analytical studies of enterprises for identifying problems and for suggesting appropriate solutions.

f   Analyse diagnostique sur le tas
d   Diagnosestudien auf dem Arbeitsplatz

1066   INDUSTRIAL COUNSELLING
Professional advice on matters concerning the various aspects of particular industry, or enter-prises, particularly relating to technical aspects, such as production engineering, plant lay-out, process know-how, manufacturing techniques, etc.

f   Consultation industrielle; Conseil industriel
d   Industrieberatung

1067   INDUSTRIAL ENGINEERING
Technical expertise involved at the plant level, including plant lay-out, process study, process control, input-output analysis.

f   Technique industrielle
d   Industrietechnik

1068   INDUSTRY PROFILES
Industry reports highlighting basic locational, market,

material input, process- and
technical expertise and investment requirements.

f   Profiles des industries
d   Industrieprofile

1069 INSTITUTIONALIZED
        TRAINING PROGRAMME
      Permanent institutional arrange-
      ments developed by a few develop-
      ment banks, as a culmination of
      their departmental ad-hoc training
      programme. It represents the
      recognition by the management
      of the importance of systematic,
      structured and pre-planned
      training as an integral part of
      organizational policy.

f   Programme institutionnel de
     formation
d   Institutionelles Ausbildungs-
     programm

1070 INVENTORY MANAGEMENT
      Determination of most economic
      inventory levels, considering cost
      of ordering, safety stock, cost
      of carrying inventory, and related
      elements, and integration with
      production scheduling and purch-
      asing policy.

f   Gestion de l'inventaire
d   Inventarverwaltung

1071 INVENTORY VALUATION;
        INVENTORY ADJUSTMENT
      A measure of the profit or loss
      which takes place as a result of
      increases or decreases in prices
      affecting the values of inventories
      held by enterprises; it is used
      to correct the overstatement or
      understatement of profits.

f   Fixation de la valeur de
     l'inventaire;
     Rectification de la valeur de
     l'inventaire
d   Wertfestsetzung des Inventars;
     Wertberichtigung des Inventars

1072 INVESTMENT
        INTELLIGENCE
      Organized data facilities on
      the basis of which investors
      can determine investments of
      their funds; these facilities
      normally provide indications
      of relative yield and rates of
      return in different investment
      outlets and investment papers.
      Several development banks
      organize these facilities for
      their own use as also for the
      use of their clientele.

f   Information de placement
d   Anlagenachrichten;
     Investierungsnachrichten

1073 INVESTMENT OPPORTUNITY
        CATALOGUE
      Information concerning invest-
      ment and trading opportunities,
      etc., identifying each investment
      report by country and by
      industrial classifications. Cards
      containing abstracts of various
      studies, market data, capital
      requirements, projected annual
      sales, production, etc., norm-
      ally published, on a commercial
      basis by a profit-earning
      organization, or as an infra-
      structure facility by a promo-
      tional agency and sometimes by
      development banks as a pro-
      motional activity.

f   Catalogue d'opportunité
     d'investissements;
     Liste d'opportunité d'investisse-
     ments
d   Katalog von Investitions-
     gelegenheiten;
     Liste von Investitionsgelegen-
     heiten

1074 JOB DESCRIPTION
      Description of the particular
      functional responsibilities of
      staff in the context of the over-
      all work flow in an enterprise.

f   Description de poste
d   Tätigkeitsbeschreibung

1075   JOB EVALUATION;
       ASSESSMENT OF FUNCTIONS
       Assessment of functional
       responsibilities of staff to
       promote efficiency and product-
       ivity.

f   Evaluation du travail
d   Arbeitsplatzbewertung

1076   JOB TRAINING
       Familiarization instructions pro-
       vided by development banks for
       fresh recruits to prepare them
       to shoulder responsibilities of the
       job they will be entrusted with.

f   Formation du travail;
       Education de poste
d   Tätigkeitsausbildung;
       Beschäftigungsausbildung

1077   LINEAR PROGRAMMING
       A mathematical technique to
       formalize decision-making
       procedures and to put them on
       a more scientific footing.

f   Programmation linéaire
d   Lineares Programmieren;
       Linearprogrammierung

1078   MANAGEMENT ACCOUNTING
       Expertise related to the provision
       of data regarding financial and
       production aspects of an enter-
       prise, mainly to provide the
       basis for control and decision-
       making to the management;
       basically a tool for management
       decision and control of day-to-day
       operation of an enterprise.

f   Comptabilité de direction
d   Managementbuchführung;
       Geschäftsleitungsbuchführung

1079   MANAGEMENT AUDIT
       Verification of the appropriate-
       ness of decision-making prccess
       and procedures employed in an
       enterprise.

f   Vérification de la direction;
       Vérification gestionnaire
d   Prüfung der Geschäftsführung

1080   MANAGEMENT
       CONSULTANCY
       Expertise related to provision
       of informed advice on the
       management aspects of an
       enterprise, e.g. provision of a
       rational organizational chart
       with work and process flow
       descriptions, line and staff
       responsibilities, reporting
       systems, control mechanism,
       etc.

f   Consultation gestionnaire
d   Managementberatung;
       Geschäftsleitungsberatung

1081   MANAGEMENT
       DEVELOPMENT
       The mechanism inbuilt within
       an organization to develop
       managerial expertise including
       the process of decision-making
       and staff initiative and the
       intelligence-support required
       thereon.

f   Développement de la direction
d   Entwicklung der Geschäfts-
       führung

1082   MANAGEMENT DEVELOP-
       MENT SERVICES
       An important function in exten-
       sion service facilities, com-
       prising provision of advice and
       assistance to existing or
       newly-promoted enterprises,
       in raising of capital, production
       planning and control, cost
       accounting and market aids.

f   Services de développement de

gérance
d   Einrichtungen zur Förderung
der Geschäftsleitung

1083 MANAGEMENT DIAGNOSIS
In-plant studies focused on present
managerial practices with a view
to rationalizing these practices.

f   Diagnostique gestionnaire
d   Diagnose der Geschäftsleitung

1084 MANAGEMENT
INFORMATION SYSTEM
Institutionalized arrangements
within an organization to inform
the management of the enterprise
periodically with key data per-
taining to all aspects of the operations to enable it to arrive at
functional decisions and to oversee day-to-day operations.

f   Système d'information de la
direction
d   Informationssystem der Geschäftsführung

1085 MANAGEMENT KNOW-HOW
The background, insight and
capabilities that are necessary
to organize and manage an
enterprise; referred particularly
in the context of modern management techniques.

f   Savoir faire gestionnaire
d   Geschäftsführungskenntnis

1086 MANAGEMENT SERVICES
Expertise made use of by
development banks, either from
within their own organization or
through outside agencies, for
rendering management counselling
for assisted enterprises in need
of such services.

f   Services de gérance;
Services d'administration
d   Managementdienste

1087 MANAGEMENT TRAINING

Programs aimed at upgrading
management know-how.

f   Formation de la direction
d   Ausbildung von Management

1088 MANAGEMENT, CREDIT
Administration of borrowed
funds in such a way as to permit
adequate liquidity with the
minimum of payments for cost
of credit.

f   Gestion de crédit
d   Kreditmanagement

1089 MANAGEMENT, FINANCIAL
Responsibilities include
development of systems and
control mechanics for profit
planning, fund management,
budgetary control, management
accounting, production cost
controls, among others.

f   Gestion financière
d   Finanzverwaltung

1090 MANAGEMENT,
MARKETING
Responsibilities include
development and application of
market research techniques
for marketing, price policy,
advertising, sales promotion,
export, forecasting and budgets,
creation of sales territories.

f   Gestion du marché
d   Marktverwaltung

1091 MANAGEMENT, PRODUCTION
Responsibilities relating to
organization, planning and
control of production, preventive
maintenance, regulation of
purchases and inventory
control, time and motion studies
and cost control measures.

f   Gestion de la production
d   Produktionsverwaltung

1092 MANAGERIAL GRID SYSTEM
A device introduced by individual enterprises or training agencies to provide knowledge about the latest developments in techniques of management or other professional disciplines to senior professionals or management personnel, on a voluntary basis, without making the participant feel that he is being trained.

f Système d'information gestionnaire
d Managerinformationssystem

1093 MARKET RESEARCH
A systematic, qualitative and quantitative analysis of past data and factors influencing demand, for arriving at an objective assessment of the volume of demand for a product in the context of expected competition, costs of sales and unit realization.

f Recherche du marché
d Marktforschung

1094 MARKETING RESEARCH
The systematic gathering, recording, and analyzing of data about problems relating to the sales and distribution of goods and services.

f Recherche d'écoulement de marchandises
d Absatzforschung

1095 OBSERVATION, FIELD; OBSERVATION, PLANT
Subjecting trainees - after they have had classroom seminars on operational techniques - to actual situations obtained in a plant floor.

f Observation sur le tas
d Feldbeobachtung

1096 OBSERVATION, ON-THE-JOB
A method used for exposing staff members of one institution to practices and procedures prevalent in other similar institutions, operating in different environments and contexts.

f Observation en cours d'emplois
d Beobachtung auf dem Arbeitsplatz

1097 OCCUPATIONAL EDUCATION; OCCUPATIONAL INSTRUCTION
Basic educational grounding oriented towards specific job opportunities; lack of such facilities in most developing countries necessitates development banking institutions to provide such orientation after recruitment.

f Formation professionnelle
d Berufsausbildung

1098 OPERATIONS RESEARCH
Area of management science which uses mathematical techniques to solve complicated operational problems; some of the techniques used are (i) linear programming; (ii) queuing theory; (iii) models and model testing; and (iv) simulation.

f Recherche opérationnelle
d Operationsresearch

1099 ORIENTATION PROGRAMME
A programme to indoctrinate new recruits on the overall functions and philosophy of the enterprise, as also on the techniques and procedures followed.

f Programme d'orientation
d Orientierungsprogramm

1100 ORIENTATION, ON-THE-JOB
A method of training fresh recruits by routing them through various departments within an organization and subsequently to

orient them in all aspects of the operations of the organization.

f Orientation en cours d'emplois
d Orientierung auf dem Arbeitsplatz

1101 PANEL;
      SYNDICATE
      A method of grouping trainees or participants under common topics of discussion or instruction.

f Syndicat;
   Comité
d Ausschuss;
   Syndikat

1102 PERFORMANCE CRITERIA
      A criteria employed by international lending agencies for evaluating the allocation and use of assistance by a development bank and the extent of resource mobilization and economic benefits achieved by the latter's operation.

f Critères d'accomplissement
d Leistungskriterien;
   Ausführungskriterien

1103 PORTFOLIO MANAGEMENT
      The process of diversifying risk while maximizing income and obtaining a wider deployment of funds.

f Gestion de portefeuille
d Portefeuilleverwaltung

1104 PRICING POLICY
      Decisions concerning various pricing alternatives keeping in view their impact on profitability.

f Politique de la fixation des prix
d Preisfestsetzungspolitik

1105 PRICING, PROMOTIONAL
      Situation when an enterprise prices its product lower than the cost of production, in order to promote the demand with a view to

maximizing its long-term profit.

f Promotion systématique de vente
d Verkaufsförderung;
   Absatzsteigerung

1106 PROCESS ENGINEERING
      Technical aspects involved in the process flow concerning manufacture of a product.

f Procédé technique
d Technisches Verfahren;
   Technischer Prozess

1107 PROCESS RESEARCH
      Documentation and laboratory research to continuously up-date and improve the processes of manufacture of a product.

f Recherche du procédé technique
d Produktionsprozessforschung

1108 PRODUCTION ENGINEERING
      Professional expertise including activities such as work-study, plant level practices, standardized norm concepts of processes applicable, capital requirement, synchronization of capacities of individual sections, process flow and job requirements.

f Production technique
d Technische Herstellung

1109 PROFESSIONALS, DEVELOP-
      MENT OF
      Opportunities and initiatives provided within the organization, supported by requisite training, for individuals working in a development bank.

f Développement des experts
d Entwicklung von Fachleuten

1110 PROFIT PLANNING AND
      BUDGETARY SYSTEM

Expertise including planning
profitability through operational
budgeting, cash budgeting,
performance of individual
divisions and departments.

f   Planification de profit et système
budgétaire
d   Profitplanung und Budgetsystem

1111 PROFITABILITY ACCOUNTING
A process of periodic accounting
geared to assessment of profit
maximization or loss minimizat-
ion.

f   Comptabilité de profit
d   Profitbuchführung;
Profitrechnung

1112 PROGRAMME PLANNING
BUDGETING SYSTEM;
PPBS
A technique employed by development agencies (originally evolved
by the USA Government) to
analyze the cost effectiveness of
their various programmes. (See:
Cost effectiveness 616)

f   Système de programme,
planification et budget
d   Programm-Planungs und Budget
System

1113 QUALITY CONTROL,
STATISTICAL
A method of estimating the quality
of the whole from the quality of
the samples taken from the whole.
The method is based upon the
laws of chance and has a sound
mathematical basis.

f   Contrôle statistique de qualité
d   Statistische Qualitätskontrolle

1114 RESEARCH AND DEVELOP-
MENT
The basic, applied and engineering
research programs including
development of prototypes and

processes undertaken by development agencies for assisting the process of modernization,
rationalization and development
of various sectors served by
them.

f   Recherche et développement
d   Forschung und Entwicklung

1115 SANDWICH COURSES
Arrangements under which
employed workers or pro-
fessionals get part-time training while being employed.

f   Cours de "sandwich"
d   "Sandwich" Kurse

1116 SIMULATION
The operation of a model which
represents an economic system,
or a project to be financed.

f   Simulation
d   Simulation

1117 SIMULATION GAMES
Operational games used to
provide experience for fresh
professionals by simulating the
real-life operations of a
development bank, preceded by
a course in theoretical training.

f   Jeux de simulation
d   Simulationsspiele

1118 SPECIALIST
A development bank professional
who has specialized in one
specific area, but does not
necessarily have expertise in
other areas, of the operations
of the institution.

f   Spécialiste
d   Fachmann;
Spezialist;
Spezialbearbeiter

1119 STANDARDIZATION
The in-built characteristics in
a modern manufacturing unit

to reproduce a given product in identical physical, dimensional and other utility, qualities.

f   Standardisation
d   Normung;
    Typisierung;
    Standardisierung

1120   STATISTICIAN
A professional trained in statistical methods; the business statistician, in addition to having a working knowledge of statistical methods, must also possess an understanding of the economic principles involved in the operations with which he is concerned.

f   Statisticien
d   Statistiker

1121   SURVEY
A technique of gathering facts and attitudes related to various aspects of the economy geared to the operations of a development bank, such as project identification, industries studies, market research, capital market studies, corporate profitability studies, etc.

f   Etude
d   Untersuchung;
    Studie

1122   SURVEY, ECONOMIC
Study devoted chiefly to the observation of the general economic situation at home and abroad, providing basic materials which constitute a background for planning future operations of enterprises.

f   Etude économique
d   Wirtschaftserhebung;
    Wirtschaftsuntersuchung

1123   SURVEY, ENTERPRISE
Study directed toward the individual enterprise directed

towards assessment of personnel aspects (management and employees); physical aspects (scale of operation, volume of production and sales); financial aspects (revenue expense position and status of finances).

f   Etude d'entreprise
d   Unternehmenserhebung;
    Unternehmensuntersuchung

1124   SYSTEMS ANALYSIS
An engineering concept related to systems flow involved in the operations of an organization or enterprise in order to specify and lay down individual systems-spread and systems-responsibilities.

f   Analyse des systèmes
d   Systemanalyse

1125   SYSTEMS MAN
A professional identified with a specific line – or staff function in the overall organization of an enterprise; also applied to professionals concerned with systems analysis.

f   Expert d'analyse des systèmes
d   Systemanalysenexperte

1126   TIME AND MOTION STUDY
A study of the time taken by an employee and the way he carries out the work assigned to him to ascertain whether the work can be simplified, so that less time be taken over it as a means of increasing efficiency.

f   Etude du temps et du mouvement
d   Zeit- und Bewegungsstudie

1127   TRAINING CENTERS,
        GOVERNMENT
Government-sponsored centers to train labor for skilled work

144

and to retrain labor that has
become redundant in declining
industries for other work. An
infra-structure facility normally
provided by governments of
developing countries to train
industrial workers and at times
professionals of national development banks to enlarge their
efficiency in the respective
professions or trades.

f   Centre gouvernemental de
    formation
d   Ausbildungsstätte der Regierung

1128 TRAINING GAP
      An imbalance in the training re-
      quirements and arrangements
      available for training professional
      experts for a development bank.

f   Lacune dans la formation
d   Ausbildungslücke

1129 TRAINING OFFICER
      Professional specialized in
      formulating programmes of
      instruction and undertaking
      training for various levels of
      professionals of a national
      development bank.

f   Chargé de la formation
d   Ausbildungsberater

1130 TRAINING POLICY
      An essential ingredient in the
      overall policy of a development
      bank to consciously foster re-
      quisite expertise for its operations
      incorporating its own orientation
      programmes and making use of
      available facilities for exposing
      its professionals to new environ-
      ments, new conditions of operations
      and new ideas.

f   Politique de formation
d   Ausbildungspolitik

1131 TRAINING PROGRAMME,
      BANK-TO-BANK;

TRAINING PROGRAMME,
INTER-BANK
Facilities of interinstitutional
exchange of staff to enable
acquaintance with each other's
working methods and operational
conditions, to mutual benefit.

f   Programme de formation
    entre banques;
    Programme de formation
    inter-bancaire
d   Bank-an-Bank Ausbildungs-
    programm;
    Interbankaires Ausbildungs-
    programm

1132 TRAINING WITHIN INDUSTRY;
      T.W.I.
      A programme of training to the
      employees of enterprises for the
      type of work on which they are
      actually engaged; a programme
      initiated in most developing
      countries through the assistance
      of the International Labor
      Organization.

f   Formation en cours d'emplois
    industriel
d   Ausbildung auf dem Industrie-
    arbeitsplatz

1133 TRAINING, IN-COUNTRY
      Facilities of training available
      for professionals of develop-
      ment banks within the country.

f   Formation nationale
d   Ausbildung im eigenem Land

1134 TRAINING, IN-WORK
      Process of imparting knowledge
      about techniques, tools and
      procedures for freshers, by
      being employed as an understudy.

f   Formation en cours d'emplois
d   Ausbildung auf dem Arbeitsplatz

1135 TRAINING, OVERSEAS;
      TRAINING, THIRD-COUNTRY
      Training facilities available to,

and made use of by, a development bank for its professionals
outside the country.

f   Formation d'outre-mer;
     Formation aux pays tiers
d   Überseeausbildung;
     Ausbildung in Drittländern

1136 TRAINING, VOCATIONAL
     That part of technical and
     commercial education devoted
     to training students in the skills
     required in their future occupatio

f   Formation professionnelle
d   Berufsausbildung

XI.
FINANCIAL ASPECTS
ASPECTS FINANCIERS
FINANZGESICHTESPUNKTE

1137 ACCOUNTS PAYABLE
An accounting item aggregating all liabilities owed by a firm to trade creditors; listed on the balance sheet under current liabilities.

f   Dettes passives;
Comptes à payer
d   Verbindlichkeiten;
Verpflichtungen;
Schulden
Buchschulden;
Kreditoren

1138 ACCOUNTS RECEIVABLE
An accounting item aggregating all amounts due to an enterprise for services rendered or commodities sold, but payment for which is expected to be received within the current or succeeding accounting period.

f   Dettes actives;
Comptes à recevoir;
Créances comptables
d   Aussenstände;
Forderungen;
Buchforderungen;
Debitoren

1139 ACCOUNT, CAPITAL
Income or expenditure relating to asset creation; changes in the composition of these items are reflected in the balance sheet.

f   Compte de capital
d   Kapitalkonto

1140 ACCOUNT, CURRENT
Income or expenditure related to the current year of an enterprise, reflected in the income statement.

f   Compte courant
d   Laufendes Konto

1141 ACCOUNT, DEVELOPMENT
Provisions made for new outlays in connection with expansion and diversification of existing lines of activities, improvement of existing facilities, or for undertaking of new lines of activities.

f   Compte d'exploitation
d   Entwicklungsunkostenkonto

1142 ACCOUNT, NOMINAL
A bookkeeping term for accounts such as cash, sales, and purchases, as distinct from the personal accounts of customers.

f   Compte nominal
d   Nominalkonto

1143 ACCOUNT, OPEN;
ACCOUNT, BOOK
Method of extending commercial credit in which the only evidence of the debt is an entry in the seller's books; it is the simplest credit instrument and is widely used in the extension of trade credit.

f   Compte ouvert
d   Offenes Konto;
     Offenstehendes Konto

1144 ACCOUNT, PROFIT AND
        LOSS;
        OPERATING STATEMENT;
        INCOME STATEMENT
      A financial statement indicating
      the financial results of the opera-
      tion of an entity during a given
      period.

f   Comptes des profits et pertes;
     Comptes des résultats
d   Gewinn und Verlustrechnung;
     Ertragsrechnung

1145 ACCOUNTING EQUATION
      A fundamental principle of
      accounting that the assets must
      equal the sum of the liabilities
      and net worth.

f   Equation de la comptabilité
d   Buchhaltungsgleichung

1146 ACCRUAL BASIS
      Method of accounting where
      entries are made at the time an
      expense was incurred or at the
      time the revenue was earned.
      (See: Cash basis 1162)

f   Base d'accumulation
d   Fälligkeitsbasis

1147 AMORTIZATION OF
        FIXED ASSETS
      Systematic assignment of the cost
      of intangible fixed assets such
      as patents, copyrights and goodwill
      to expenses.

f   Amortissement de l'actif
d   Amortisation des Vermögens-
     bestandes

1148 AMORTIZATION OF A LOAN
      Repayment of principal amount
      of borrowings over a given period
      of time.

f   Amortissement d'un emprunt
d   Amortisation einer Anleihe

1149 ANNUITY
      Process of amortizing a loan
      by an investor in a sum of
      money to be received annually
      over a period of time. The
      amount includes principal as
      well as interest payments; the
      principal component increasing
      while the interest component
      declining.

f   Annuité;
     Rente annuelle
d   Annuität;
     Jahresrente

1150 APPROPRIATION
      Apportioning out of annual
      earnings for committed outflows.

f   Affectation
d   Zuwendung

1151 APPROPRIATION ACCOUNT
      Individual heads of commit-
      ments against each of which net
      profits are apportioned.

f   Compte d'affectation
d   Zuwendungskonto

1152 AUDIT
      Verification of the authenticity
      of financial transactions and
      their appropriateness.

f   Vérification des comptes
d   Buchprüfung

1153 BALANCE SHEET
      A statement indicating assets,
      liabilities and net worth status
      of an enterprise or financing
      company, at some particular
      date; a statutorily enjoined
      obligation on all non-proprietory
      entities in most countries.

f   Bilan
d   Bilanz

1154 BALANCE, TRIAL
A means of checking the internal
consistency and authenticity of
statements of accounts.

f   Bilan provisoire
d   Zwischenbilanz

1155 BUDGETARY CONTROL
The process of checking actual
results against targets planned
earlier.

f   Contrôle budgétaire
d   Budgetkontrolle

1156 BUDGET;
BUDGETING
Process of planning the income
and expenditures of an enterprise
for a given period in the future.

f   Budget;
Planification du budget
d   Budget;
Budgetplanung

1157 CAPITAL ALLOWANCES
The proportion of annual profit
(gross) allowed by tax authorities
as a deduction to cover charges
such as special depreciation and
other incentive allowances prior
to computation of taxable income.

f   Déduction;
Remise;
Bonification
d   Nachlass;
Abzug

1158 CAPITAL APPRECIATION
Increase in the market value of
equity capital; or, increase in
the money value of capital assets.

f   Accroissement du capital
d   Kapitalwertzunahme

1159 CAPITAL BUDGETING
Process of formulating the
financial programme of a company
in keeping with the envisaged

operational programme; this includes provision for expansion
of existing production facilities
and creation of new ones.

f   Budget de capital;
Budget des capitaux
d   Kapitalbudget;
Entwicklungsbudget

1160 CAPITAL LOSS
Erosion of the equity of an
enterprise by successive losses
in operations.

f   Perte de capital
d   Kapitalverlust

1161 CASH BALANCE
Resources kept liquid and
readily available for use.

f   Solde liquide;
Solde de caisse
d   Barbestand;
Kassensaldo

1162 CASH BASIS
Method of recording receipts
and expenditures when proceeds
are collected or disbursed.
(See: Accrual basis 1146)

f   Base d'espèces;
Base de caisse;
Base comptant
d   Kassenbasis;
Barschaftsbasis

1163 CASH CUSHION
Volume of liquidity maintained
in addition to overdrafts and
other short term credit
facilities.

f   Espèces en caisse à court
terme
d   Kurzfristiges Barvoratsvolumen

1164 CASH GENERATION
The net cash inflow arising
from an investment or in an
enterprise as a result of its

operation in a given period.

f Génération d'espèces
d Kapitalschaffung
Kapitalerzeugung

1165 CHARGE, CAPITAL
Provisions in the profit and loss
account for payment of interest
on borrowed capital, repayment
of annual principal borrowed and
depreciation charges on fixed
assets.

f Coût de capital
d Kapitalspesen

1166 CHARGE, COMMITMENT
Fee charged by the lender to the
borrower on the undisbursed part
of the credit line or loan.

f Droit d'un engagement financier
d Gebühr für eine finanzielle
Verbindlichkeit

1167 COST OF SALES;
COST, SELLING
Costs incurred in creating,
retaining or expanding, a market
for a product. These costs include
the cost of advertising, earnings
and expenses of commercial
travellers, costs of market
research; and the various inducements by way of stamps, give-
aways and specially-reduced prices
offered by firms to attract
customers.

f Coût de vente
d Verkaufskosten

1168 COST, AVERAGE
Distribution of cost of production
amongst individual units on the
basis of arithmetical average.

f Coût moyen
d Durchschnittskosten

1169 COST, DIRECT;
COST, PRIME

A cost which can be consistently
identified with a specific unit
of output.

f Coût direct
d Direkte Kosten

1170 COST, FIXED;
OVERHEAD
Cost which does not vary with
changes in a firm's output within
reasonable limits, e.g. the cost
of plant and management.

f Coût fixe
d Fixe Kosten

1171 COST, FULL
A concept employed in costing,
comprises the total variable
costs involved in the production
of a particular unit plus the
appropriate portion of the fixed
costs. (See: Full cost pricing
1211)

f Coût total d'un produit
d Selbstkosten eines Produktes

1172 COST, HISTORICAL
Actual cost of the assets at the
time acquired.

f Coût historique
d Historische Kosten;
Anschaffungskosten

1173 COST, INDIRECT;
INDIRECT MANUFACTURING
EXPENSE
A cost item which cannot be
consistently identified with a
specific product unit; it includes
all fixed costs, is joint in nature
and can be apportioned to
different products only by a
rough approximation; e.g. wages
of supervisors, power, maintenance, taxes, etc. (See: Cost,
variable 1183)

f Coût indirect
d Indirekte Kosten

150

1174 COST, JOINT
Expenditures on goods and services which cannot be identified with a single specific commodity produced or services rendered.

f   Coût conjoint
d   Gemeinsame Kosten

1175 COST, LONG-RUN AVERAGE
The lowest practicable average cost of producing a commodity, within the current state of technical knowledge and managerial ability, after adequate time has been allowed to make all the necessary adjustments.

f   Coût moyen à long terme
d   Langfristige Durchschnittskosten

1176 COST, MARGINAL
The additional cost that a producer incurs for making an additional unit of output.

f   Coût marginal
d   Grenzkosten

1177 COST, OUTAGE
Costs represented by the non-availability of services or facilities for any reason (plant breakdown, overhead), or for failure to complete project construction according to schedule.

f   Coût de retard
d   Verzugskosten

1178 COST, REPLACEMENT
Cost involved in the replacement of the existing set of fixed assets with another set of equal productive capacity.

f   Frais de remplacement;
    Coût de substitution
d   Wiederbeschaffungskosten;
    Ersatzkosten;
    Substitutionskosten

1179 COST, RUNNING
Operating costs, which include the cost of raw materials and power, labor and supervision. It excludes capital charges and other overheads. (See: Cost, variable 1183)

f   Coût d'exploitation
d   Betriebskosten

1180 COST, STANDARD
A system whereby predetermined costs are developed and used as a basis for comparison with actual costs in order to overcome the limitations of historical cost.

f   Coût courant;
    Coût forfaitaire
d   Standardkosten

1181 COST, SUPPLEMENTARY
The cost of production which does not vary with current output; the overhead necessarily incurred by a firm whether in production or not.

f   Coût supplémentaire
d   Zusatzkosten

1182 COST, TOTAL PRODUCTION
The total sum of a firm's fixed and variable costs in the production of a particular output.

f   Coût total
d   Gesammtkosten

1183 COST, VARIABLE
Items of costs which vary with quantity of output, e.g. the cost of labor and raw materials.

f   Coût variable
d   Variable Kosten

1184 CREDIT, TRADE
A credit advanced to an enterprise by suppliers.

f   Crédit de commerce

d   Handelskredit

1185 DEBT SERVICING
The payment of interest on a debt,
plus whatever installments of
the principal are due.

f   Service des dettes
d   Schuldendienst

1186 DEBTS, BAD
Receivables not likely to be
recovered.

f   Créances douteuses
d   Zweifelhafte Forderungen;
     Zweifelhafte Aussenbestände;
     Zweifelhafte Schulden

1187 DEBTS, DOUBTFUL
Receivables whose recovery is
uncertain.

f   Dettes véreuses
d   Unsichere Forderungen

1188 DEFERRED PAYMENTS
Supplies and procurements made
earlier, payments whereof are
provided in the current financial
year.

f   Paiements différés
d   Zahlungsaufschiebung

1189 DEFICIT
The amount by which liabilities
exceed assets, or expenditures
exceed revenues.

f   Déficit
d   Defizit

1190 DEPLETION
Reduction in the volume of fixed
assets by obsolescence or im-
proper maintenance and of natural
resources by extraction. (See:
Depletion allowance 1191)

f   Epuisement;
     Réduction
d   Erschöpfung;
     Reduzierung

1191 DEPLETION ALLOWANCE
A tax allowance extended to the
owners of exhaustible natural
resources.

f   Allocation pour épuisement
d   Vergütung für Reduzierung

1192 DEPRECIATION
Annual provision for replacing
assets, computed on the basis
of its expected economic life,
either by the straight line
method, or reduced balance
method. (See: Depreciation
allowance 1193)

f   Dépréciation
d   Abschreibung;
     Wertminderung;
     Wertverlust

1193 DEPRECIATION ALLOWANCE
A tax allowance to enterprises
on the amount paid for new
machinery spread over a period
of time, generally rather shorter
than the expected life of the
machine.

f   Allocation pour dépréciation
d   Vergütung für Abschreibung

**1194 DEPRECIATION,
       ACCELERATED**
A practice whereby for tax
purposes a firm is permitted
to depreciate a new machine
over a shorter period than that
for which it is likely to be
employed, with possibly a much
larger allowance for the first
few years than for subsequent
years.

f   Dépréciation accélérée
d   Beschleunigte Abschreibung

**1195 DEPRECIATION, REDUCED
       BALANCE**
A method of depreciating fixed
assets whereby a higher
percentage annual rate may be

provided in the initial years and a progressively lower rate in subsequent years; the base for calculating the rate, however, is the depreciated value of the successive years and not the original value. This method of depreciation allowance is adopted mainly for purposes of initial tax-relief, or to provide for the initial liquidity needs of the enterprise.

f   Dépréciation de moins-value
d   Geometrisch-degressive Ab-
    schreibung

1196 DEPRECIATION, STRAIGHT
      LINE
      A method of amortizing fixed assets whereby the annual rate is derived from dividing the value of assets by the number of years of economic life assumed. This method does not provide any elbow-room for varying the depreciation rate to suit business conditions.

f   Dépréciation linéaire
d   Lineare Abschreibung

1197 DISINVESTMENT
      A situation wherein the net capital stock of an enterprise in a given period suffers a reduction.

f   Désinvestissement;
    Investissement négatif
d   Negative Investition

1198 DIVIDEND
      The amount distributed to stock-holders out of net earnings.

f   Dividende
d   Dividende;
    Gewinnanteil

1199 DIVIDEND COVER
      The number of times dividend payment is covered by a company's earnings.

f   Couverture de dividende
d   Dividendendeckung

1200 DIVIDEND RATE
      The amount of distributed profit as a percentage of the nominal value of the share capital to which it relates.

f   Taux de dividende
d   Dividendenrate

1201 DIVIDEND, CASH
      Dividend on equity disbursed in cash.

f   Dividende en espèces
d   Bardividende;
    Bargewinnanteil

1202 EARNINGS, NET
      Total income after allowing for cost of borrowings, depreciation and taxes.

f   Revenus nets
d   Reinverdienst;
    Reingewinn

1203 EARNINGS, RETAINED;
      UNDISTRIBUTED PROFITS
      The excess of a company's post-tax income over all dividends distributed to stock-holders; profits ploughed back.

f   Revenu retenu
d   Zurückbehaltener Gewinn

1204 ESCALATOR CLAUSE
      A contractual provision pro-viding for automatic increases in prices or payments for services.

f   Echelle mobile
d   Gleitklausel

1205 EXPENDITURE, CAPITAL
      Investments on acquisition of fixed assets.

f   Dépense de capital
d   Kapitalausgaben

1206 EXPENSES, MANAGEMENT
Item of expenses normally
assigned for expenditures incurred by the directors and
senior executives.

f   Dépenses de l'administration
d   Managementausgaben

1207 EXPENSES, OPERATING
Direct and indirect costs
associated with the normal operation of an enterprise distinguished
from capital expenditure - or
developmental costs and provisions,
excluding financial costs.

f   Dépenses d'exploitation
d   Betriebsausgaben

1208 FINANCIAL RETURN;
        FINANCIAL YIELD
As opposed to social return; all
measurable income of an enterprise in terms of money.

f   Rendement financier
d   Finanzieller Ertrag

1209 FINANCIAL STATEMENTS
Statements of accounts such as
balance sheet, audited or pro-
forma, profit and loss account and
cash- and fund flow, schedules
supporting these statements, relating to the operation of an enterprise for a period just completed,
or for a given future period.

f   Déclaration financière;
    Déposition financière
d   Finanzerklärung;
    Finanzielle Erklärung

1210 FINANCIAL YEAR
Period of twelve months adopted
for accounting purposes, may be
calendar year or otherwise.

f   Exercice financier;
    Année financière;
    Année budgétaire;
    Année d'exploitation

d   Rechnungsjahr;
    Finanzjahr;
    Betriebsjahr;
    Geschäftsjahr

1211 FULL COST PRICING
A method of pricing whereby
average direct costs for labor
and materials forms the basis
with a proportionate allowance
for overheads; the overhead
costs are calculated assuming
less than full capacity operation
of the plant. (See: Cost, full
1171)

f   Détermination du coût total
    d'un produit
d   Selbstkostenpreisfestsetzung

1212 GUARANTEE FUND
Provision made by development
banks as a cushion against
risks involved in activities
related to extension of gurantees
against payments, supplies
of plant and equipment, processes or performances.

f   Fonds de garantie
d   Kreditfonds

1213 GUARANTEE, OUTSTANDING
Guarantee obligations yet to
be retired.

f   Garantie à recouvrir
d   Aussenstehende Bürgschaft

1214 ILLIQUIDITY
Lack of cash for meeting normal
day-to-day working capital
requirements.

f   Manque de liquidité
d   Zahlungsunfähigkeit

1215 INCOME, EARNED
An accounting term which refers
to the income that results when
goods are disposed of, or when
services are rendered.

f   Revenu gagné
d   Verdientes Einkommen

1216 INCOME, GROSS;
       REVENUE, GROSS
      The total income from all sources
      before deduction of tax obligations.

f   Revenu brut
d   Bruttoeinkommen;
    Bruttoertrag;
    Bruttoeinkünfte

1217 INCOME, NET;
       REVENUE, NET
      Term used synonymously with
      net profits.

f   Revenu net
d   Nettoeinkommen;
    Nettoertrag;
    Nettoeinkünfte

1218 INCOME, OPERATING
      Term useful as a measure to
      assess the earning capacity of
      total funds invested; derived by
      deducting from gross earnings
      operating expenses.

f   Revenu d'exploitation
d   Betriebseinkommen;
    Geschäftseinkommen

1219 INCOME, RETAINED
      Earnings retained within the
      enterprise after meeting all
      obligations including payments
      of dividends.

f   Revenu retenu
d   Zurückbehaltener Gewinn

1220 INCOME, UNEARNED
      A term denoting income derived
      from investments as opposed to
      the normal operational activities
      of the enterprise.

f   Revenu non-gagné
d   Nicht erarbeitetes Einkommen

1221 INDEBTEDNESS

The volume of outstanding
long-term borrowings.

f   Endettement
d   Verschuldung

1222 INTEREST DURING
       CONSTRUCTION
      Interest payments accrued
      during the implementation
      period of the project.

f   Intérêts pendant la construction
d   Zinsen während der Konstruk-
    tionsperiode

1223 INTEREST, ACCRUED
      Interest on long term borrowed
      funds which is due and to be
      paid or collected.

f   Intérêts cumulés;
    Intérêts courus
d   Angefallene Zinsen;
    Aufgelaufene Zinsen

1224 INTEREST, GROSS
      The amount of interest accrued
      and/or received before taxes.

f   Intérêts bruts
d   Bruttozinsen

1225 INTEREST, IMPUTED
      Opportunity or alternative cost
      of invested capital. Development
      banks obliged to undertake
      non-profit-earning investments
      seek to impute such cost of
      investment to arrive at a correct
      position of the financial results
      of their operations and if
      possible, to recover such cost
      from the government.

f   Intérêts imputés
d   Unterstellte Zinsen

1226 INVESTMENT PORTFOLIO
      The range and variety of invest-
      ments of a development bank,
      underwriting and guarantee
      obligations and equity

investments, in a variety of
industry-lines.

f   Portefeuille d'investissement
d   Investitionsportefeuille

1227 LIQUIDITY
The ability of an enterprise to
meet its short-term liabilities;
a reflection of its current assets
portfolio.

f   Liquidité
d   Liquidität;
Verfügbarkeit von Kapital

1228 LOANS OUTSTANDING
The totals of loans sanctioned and
disbursed by a development bank
at a point of time.

f   Emprunts à recouvrir
d   Aussenstehende Anleihen

1229 LOAN PORTFOLIO
Totality of outstanding loans,
approved and committed by a
development bank. (See: Investment portfolio 1226)

f   Portefeuille d'emprunts
d   Anleiheportefeuille

1230 MATURITY
The date upon which a loan is due
for repayment.

f   Echéance
d   Fälligkeit

1231 OPERATING BUDGET
A formal quantitative expression
of management plans.

f   Budget d'exploitation
d   Betriebsbudget

1232 OPERATING LOSS
Revenue loss incurred before
providing for interest and depreciation.

f   Déficit d'exploitation
d   Geschäftsverlust;
Betriebsverlust

1233 PAYMENT, CONTRACTUAL
A fixed amount payable by an
enterprise, for payment against
supplies or services as provided
for under a contract.

f   Paiement contractuel
d   Kontraktuelle Zahlung

1234 PETTY CASH;
       TILL MONEY;
       IMPREST FUND
The relatively small amount of
cash an enterprise keeps to
meet day-to-day obligations.

f   Petite caisse
d   Kleine Kasse

1235 PORTFOLIO ROTATION
A measure of the frequency with
which a development bank, a
finance or investment institution, revolves its investible
resources amongst types and
varieties of investment outlets.

f   Roulement de portefeuille
d   Portefeuilleturnus

1236 PROFIT
Net earnings after all costs of
production including depreciation
and direct taxes.

f   Profit;
     Bénéfice;
     Gain
d   Gewinn;
     Profit

1237 PROFIT, GROSS
Profit before selling expense,
depreciation, interest payments,
management expenses, and
taxes.

f   Bénéfice brut;
     Profit brut
d   Bruttogewinn

1238 PROFIT, NET
Profit after all payment of
obligations, including taxes,

available for distribution. (See: Income, net 1217)

f Bénéfice net;
 Profit net
d Nettogewinn

1239 PROFIT, OPERATING
 The difference between the gross profit and the operating expenses. (See: Income, operating 1218)

f Bénéfice d'exploitation;
 Profit d'exploitation
d Betriebsgewinn;
 Geschäftsgewinn

1240 PROFIT, UNDISTRIBUTED
 Residual of earnings after payment of dividends.

f Bénéfice non distribué;
 Profit non distribué
d Unverteilter Gewinn;
 Einbehaltener Gewinn

1241 RATIO, INVENTORY-SALES
 A measure representing the relationship between a company's stock of goods and its sales in a given period; this ratio is a useful forecasting tool.

f Taux d'inventaire-vente
d Inventar-Verkaufsverhältnis

1242 RATIO, OVERDUES;
  RATIO, OUTSTANDING
 A measure representing the relationship between a development bank's loan installment that have fallen due, but not actually received and outstanding loan amounts or totals of installments due at a point of time.

f Taux d'arrérages;
 Taux d'arriérés
d Verhältnis der Zahlungsrückstände

1243 RATIO, SELF-FINANCING
 The amount of capital required for new investment by an organization obtained from its own savings (i.e. from depreciation funds, profits and surplus) expressed as a percentage of total capital requirements.

f Taux de financement des ressources internes
d Selbstfinanzierungsrate

1244 REBATE
 A percentage deduction allowed on stipulated interest rate for prompt and regular payment.

f Rebais;
 Remboursement;
 Ristorne;
 Escompte
d Preisnachlass;
 Rabatt;
 Abzug

1245 REBATE, DEFERRED
 Rebates granted on prices for services, or commodities, on a deferred basis as an incentive of encouraging customers to buy exclusively from a particular firm; a technique of sales promotion.

f Rebais différé
d Aufgeschobener Nachlass

1246 SOLVENCY
 The ability of an enterprise to meet its debt obligations.

f Solvabilité
d Zahlungsfähigkeit;
 Solvenz

1247 SOLVENCY, ACTUAL
 The ability of an enterprise to cover all its liabilities in the event of·liquidation.

f Solvabilité actuelle
d Tatsächliche Zahlungsfähigkeit

1248 SOLVENCY, TECHNICAL
The ability of an enterprise to
pay its debts as they come due.

f Solvabilité technique
d Technische Zahlungsfähigkeit

1249 STATEMENTS, COMPARATIVE
Statements of performances of
the current period in comparison
to the previous ones of one
enterprise, or of one entity with
similar others for the same or
comparable periods.

f Exposé comparatif;
Etat comparatif;
Relevé comparatif
d Vergleichende Finanzerklärung

1250 STATEMENTS, CONSOLIDATED
Reflect the financial position of
a parent unit and its subsidiary
as a single business enterprise.

f Exposé consolidé;
Etat consolidé;
Déclaration consolidée;
Relevé consolidé
d Konsolidierte Finanzerklärung

1251 SUBSIDIZING ADMINISTRATIVE
EXPENSES
Process of defraying part of the
annual operational expenses by
the government or other developmental authorities in return for
performing certain functions not
normal for development banks on
behalf of the government or
authorities concerned.

f Subvention de dépenses administratives;
Subvention de frais de gérance
d Subvention von Verwaltungsausgaben

1252 WORKING CAPITAL, NET
Permanent element in the
components of working capital;
measured as the difference
between current liabilities and
current assets.

f Capital d'exploitation, net;
Fonds de roulement, net
d Nettobetriebskapital;
Nettogeschäftskapital

1253 WORKING CAPITAL,
START-UP
Liquidity requirements involved in commencement of
operations.

f Capital d'exploitation de
commencement
d Startbetriebskapital;
Anfangsgeschäftskapital

1254 WRITE-DOWN
Adjusting the value of assets
downwards to conform to their
present estimated value.

f Réduction du capital
d Kapitalherabsetzung

1255 WRITE-OFF
The act of removing an asset
from the books of a company.

f Déduction d'une certaine somme
pour l'usure
d Kapitalabschreibung

1256 WRITE-UP
The process by which an
asset's book value is increased
to its present appraised value.

f Accroissement du capital
d Kapitalwertzunahme

1257 YIELD LEVEL
Rate of return on investment,
measured in terms of total
capital employed, or total assets,
or total sales.

f Niveau de rendement
d Ertragsniveau

ENGLISH

ENGLISH

Absorption 834
Acceptance, bank 751
- , bankers' 751
- , trade 752
Acceptance credit 775
Accomodation-bill 222
Account, book 1143
- , capital 1139
- , current 1140
- , goodwill 861
- , nominal 1142
- , open 1143
- , profit and loss 1144
Accounting 1037
Accounting equation 1145
Accounts, payable 1137
-, receivable 1138
Accrual basis 1146
Accumulation 207
ADB 392, 394
Advances, self-liquidating 467
Adviser, economic 952
- , financial 953
- , technical 954
Agency, autonomous
- , coordinating 382
Agency marketing 468
Agro-business establishment 383
Agro-industry 50
Allotment of shares 753
Amalgamation 754
Amortization of a loan 1148
- of fixed assets 1147
Analysis, activity 1025
- , cost benefit 575
- , credit 576
- , critical path 1026
- , cross-section 577
- , demand 578
- , distribution cost 1027
- , efficiency 1028
- , industry potential 1029
- , input-output 1030
- , inter-industry 1030
- , investment-effectiveness 579
- , net work 1026
- , probability 580
- , production cost 1032
- , product profitability 1031
- , ratio 581
- , systems 1124

Annual return 755
Annuity 1149
Apex institution 384
Application money 862
Applied research 1033
Appraisal, collateral 582
- , credit worthiness 583
- , economic 584
- , financial 585
- , management 586
- , market 587
- , technical 588
Appraiser 956
Appropriation 1150
Appropriation account 1151
Arbitrage, stock 208
Area, backward 2
Area development 1
Area seminar 1034
Area surveys 589
Articles of association 756
- of incorporation 756
- of partnership 756
Assessment of functions 1075
Asset 863
Asset appreciation 864
Assets, current 866
- , earning 867
- , fixed 868
- , floating 866
- , frozen 869
- , intangible 870
- , liquid 871
- , net 872
- , net equity 873
- , non-current 868
- , quick 874
- , ready 874
- , slow 875
- , sundry 876
- , tangible 877
- , wasting 878
Assets coverage, fixed 879
- of a bank 865
Assignment 757
Association clause 758
At par 209
- the market 210
Audit 1152
Audit, operational 1035
Auditor 957

161

Auditor, external 958
- , internal 959
Authorized clerk 211
Automation 1036
Averaging 212
Backward area 2
Backwardation 213
Backwash effects 3
Balance, trial 1154
- of payments deficit 4
- of trade 5
Balance sheet 1153
Bank 385
- , African development 392
- , agricultural development 393
- , Asian Development 394
- , central 387
- , commercial 388
- , cooperative 389
- , correspondent 390
- , development 391
- , discount 449
- , export-import 397
- , industrial development 395
- , Inter-American Development 396
- , investment 398
- , land mortgage 399
- , managing 400
- , merchant 401
- , mutual savings 402
- , post office savings 403
- , private 404
- , savings 405
- , State 406
- , trade 407
- , trading 407
- , World 453
Bank acceptance 751
Bankability of a project 590
Bank charter 960
Bank credit 214
Bank discount 215
Bank draft 216
Banker, development 961
- , investment 962
Banker's draft 216
Banker's reference 591
Banking 469
- , branch 410
- , group 411
- , investment 523

Banking, unit 412
Banking facilities 408
Banking institution 385
Banking syndicate 409
Banking system 217
Bank of issue 386
Bank rate 179
Bankruptcy 759
Bear 218
Bear raid 219
Benefits, direct, primary 592
- , indirect, secondary 593
- , induced 594
- , national 595
- , net 596
- , stemming 597
Best profit equilibrium 598
Bid and offer 220
Bidding, competitive 760
- , international 760
Bill, accomodation- 222
- , commercial 761
- , due 273
- , time- 223
- , trade- 224
- of credit 824
- of exchange 761
- of exchange, sight 762
- of exchange, term 763
- of lading 764
Bills discounted 221
Black market 6
Blue chips 225
Board of directors 963
Bond 226
Bonds, adjustment 228
- , baby 229
- , bearer 230
- , callable- 231
- , collateral trust- 232
- , convertible 234
- , coupon- 233
- , debenture 262
- , funding 235
- , general mortgage 236
- , gilt-edged 331
- , guaranteed 237
- , income 238
- , junior 239
- , legal 240
- , mortgage 241

ENGLISH

Bonds, non-negotiable 246
- , open-end 242
- , participating 243
- , perpetual 244
- , piggy 229
- , redeemable 245
- , registered 246
- , serial 247
- , tax exempt 248
Bond yield 227
Bonus, cum 776
Bonus issue 344, 900
Book-keeping 1037
Boom 7
Borrowing base 880
- capacity 880
- power 881
Bourse 413
Breakeven point 599
Broker, bill 415
- , floor 416
- , foreign exchange 417
- , placing 418
- , share 414
- , specialist 419
Brokerage 249
Bucket shop 250
Budget 1156
- , operating 1231
Budgetary constraints 101
- control 1155
Budgeting 1156
- , capital 1159
Building society 420
Bull 251
Business school 1038
By-laws of the charter 964
Call 882
Callable capital 882
- loan 535
Call loan 307
Call money 307
Capacity, excess 600
- , installed 601
- , investment adsorptive 71
- , maximum 601
Capital, authorized 885
- , auxiliary 886
- , callable 882
- , cost of 603
- , debt 887

Capital, employed 888
- , fixed 604
- , institutional 605
- , instrumental 886
- , issued 889
- , loan 887
- , net 872
- , nominal 890
- , optional 606
- , owners' 891
- , paid-in 895
- , paid-up 895
- , producers' 892
- , productivity of, 683
- , real 892
- , registered 885
- , reserve 893
- , return on 730
- , risk 898
- , share 894
- , social overhead 68
- , stock 894
- , subscribed 895
- , uncalled 896
- , unimpaired 897
- , venture 898
Capital allowance 1157
Capital appreciation 1158
Capital budgeting 1159
Capital flight 8
Capital formation 9
Capital gearing 883
Capital goods 33
Capital inflow 10
Capitalism, subsidized 94
Capitalization 899
Capitalization issue 900
Capitalization of reserves 902
Capitalization ratio 901
Capital loss 1160
Capital market promotion 470
Capital participation 884
Capital rationing 102
Capital recovery factor 602
Capital structure 899
Capital subscription 884
Captive unit 11
Career planning 1039
Carry-over 252
Case study 1040
Cash balance 1161

Cash basis 1162
Cash cushion 1163
Cash-flow 607
- , discounted 609
Cash-flow forecast 608
Cash generation 1164
Catalytic function 471
Cats and dogs 253
Census of industrial production 12
Certificate of deposit 254
- of incorporation 765
- of indebtedness 255
Chamber of commerce 421
Charge, capital 1165
- , commitment 1166
- , fixed 766
- , floating 767
Charter of incorporation 960
Checklist 610
Chief engineer 1002
CIF 611
Clearing 256
Clearing house 447
Collateral 612
Commission 257
Common stock 353
Company 422
- , affiliated 423
- , associated 423
- , client 769
- , closed-end investment 424
- , commercial credit 425
- , consumer finance 426
- , factoring 427
- , finance 428
- , highly geared 917
- , holding 429
- , investment 430
- , joint stock 431
- , limited 432
- , limited liability 432
- , multinational 434
- , open-end investment 435
- , personal finance 426
- , public limited 433
- , sales finance 425
- , small business investment 436
- , small-loan 426
Company promoter 613
Company reconstruction 768
Company reorganization 768

Comprehensive professional
  personality 1041
Computer 1042
Consols 258
Construction schedule 614
Consultancy, professional 1043
Consultant, industrial 965
- , management 966
- , technical 965
Consultative group 967
Consulting engineer 965
Consulting firm 968
Consumer councils 13
Consumer-goods 34
Contango 252
Contingencies 615
Contingent expenses 615
Contingent reserves 939
Continuation 252
Contract 259
Contract note 103
Controlling share ownership 817
Convertibility, currency 118
Conveyance 104
Cooperant factors 14
Cooperative, agricultural credit 437
Cornering the market 260
Corporation 422
- , agricultural mortgage 438
- , industrial and commercial
  finance 439
- , private 440
- , public 441
- , thin 946
Cost, alternative 625
- , average 1168
- , direct 1169
- , external 622
- , factor 623
- , fixed 1170
- , full 1171
- , historical 1172
- , indirect 1173
- , indirect foreign exchange 624
- , joint 1174
- , long-run average 1175
- , marginal 1176
- , opportunity 625
- , outage 1177
- , prime 1169
- , private opportunity 626

ENGLISH

Cost, replacement 1178
- , running 1179
- , selling 1167
- , social 627
- , social opportunity 628
- , standard 1180
- , supplementary 1181
- , total production 1182
- , transfer 629
- , variable 1183
Cost accounting methods 1044
Cost control 1045
Cost control techniques 1046
Cost effectiveness 616
Cost estimates 617
Costing 1047
Cost of capital, opportunity 619
Cost of investment, opportunity 620
Cost of production 621
Cost of purchase 771
Cost of sales 1167
Cost overruns 770
Cost-plus contract 772
Cost price 618
Counselling programme 472
Counter guarantee 473
Counterpart funds 105
Coupon payment 261
Covenant, financial 106
- , restrictive 107
Cover 773
Crash programme 774
Credit, acceptance 775
Credit, commercial 476
- , consumer 477
- , deferred 478
- , documentary 479
- , hire purchase 480
- , installment 481
- , mortgage 482
- , revolving 483
- , rollover 483
- , supervised 484
- , supplemental 498
- , suppliers' 485
- , trade 1184
- , trading capital 486
- , working capital 486
Credit control 108
- , selective 109
Credit creation 110

Credit facilities 111
Credit guarantee 113
- guarantee, export 137
Credit inflation 112
Credit insurance services 474
Credit line 928
Credit on mortgage 482
Credit restriction, quantitative 114
Credit shift 115
Credit squeeze 116
Credit standard 630
Credit status 630
Credit substitutes, provision of 475
Creditworthiness 631
c.r.f. 602
Cum bonus 776
Cum dividend 777
Cum interest 778
Cum rights 779
Cumulative voting 780
Currency, hard 119
- , over-valued 120
- , soft 121
Currency appreciation 117
Currency convertibility 118
Customs, tariff 122
Cut-off point 632
Cybernetics 1048
Data bank 1049
Data file 1049
DCF 609
Debenture 262
- , convertible 263
- , fixed 264
- , irredeemable 265
- , mortgage 266
- , naked 267
- , simple 267
Debenture bonds 262
Debt ceiling 903
Debt instruments 268
Debt limit 903
Debts, bad 1186
- , doubtful 1187
- , floating 904
- , funded 905
- , junior 906
- , senior 907
Debt service coverage 633
Debt servicing 1185

Decentralized industrial development 15
Decision making 969
Decision-making process 970
Deed of arrangement 781
Deed of suretyship 189
Deed of trust 145
Deferred payments 1188
Deficit 1189
Deficit financing 123
Deflation 16
Deflator 1050
Delegation of authority 1051
Demand, aggregate 634
– , derived 635
– , effective 634
Department, accounting 971
– , credit 972
– , disbursement 973
– , end-use 974
– , engineering 975
– , follow-up 974
– , legal 976
– , loan 972
– , market research 977
– , operations 978
– , projects 979
– , securities 980
– , technical 975
Depletion 1190
Depletion allowance 1191
Deposit, fixed 269
– , term 269
Depreciation 1192
– , accelerated 1194
– , reduced balance 1195
– , straight line 1196
Depreciation allowance 1193
Depth interview 1052
Devaluation 124
Developing countries 17
Development administration 981
Developmental activities 487
Development areas 18
Development bank expert 982
Development of professionals 1109
Development scheme 19
Dilution 270
Disbursement 488
Discount 271
Discount bank 449

Discount house 449
Discount rate 180
Discretionary orders 272
Disinflation 20
Disinflationary policy 125
Disinvestment 1197
Diversification, industrial- 21
– , product- 21
Diversification of risk 489
Diversity factor 782
Dividend 1198
– , accumulative 786
– , cash 1201
– , cum 777
– , cumulative 786
– , government-guaranteed 787
– , gross 788
– , interim 789
– , non-cumulative 790
– , optional 791
– , ordinary 792
– , tax-free 793
Dividend cover 1199
Dividend limitation 783
Dividend mandate 784
Dividend rate 1200
Dividend warrant 785
Documentation 794
Drawback facilities 795
Due bill 273
Dummy 274
Dumping 796
Duties, countervailing 126
– , customs 127
– , excise 128
– , import 129
Earnest money 636
Earnings, net 1201
– , retained 1203
Economic democracy 22
– efficiency, promotion of 490
– indicators 637
Economics division 983
Elasticity, income 642
Elasticity of demand 638
– of evaluation 639
– of substitution 640
– of supply 641
Eligible papers 336
Enterprise, free- 23
– , private 442

ENGLISH

Enterprise, public 443
Entrepreneur 643
- development 491
Environmental engineering 24
Equities 908
Equity 909
- , non-voting 910
- , return on 731
- , shareholders' 909
Equity investment 492
- investment, limit for 532
Equity participation 493
Equity sales 494
Escalator clause 1204
Eurodollars 275
Ex-bonus 797
Ex-capitalization 798
Exchange control 130
Exchange management 131
Exchange restrictions 132
Exchange stability 133
Ex-coupon 799
Ex-dividend 800
Executive committee 1000
- development programme 1053
Expenditure, capital 1205
- , development 134
- , government 135
Expenses, contingent 615
- , management 1206
- , operating 1207
- , pre-formation 644
- , preliminary 644
- , pre-operative 644
- , project development 645
Export bonus 136
Export credit guarantee 137
Export credit insurance 138
Export finance assistance 495
Export incentives 139
Export intelligence 984
Export license 140
Export permit 140
Exports, foregone 25
Export unit realization 26
Exposure 911
Ex-right 801
Extension facilities 802
External economy 27
- economy, pecuniary 28
- economy, technological 29

External training assistance 1054
Extra-mural courses 1055
Factor proportions 30
Feasibility study 646
- study, economic 647
- study, financial 648
- study, managerial 649
- study, technical 650
Field staff 985
Finance, balancing 498
Finance house 428
Financial analyst 986
- capacity 651
- counselling 1056
- institutions 444
- intermediaries 444
- projections 652
- reporting 1057
- return 1208
- statements 1209
- year 1210
- yield 1208
Financing, accounts receivable 496
- , agricultural 497
- , balancing equipment 499
- , concessional 500
- , consortia 501
- , conventional 502
- , development 503
- , joint 504
- , long-term 505
- , medium-term 506
- , parallel 507
- , public utility 508
- , short-term 509
- , subsidized 510
Fiscal policy 141
Fixed capital 868
Floatation 912
Forecasting 1058
- , long-term 1059
- , multi- 1060
- , sales 1061
- , short-term 1062
Foreclosure 803
Foreign exchange control 130
Foreign exchange earnings 653
Foreign exchange effect 654
Foreign exchange reserves,
  depletion of 31

Foreign exchange savings 653
Foreign trade policy 142
Forward exchange 276
Forward trading contract 277
Free enterprise 23
Free limit 511
Free trade zone 32
Full cost pricing 1211
Fund, imprest 1234
- , mutual 435
- , revolving 913
- , sinking 914
Funded government securities 258
Funding 915
- operation 915
Funds, counterpart 105
- , investible 70
- , managed 549
Generalist 1063
Gestation period 655
Gilt-edged bonds 331
- investment 278
Glut 804
Going concern 805
Goods, capital 33
- , consumer 34
- , intermediate 35
Goodwill 806
Grace period 807
Growth-oriented policy 36
Guarantee, credit 113
- , investment 147
- , outstanding 1213
Guarantee charges 656
Guarantee cover 657
Guarantee fund 1212
Guarantee societies 445
Guarantor 808
Hedge 279
Highly geared company 917
House, accepting 446
- , bankers' clearing 447
- , clearing 447
- , confirming 448
- , discount 449
- , export commission 450
- , hire purchase finance 451
IBRD 453
IDA 454
Identification of projects 512
IFC 455

Illiquidity 1214
Import ban 143
Import quota 144
Import substitution 513
Imprest fund 1234
Income, earned 1215
- , gross 1216
- , net 1217
- , operating 1218
- , retained 1219
- , unearned 1220
Income distribution 37
Income statement 1144
Indebtedness 1221
Indent 809
- , closed 810
- , open 811
Indenture 145
Index number 40
- of industrial production 38
- of prices and output 39
Indirect manufacturing expense 1173
Industrial counselling 1066
- credit and investment corporation 395
- design centre 41
- development, decentralized 15
- education 42
- engineering 1067
- estate 43
- estate, ancillary 44
- estate, functional 45
- estate, single-trade 46
Industrialization, spread effect of 91
Industrial licensing 47
- migration 48
- park 43
- production, index of 38
- promotion agency 49
Industry, agro- 50
- , by-product 51
- , capital-intensive 52
- , capital-light 53
- , cottage 54
- , domestic 54
- , export 55
- , feeder 56
- , home 54
- , infant 57

ENGLISH

Industry, key 58
- , market-oriented 59
- , regulated 60
- , skill-oriented 61
- , small-scale 62
Industry centre, prototype 63
Industry profiles 1068
Industry status, pioneer 64
Inflation 65
- , credit 112
- , galloping 66
- , hyper- 66
- , runaway 66
Inflationary gap 67
Information system 812
Infra-structure 68
- , financial 69
In-plant counselling 1064
- diagnostic studies 1065
Inscribed shares 368
Insolvency 813
- , technical 814
Institutional finance 146
- investors 452
Institutionalized training programme 1069
Insufficiency gap 658
Insurance coverage 815
Interest, accrued 1223
- , controlling 817
- , cum 778
- , gross 1224
- , imputed 1225
Interest during construction 1222
Interest rate 514
- rate, concessional 519
- rate, effective 516
- rate, foreign currency 517
- rate, market 280
- rate, natural 281
- rate, nominal 282
- rate, penalty 518
- rate, prime 283
- rate, pure 284
- rate, subsidized 519
Interest rate ceiling 515
Interest spread 520
- spread, negative 521
Intermediate goods 35
International bank for reconstruction and development 453

International development association 454
- finance corporation 455
Inter-project coordination 816
Inventory 818
Inventory adjustment 1071
Inventory management 1070
Inventory turnover 819
Inventory valuation 1071
Investible funds 70
Investment 522
- , autonomous 74
- , equity 492
- , gilt-edged 278
- , gross fixed 918
- , induced 75
- , return on 732
- , token 527
Investment absorptive capacity 71
Investment allocation criteria 659
Investment banking 523
Investment center 456
Investment climate 72
Investment counsellor 987
Investment guarantee 147
Investment incentives 148
Investment intelligence 1072
Investment manager 953
Investment opportunity catalogue 1073
Investment plan 524
Investment policy 525
Investment portfolio 1226
Investment priorities 73
Investment strategy 526
Investment trust 430
Investor confidence 76
Investors, institutional 452
Issue, bonus 900
- , capitalization 900
- , conversion 286
- , defensive 287
- , hot 288
- , oversubscribed 820
- , public 821
- , scrip 900
- , tap 149
- , undersubscribed 822
Issue by tender 285
Issuing bank 386
Jobber 419

Jobber, stock 419
Jobber's turn 289
Job description 1074
Job evaluation 1075
Job training 1076
Joint venture 660
Junior lien bonds 239
Junior loans 906
Law, banking 153
- , bankruptcy 154
- , blue-sky 155
- , company 156
- , foreign capital investment 157
- , mercantile 158
Law enforcement procedures 150
Law of contracts 151
Law of partnership 152
Legal aid 159
- counsel 988
- impediments 160
- list 290
- officer 988
Legislation, incentive 161
- , pioneer industry 162
Lending, commercial 529
- , indigenous 530
- , rural 531
Lending operations 528
Letter of allotment 823
- of credit 824
- of hypothecation 163
- of regret 825
- of renunciation 826
Leverage 919
- , real 920
Liability, contingent 922
- , current 926
- , limited 923
- , long-term 924
- , secured 925
- , short-term 926
- , unsecured 927
- of a company 921
Lien 164
Life, economic 661
- , useful 662
Limit for equity investment 532
Limiting factor 827
Line and functional organization 990
- and staff organization 991
Linear programming 1077

Line of credit 928
Line relationship 989
Linkage 77
- , backward 78
- , forward 79
Liquidation 828
Liquidity 1227
- preference 165
Loan, bridging 534
- , call 535
- , clean 548
- , conversion 536
- , debenture 537
- , factory type 538
- , foreign currency 539
- , hard 540
- , hard currency 541
- , local currency 542
- , personal 543
- , secured 544
- , soft 500
- , soft currency 545
- , sub- 546
- , subordinated 929
- , tied 547
- , unsecured 548
Loan committee 992
Loan contract 829
Loan conversion 915
Loan on debentures 537
Loan portfolio 1229
Loan programme, small 533
Loans, junior 906
Loans outstanding 1228
Loans, senior 907
Loan servicing 663
Managed funds 549
Management, commercial 994
- , corporate 995
- , credit 1088
- , financial 1089
- , marketing 1090
- , middle 996
- , modern 997
- , office 998
- , production 1091
- , tradition-oriented 999
Management accounting 1078
Management audit 1079
Management consultancy 1080
Management development 1081

Management development services 1082
Management diagnosis 1083
Management information system 1084
Management interests 993
Management know-how 1085
Management services 1086
Management training 1087
Managerial grid system 1092
Managing board 1000
Managing director 1001
Managing engineer 1001
Manipulation 291
Margin, safety 292
Margin money 664
Market, active 295
- , bear 296
- , black 6
- , buyers' 297
- , capital 298
- , cash 306
- , discount 299
- , foreign exchange 300
- , money 301
- , mortgage 302
- , narrow 303
- , new issue 304
- , over-the-counter 305
- , physical 306
- , sellers' 831
- , spot 306
- , thin 303
- , trading 305
Market for securities 293
Marketing agency 468
Marketing research 1094
Market research 1093
Market researcher 1003
Market services, capital 294
Market share 665
Mark-up 830
Maturity 1230
- of a loan 832
Memorandum of association 833
Merger 834
Mission, appraisal 1004
- , bank 1005
- , fact-finding 1006
- , project preparation 1007
- , reconnaissance 1008

Model schemes 666
Modernization 835
Monetary policy 166
Money, call 307
- , cheap 167
- , dear 168
- , earnest 636
- , easy 167
- , funk 169
- , hot 169
- , margin 664
- , near 308
- , tight 168
- at call and short notice 307
Monitoring system 836
Mortgage 170
- , closed 171
Mortgage instrument 837
Multiplier 172
Mutual fund 435
Nationalization 173
Negotiable 309
- instrument 310
- paper 310
Net capital 872
Net worth 930
Nominee 311
Non-cumulative 312
Objects clause 838
Observation, field 1095
- , on-the-job 1096
- , plant 1095
Obsolescence 839
Occupational education 1097
- instruction 1097
Offer for sale 841
Official receiver 842
Off the shelf goods 840
One-man business 1011
Open market operations 174
Operating budget 1231
- loss 1232
- statement 1144
Operational problem 843
Operations officer 1009
Operations research 1098
Organization chart 1010
Orientation, on-the-job 1100
Orientation programme 1099
Ordinary shares 908
Outlays, private 80

Outlays, public 81
Output, gross 667
- , net 668
Over-capitalization 931
Overdraft 550
Overhead 1170
Over-subscription 932
Owner-manager 1011
Ownership, government 1012
- , mixed 1013
- , private 1014
Panel 1101
Parity 175
- , indirect 82
Pay-back 669
Payment contractual 1233
Pay-off 669
Pay-out period 669
Performance criteria 1102
Performance guarantee 551
PERT 1026
Petty cash 1234
Placing 313
- , private 314
Policy statement 552
Population explosion 83
Portfolio 933
Portfolio management 1103
Portfolio rotation 1235
Post-finance supervision 553
PPBS 1112
Pre-investment services 554
Premium 315
Present value 670
Present value method 671
Present worth 670
Present worth factor 672
Price, accounting 673
- , anticipated 674
- , competitive 675
- , demand 676
- , factor 677
- , imputed 678
- , international 682
- , market 679
- , shadow 680
- , social demand 681
- , world market 682
Price control 176
Prices, closing 316

Prices, coming-out 317
- , opening 318
Price stabilization 177
Pricing, promotional 1105
Pricing policy 1104
Prior charges 934
Procedure, incorporation 844
Procedures, tender 555
Process engineering 1106
Process research 1107
Procurement, sources of 845
Procurement policy 556
Production engineering 1108
Productivity of capital 683
Products, joint 684
Profit 1236
- , gross 1237
- , net 1238
- , operating 1239
- , undistributed 1240
Profitability 687
- , commercial 688
Profitability accounting 1111
Profit expectation 685
Profit margin 846
Profit maximation 847
Profit planning and budgetary
    system 1110
Profit sharing 686
Profit taking 319
Programme-based assistance 557
Programme evaluation and review
    technique 1026
Programme planning budgeting
    system 1112
Project 689
- , cut-off 694
- , self-liquidating 695
- , shadow 696
- , "time slice" 697
Project appraisal 691
Project-based assistance 558
Project cost 690
Project director 1015
Project economist 1016
Project engineer 1017
Project evaluation 691
Project evaluation officer 1018
Project evaluator 1018
Project formulation 559
Project line 560

Project location 692
Project manager 1015
Project selection 693
Promissory note 320
Promotional activities 487
Prospectus 848
Protection 178
Proxy 849
Public sector 84
Public utility 85
Public works 86
Punter 321
P.W.F. 672
Pyramiding 322
Quality control, statistical 1113
Quotation 323
Rate, bank 179
- , borrowing 561
- , capacity utilization 698
- , commercial loan 562
- , discount 180
- , dividend 1200
- , lending 563
- , operating 698
- , rediscounting 180
Rate of exchange, fixed 182
- of exchange, flexible 181
- of exchange, free 183
- of exchange, multiple 184
Rate of return 699
- of return, discounted 701
- of return, fair 702
- of return, internal 703
- of return, social 704
- of return on invested capital 700
Ratio, acid test 705
- , average capital-output 706
- , banker's 709
- , benefit cost 707
- , capital-output 708
- , common stock 935
- , concentration 564
- , current 709
- , current position 709
- , cut-off 710
- , debt capitalization 723
- , debt-equity 711
- , debt-service 712
- , debt-to-net-worth 713
- , depreciation-reserve 714
- , derived 715

Ratio, dynamic 716
- , fixed asset coverage 717
- , incremental capital-output 720
- , inventory-sales 1241
- , investment coverage 718
- , liquidity 705
- , loan safety 719
- , marginal capital-output 720
- , operating cost 721
- , outstanding 1242
- , overdues 1242
- , pay-out 722
- , portfolio 723
- , product-capital 724
- , profitability 725
- , quick 705
- , self-financing 1243
- , solvency 726
- , static 727
Rebate 1244
- , deferred 1245
Recoupment period 669
Redemption 936
Redemption date 937
Redeployment 850
Rediscount 324
Rediscounting 565
Refinancing 565
Regional development 1
Reporting system 851
Research and development 1114
Reserves 938
- , contingency 939
- , depreciation 940
- , excess 941
- , free 942
- , legal 943
- , minimum legal 944
- , statutory 943
Resource mobilization 566
Return, annual 755
- , economic 728
- , social 728
Return on assets 729
- on capital 730
- on equity 731
- on investment 732
- on sales 733
Revalorization 185
Revaluation 185
Revenue, gross 1216

Revenue, net 1217
Rigging 325
Rights, conversion 853
- , cum 779
Rights letter 852
Rights on 779
Risk, business 734
- , calculated 568
- , commercial 734
- , credit 569
- , economic 735
- , financial 736
- , foreign exchange 570
- , lending 736
- , political 737
Risk spread 567
Round lot 326
Rural banking expert 1019
Safety margin 292
Sales, return on 733
Sales mix problem 738
Sales potential 739
Sales promotion 854
Sandwich courses 1115
Savings, compulsory 187
- , corporate 186
- , forced 187
- , foreign exchange 653
Savings and loan association 457
Savings investment gap 188
Savings ratio 87
Scrip 327
Scrip issue 900
Sectors, organized 88
- , unorganized 89
Securities 328
- , approved 336
- , convertible 329
- , digested 330
- , funded government 258
- , government 331
- , irredeemable 332
- , listed 333
- , marketable 334
- , second-hand 335
- , trustee 336
- , undigested 337
- , unlisted 338
Security 612
Security arrangement 740
Security margin 741

Selling short 339
Senior loans 907
Sensitivity test 742
Settlement day 340
Share broker 414
Share certificate 341
Share option 342
Shares, authorized 367
- , bonus 344
- , callable 345
- , convertible 346
- , cumulative 347
- , cumulative preference 348
- , deferred 349
- , deferred management 350
- , inscribed 368
- , multiple voting 351
- , no-par-value 352
- , ordinary 353, 908
- , paid-up 354
- , preference 355
- , preference participating 356
- , preferred 355
- , watered 370
Shares and stocks 343
Simulation 1116
Simulation games 1117
Skill formation facilities 90
Small business 62
Social overhead capital 68
Soft loan 500
Sole proprietor 1011
Solvency 1246
- , actual 1247
- , technical 1248
Sources, external 743
- , internal 744
Specialist 1118
Speculation 357
Spin-off method 358
Splitting 359
Split-up 359
Spot payment 360
Spot purchase 361
Spread effect of industrialization 91
Staff, expatriate 1021
- , follow-up 1022
- , reviewing 1022
- , supervisory 1022
Staff turnover 1020
Stag 362

Stagflation 92
Standardization 1119
Stand at a discount, to 271
Statements, comparative 1249
- , consolidated 1250
Statistician 1120
Stock, authorized 367
- , common 353
- , cash price of 369
- , inscribed 368
- , spot price of 369
- , watered 370
Stock arbitrage 208
Stock conversion 363
Stock dividend 364
Stock exchange introduction 365
Stock split 369
Stock turn 366
Stock turnover 819
Straddle 371
Sub-contracting system 93
Subsidized capitalism 94
Subsidizing administrative expenses
  1251
Supervision of projects 571
Supplemental credit 498
Supply, aggregate 745
Surety bond 189
Surtax 190
Survey 1121
- , economic 1122
- , enterprise 1123
Switching 372
- anomaly 373
- coupon 374
- policy 375
Syndicate 458, 1101
Systems analysis 1124
Systems man 1125
Talon 945
Task force 1023
Tax, capital gains 194
- , corporation 195
- , development 196
- , interest equalization 197
- , undistributed profits 198
Taxability 199
Taxable capacity 199
Taxation, double 200
- , multiple 201
Tax concession 191

Tax credit 191
Taxes, indirect 202
Tax haven 192
Tax incentive 193
Tax relief 191
Technical advisory services 572
Technology, capital-intensive 95
- , intermediate 96
- , labor-intensive 97
Tender documents 855
Tender specification 856
Tenor 376
Thin corporation 946
Thrift institution 459
Till money 1234
Time and motion study 1126
Time-bill 223
Title deed 203
Trade-bill 224
Trade organization 460
Training, in-country 1133
- , in-work 1134
- , overseas 1135
- , third-country 1135
- , vocational 1136
Training centers, government 1127
Training gap 1128
Training officer 1129
Training.policy 1130
Training programme, bank-to-bank
  1131
- programme, inter-bank 1131
Training within industry 1132
Transfer deed 203
Transfer earnings 98
Transfer of shares 857
Treasury bill 204
Treasury note 205
Trust 461
- , closed-end 462
- , fixed 463
- , investment 430
- , unit 464
Trust company 461
Trustee, public 858
Trust indenture 145
Turnover 859
T.W.I. 1132
Under-capitalization 947
Undervaluation 206

Underwriter 465
- , sub- 466
Underwriting 573
Undistributed profits 1203
Unit, ancillary 99
- , parent 100
Unsecured creditor 860
Usance 377
Usury 378
Valuator 956
Value, book 948
- , break-up 949
- , capitalized 950
- , issue 379
- , market 951
- , nominal 379
- , par 379
Value added 746

Viability, financial 747
- , overall 748
- , technical 749
Warrant 380
Wash sales 381
Watered shares 370
Winding-up 828
Withdrawal procedures 574
Working capital, net 1252
- capital, start-up 1253
Work process chart 1024
World bank 453
Write-down 1254
Write-off 1255
Write-up 1256
Xd 800
Xr 801
Yield level 1257
Yield method 750

FRENCH

FRANÇAIS

Accaparement du marché 260
Accréditif automatiquement
  renouvelable 483
- documentaire 479
Accroissement du capital 1158, 1256
Accumulation 207
Achalandage 806
Achat du disponible 361
Acompte de dividende 789
- sur dividende 789
Acte constitutif 765
- constitutif d'une société 833
- d'association 756
- de caution 189
- de cession 757
- de société 833
- de transfert 757
- translatif de propriété 203
Actif 863
- courant 866
- de capacité d'acquérir 867
- d'exploitation 867
- disponible 871, 874
- divers 876
- indisponible 875
- intact 873
- liquide 871
- net 872, 930
- périssable 878
Action gratuite 344
- provisoire 327
Actions autorisées 367
- avec droit de vote multiple 351
- cumulatives 347
- de capital 353
- de préférence 355
- de priorité 355
- de priorité cumulatives 348
- différées 349
- libérées 354
- nominatives 368
- ordinaires 353, 908
- privilégiées 355
- privilégiées cumulatives 348
- privilégiées de participation 356
- sans valeur nominale 352
Activités de développement 487
- de promotion 487
Administrateur gérant 1001
- officiel de faillite 842
Administration de développement 981

Administration de devises 131
- d'un bureau 998
- d'un office 998
- moderne 997
- moyenne 996
- traditionelle 999
Affaiblissement de la monnaie 124
Affaire qui marche 805
- roulante 805
Affectation 1150
Afflux des capitaux 10
Agence autonome 955
- de coordination 382
- de promotion industrielle 49
- de recouvrement de créances 427
"Agency marketing" 468
Agent de banque 414
- de bourse 416
- de change 417
- de placement 418
Aide externe à la formation 1054
Allocation pour dépréciation 1193
- pour épuisement 1191
Amortissement 936
- de l'actif 1147
- d'un emprunt 1148
Analyse coût-bénéfice 575
- d'activité 1025
- de coût de production 1032
- de crédit 576
- de demande 578
- d'efficacité 1028
- d'efficacité d'un investissement
  579
- de probabilité 580
- de rendement 1028
- de rentabilité par produit 1031
- de secteurs croisés 577
- des systèmes 1124
- de taux 581
- diagnostique sur le tas 1065
- du potentiel industriel 1029
- intersectorielle 1030
Année budgétaire 1210
- d'exploitation 1210
- financière 1210
Annuité 1149
Anomalie de "switch" 373
Anti-inflation 20
Appel à la souscription publique 848
Appréciateur 956
Arbitrage en bourse 208

179

Arbitrage sur valeurs 208
Argent abondant 167
- à vue 307
- "chaud" 169
- cher 168
- remboursable sur demande 307
Arrangement de couverture 740
- de sécurité 740
Arrhes 664
Article de société 758
Assistance à titre d'un projet spécifique 558
- à titre d'un programme 557
- au financement d'exportation 495
- juridique 159
Association 458
- de Développement International 454
- d'épargne 459
Assurance de crédit de l'exportation 138
Attaque des baissiers 219
- du découvert 219
Au marché 210
- pair 209
Automation 1036
Avance 488
Avec dividende 777
- droit 779
- intérêt 778
- prime 776
Avis de répartition 823
Avoirs bloqués 869
- immobilisés 869
Baissier 218
Balance commerciale 5
Bancable 309
Banquabilité d'un projet 590
Banque 385
- Africaine de Développement 392
- Asiatique de Développement 394
- à succursales 410
- à unité 412
- centrale 387
Banque commerciale 388, 407
- coopérative 389
- d'acceptation 446
- de circulation 386
- de commerce 388, 407
- de confirmation 448
- de correspondance 390
- de développement 391

Banque de développement agraire 393
- de développement industriel 395
- d'émission 386
- de placement 398, 523
- de placement et de direction 401
- d'escompte 449
- d'Etat 406
- d'exportation-importation 397
- directoriale 400
- foncière 399
- gestionnaire 400
- Inter-américaine de Développement 396
- Mondiale 453
- nationale 406
- privée 404
Banqueroute 759
Banquier de développement 961
- de placement 962
- d'investissement 962
Base comptant 1162
- d'accumulation 1146
- de caisse 1162
- de crédit 880
- d'espèces 1162
Bénéfice 1236
- brut 1237
- d'exploitation 1239
- net 1238
- non distribué 1240
Bénéfices de procédé additionnel 597
- directs et primaires 592
- d'opération de finissage 597
- indirects et secondaires 593
- induits 594
- nationaux 595
- nets 596
Biens de consommation 34
- d'équipement 33
- disponibles 840
- intermédiaires 35
Bilan 1153
- provisoire 1154
Billet à ordre 320
- de banque 751
- de commerce 752
- de complaisance 222
- du Trésor 205
- du Trésor à court terme 204

FRANÇAIS

Billet simple 320
Bonification 1157
Bons de petite épargne 229
Bordereau d'achat 103
- de courtage 103
Bourse 413
Brut investissement fixe 918
Budget 1156
- de capital 1159
- des capitaux 1159
- d'exploitation 1231
Bureau du contentieux 976
- d'un courtier marron 250
Caisse d'épargne 405
- d'épargne de la poste 403
- d'épargne mutuel 402
Candidat désigné 311
- nommé 311
Capacité contributive 199
- d'absorption des investissements 71
- de crédit 880
- financière 651
- maximum 601
- montée 601
Capital-actions 894, 909
- dilués 370
- sans droit de vote 910
Capital appelé 882
- auxiliaire 886
- déclaré 885
- d'emprunt 887
- de participation 884
- de production 892
- de propriétaire 891
- de réserve 893
- de risque 898
- de roulement 888
- d'établissement 894
- d'exploitation de commencement 1253
- d'exploitation, net 1252
- d'option 606
- effectif 895
- émis 889
- fixe 604, 868
- initial 894
- institutionnel 605
- intact 897
Capitalisation 899
- des réserves 902
Capitalisme subventionné 94

Capital mis en circulation 889
- mobilisé 604
- nominal 885, 890
- non appelé 896
- originaire 894
- réel 892, 895
- social 890
- souscrit 895
- versé 895
Capitaux fixes 604, 868
Carte d'organisation 1010
- du procédé de travail 1024
Catalogue d'opportunité d'investissements 1073
Centre de dessin industriel 41
- d'industrie prototype 63
- d'information des investissements
   456
- d'informations techniques 1049
- gouvernemental de formation 1127
Certificat 380
- d'action 341
- d'endettement 255
- de prise de charge 764
- de sortie 140
- d'inscription hypothécaire 163
- d'obligation 226, 262
- nominatif 327
Cession de titres 857
Chambre de commerce 421
- de compensation des banquiers 447
Changement des actions 366
Changes à terme 276
Chargé de la formation 1129
Charge fixe 766
- flottante 767
Charte d'Incorporation 960
Chef d'exploitation 1001
Chemin critique 1026
Chiffre d'affaires 859
- indicateur 40
"Ciel d'impôt" 192
CIF 611
Clause de l'objectif de l'entreprise
   838
- de société 758
Clerc autorisé 211
Clientèle 806
Climat d'investissements 72
Comité 1101
- de directeurs 963

Comité des prêts 992
Commande de marchandises 809
Commerçable 309
Commissaire des comptes 957
Commission 257
- de placement 249
Compagnie 422
- de finance 428
Comptabilité 971, 1037
- de direction 1078
- de profit 1111
Compte courant 1140
- d'affectation 1151
- de capital 1139
- de clientèle 861
- de fonds de commerce 861
- d'exploitation 1141
- nominal 1142
- ouvert 1143
Comptes à payer 1137
- à recevoir 1138
- des profits et pertes 1144
- des résultats 1144
Concordat 781
Confiance de capitaliste 76
Connaissement 764
Conseil d'administration 1000
- de consommateurs 13
- de gérants 1000
- industriel 1066
Conseiller d'entreprise 966
- économique 952
- technique 954
Consortium de banques 411
Consultant d'investissements 987
Consultation financière 1056
- gestionnaire 1080
- industrielle 1066
- professionnelle 1043
- sur le tas 1064
Contingent d'importation 144
Contraints budgétaires 101
Contrat 259
- d'arrangement 781
- d'association 756, 833
- de changes à terme 277
- de garantie 189
- de prêt 829
- de société 756, 765
- financier 106
- restrictif 107

Contre-garantie 473
Contribution indirecte 202
Contrôle budgétaire 1155
- d'après financement 553
- de cours de change 130
- de coût 1045
- de crédit 108
- de projets 571
- des prix 176
- de taux du change 130
- d'exploitation 1035
- sélectif de crédit 109
- statistique de qualité 1113
Convention financière 106
- restrictive 107
Conversion d'actions 363
- d'un emprunt 915
Convertibilité de devises 118
Coopérative agricole de crédit 437
- d'épargne et de prêt 457
Coordination entre projets 816
Corporation du droit civil 440
- du droit public 441
- d'une faible capitalisation 946
- d'utilité publique 85
- Financière Internationale 455
Cotation 323
Cote 323
Coupon attaché 777
- de dividende 785
- de "switch" 374
Cours 323
- de clôture 316
- de "sandwich" 1115
- du change fixe 182
- du change flexible 181
- du change libre 183
- du change multiple 184
Courses externes 1055
Courtage 249, 257
Courtier de bourse 417
- d'escompte 415
Coût alternatif 625
- alternatif de capital 619
- alternatif d'investissements 620
- alternatif privé 626
- alternatif social 628
- , assurance et fret 611
- conjoint 1174
- courant 1180
- d'acquisition 771

FRANÇAIS

Coût de capital 603, 1165
- de cession 629
- de facteur 623
- de la production 621
- de retard 1177
- de substitution 1178
- de vente 1167
- d'exploitation 1179
- direct 1169
- d'un projet 690
- et contrat 772
- externe 622
- fixe 1170
- forfaitaire 1180
- historique 1172
- indirect 1173
- indirect des devises 624
- marginal 1176
- moyen 1168
- moyen à long terme 1175
- social 627
- supplémentaire 1181
- total 1182
- total d'un produit 1171
- variable 1183
Couverture 773
- d'assurance 815
- de dividende 1199
- de garantie 657
- des capitaux fixes 879
- de service de dettes 633
Créance garantie 925
- sans garantie 927
Créances comptables 1138
- douteuses 1186
Créateur de société 613
Création de crédit 110
Crédibilité 631
Crédit bancaire 214
- commercial 476
- contrôlé 484
- d'approvisionnement 485
- de banque 214
- de commerce 1184
- de consommation 477
- de liquidation de soi-même 467
- de paiement partiel 481
- de roulement 486
- de vente à tempérament 480
- de versements échelonnés 481
- différé 478

Crédit documentaire 479
- en blanc 548
- en devises 539
- en monnaie forte 541
Créditeur sans garantie 860
Crédit hypothécaire 482
- nanti 544
- par acceptation 775
- par acceptation renouvelable 483
- remboursable sur demande 535
- supplémentaire 498
- sur titres 479
Critères d'accomplissement 1102
- d'allocation des investissements 659
Curateur publique 858
Cybernétiques 1048
Date d'amortissement 937
Débit prioritaire 934
Déboursement 488
Décalage entre épargnes et investissements 188
Déclaration consolidée 1250
- financière 1209
Découvert 550
Déduction 1157
- d'une certaine somme pour l'usure 1255
Déficit 1189
- de la balance des paiements 4
- d'exploitation 1232
Déflateur 1050
Déflation 16
Délai de grâce 807
Délégation de banque 1005
- de pouvoirs 849
- des compétences 1051
- d'évaluation 1004
Demande agrégée 634
- dérivée 635
- effective 634
- et offre 220
Démocratie économique 22
Département de déboursement 973
- de "follow-up" 974
- de projet 979
- de recherche du marché 977
- des crédits 972
- de titres 980
- d'opération 978
- économique 983

Département opératoire 978
- technique 975
Dépassement de souscriptions 932
Dépense de capital 1205
Dépenses de développement 134
- de développement de projet 645
- de l'administration 1206
- d'exploitation 1207
- gouvernementales 135
- imprévues 615
- préalables 644
- préliminaires 644
- préparatoires 644
- privées 80
- publiques 81
Déplacement de crédit 115
Déposition financière 1209
Dépôt à terme 269
- à terme fixe 269
- de garantie 636
Dépréciation 1192
- accélérée 1194
- de moins-value 1195
- des changes 124
- linéaire 1196
"Depth Interview" 1052
Dernier cours 316
Description de poste 1074
Désinvestissement 1197
Désuétude 839
Détermination du coût total d'un
    produit 1211
Dette à court terme 926
- à long terme 924
- chirographaire 927
- consolidée 905
- flottante 904
- fondée 905
Dettes actives 1138
- de dernière priorité 906
- de première priorité 907
- d'une entreprise 921
- passives 1137
- véreuses 1187
Dévaluation de la monnaie 124
Développement de la direction 1081
- des entrepreneurs 491
- des experts 1109
- d'une région 1
- industriel décentralisé 15
- régional 1

Devis appréciatif 617
Devise forte 119
Diagnostique gestionnaire 1083
Digne de crédit 631
Dilution des titres 270
Directeur de placement 953
- de projet 1015
- d'investissement 953
- technique 1002
Disponibilité 871
Disposition de biens 104
Distribution des revenus 37
Diversification de risque 489, 567
- des produits 21
- industrielle 21
Dividende 1198
- brut 788
- cumulatif 786
- d'action 364
- d'option 791
- en espèces 1201
- net d'impôts 793
- non-cumulatif 790
- ordinaire 792
Documentation 794
Documents de soumission 855
Donneur de caution 808
Double imposition 200
- taxation 200
Droit commercial 158
- compensateur 126
- de commission 257
- de consommation 128
- de conversion 853
- de faillite 154
- d'engagement financier 1166
- de rétention 164
Droits d'entrée 129
"Dumping" 796
Ecart inflationniste 67
Echange de titres 358
Echéance 376, 1230
- d'un prêt 832
Echelle mobile 1204
Echelonnement de taux d'intérêt 520
- négatif de taux d'intérêt 521
Ecole commerciale 1038
Economie externe 27
- externe pécuniaire 28
- externe technologique 29
Economiste de projet 1016

FRANCAIS

Education de poste 1076
Effet à terme 223
- commercial 761
- de banque 751
- de commerce 224
- de devises 654
- de propagation industrielle 91
Effets de remous 3
- escomptés 221
Efficacité de coût 616
Elaboration d'un projet 559
Elasticité de demande 638
- de revenus 642
- de substitution 640
- d'évaluation 639
- d'offre 641
Emission "chaude" 288
- comme déterminée dans l'offre 285
- de capitalisation 900
- de conversion 286
- défensive 287
- directe du Gouvernement 149
- d'obligations 912
- excessive 822
- publique 821
Empêchements légales 160
Emplacement d'un projet 692
Emprunt de conversion 536
- d'obligations 537
Emprunt-obligations 537
Emprunts à recouvrir 1228
Enchères internationales 760
Encombrement du marché 804
Endettement 1221
Engagement contractuel 145
- éventuel 922
- garanti 925
- limité 923
En moyenne 212
Entrepreneur 643
Entreprise à grande intensité de
   dettes 917
- de client 769
- de service public 85
- en participation 660
- privée 442
- publique 443
Epargnes corporatives 186
- forcées 187
Epuisement 1190
- des réserves en devises 31

Equation de la comptabilité 1145
Equilibre de profit optimum 598
Escompte 1244
- commercial 215
- de banque 215
- officiel 179
Escompter 271
Escompteur 415
Espèces en caisse à court terme
   1163
Estimateur 956
Etablissement agro-industriel 383
- bancaire 385
- du prix de revient 1047
Etat comparatif 1249
- consolidé 1250
- de crédit 630
- estimatif 617
Etre au-dessous du pair 271
Etude 1121
- de cas 1040
- d'entreprise 1123
- de praticabilité 646
- de praticabilité directoriale 649
- de praticabilité économique 647
- de praticabilité financière 648
- de praticabilité gestionnaire 649
- de praticabilité technique 650
- du temps et du mouvement 1126
- économique 1122
Etudes de la région 589
Etude sur les possibilités de
   réalisation 646
Eurodollars 275
Evaluateur de projet 1018
Evaluation de bon état de crédit 583
- de garantie 582
- de la gestion 586
- du marché 587
- d'un projet 691
- du travail 1075
- économique 584
- financière 585
- technique 588
Examen de sensitivité 742
Excédent de capacité 600
- de coût 770
Ex-dividende 800
- extraordinaire 797
Ex-droit 801

Exécution sur les biens immeubles 803
Ex-émission de capitalisation 798
Exemption d'impôts 191
Exercice financier 1210
Exigibilités 926
Expectation de profit 685
Expert compréhensif 1041
- comptable 957
- comptable externe 958
- comptable interne 959
- d'analyse des systèmes 1125
- de banque rurale 1019
- d'une banque de développement 982
- financier 986
- financier de développement 961
Explosion démographique 83
- des naissances 83
Exportations manquées 25
- renoncées 25
Exposé comparatif 1249
- consolidé 1250
Exposition 911
Facilités d'anti-pollution 24
- de banque 408
- de crédit 111
- de remboursement 795
- de ristourne 795
- d'extension 802
Facteur de diversité 782
- de la récupération du capital 602
- de valeur actuelle 672
- limitant 827
Facteurs coopérants 14
Faculté de réunir sur un seul candidat plusieurs voix 780
Faillite 759
Faire la contrepartie 279
Fiduciaire publique 858
Financement à court terme 509
- à long terme 505
- à moyen terme 506
- commun 504
- conventionnel 502
- de concession 500
- de consortium 501
- de créances 496
- de dettes actives 496
- de développement 503
- des entreprises de service public 508

Financement des machines 499
- du capital de roulement 538
- du secteur agricole 497
- en participation 504
- institutionel 146
- parallèle 507
- par déficit budgétaire 123
- pour combler une lacune 534
- subventionné 510
Fixation de la valeur de l'inventaire 1071
Fonction catalytique 471
Fonctionnaire d'opération 1009
Fondateur de société 613
Fonds administrés 549
- consolidés 258
- d'amortissement 914
- de commerce d'une maison 806
- de contre-partie 105
- de garantie 1212
- de roulement, net 1252
- d'investissements 464
- investibles 70
- renouvelable 913
- social 885
Formation aux pays tiers 1135
- de la direction 1087
- d'outre-mer 1135
- du capital 9
- du travail 1076
- en cours d'emplois 1134
- en cours d'emplois industriel 1132
- industrielle 42
- nationale 1133
- professionnelle 1097, 1136
Formulation d'un projet 559
Formule politique 552
Fractionnement des actions 359
Frais de remplacement 1178
Franchise d'imposition 191
Fuite des capitaux 8
Fusion 754
Fusionnement 754
Gage hypothécaire 170
Gain 1236
Garant 808
Garantie 612, 773
- à recouvrir 1213
- d'accomplissement 551
- de crédit 113
- de crédits à l'exportation 137

FRANÇAIS
Garantie d'émission 573
- d'exécution 551
- d'investissement 147
Généraliste 1063
Génération d'espèces 1164
Gestion commerciale 994
- de crédit 1088
- de la production 1091
- de l'inventaire 1070
- de portefeuille 1103
- du marché 1090
- d'une société 995
- financière 1089
- moyenne 996
Gratification pour l'exportation 136
Groupe consultatif 967
Hausse rapide 7
Haussier 251
Homme de paille 274
Hypothèque 170
- fermée 171
Identification des projets 512
Immunité fiscale 191
Impôt de développement 196
- de péréquation d'intérêts 197
- indirect 202
- sur l'accroissement de fortune 194
- sur la fortune acquise 194
- sur les bénéfices non distribués 198
- sur les sociétés 195
Indicateurs économiques 637
Indice de la production industrielle 38
- des prix et de la production 39
Industrie à domicile 54
- agronome 50
- agronomique 50
Industrie-clef 58
Industrie dans son enfance 57
- d'embranchement 56
- de produits secondaires 51
- de sous-produits 51
- d'exportation 55
- intense en capital 52
- non-intense en capital 53
- orientée à la compétence technique 61
- orientée au marché 59
- réglementée 60
Inflation 65
- de crédit 112

Inflation en cours 66
Information de placement 1072
- d'exportation 984
Infrastructure 68
- monétaire 69
Ingénieur conseil 965
- de projet 1017
Insolvabilité 813
- technique 814
Instrument hypothécaire 837
Instruments de dette 268
Intensité de crédit 883
- de dettes à long terme 919
Interdiction d'importation 143
Intérêt décisif 817
Intérêts bruts 1224
- courus 1223
- cumulés 1223
- gestionnaires 993
- imputés 1225
- pendant la construction 1222
Introduction de bourse 365
Inventaire 818
Investigateur du marché 1003
Investissement 522
- au capital originaire 492
- autonome 74
- induit 75
- négatif 1197
- symbolique 527
Investisseurs institutionnels 452
Jeux de simulation 1117
Joueur à la baisse 218
Jour de liquidation 340
- du réglement 340
Jurisconsulte d'une banque 988
Lacune dans la formation 1128
- d'insuffisance 658
La petite industrie 62
Législation pour l'industrie pilote 162
- stimulante 161
- sur les faillites 154
Le passif exigible 926
Lettre de change 761
- de change à terme 763
- de change à vue 762
- de crédit 824
- de renonciation 826
- de répartition 823

Lettre de répartition des nouvelles
     émissions 852
- d'une somme exigible 273
- négative 825
Lettres de gage 241
Liberté d'entrepreneur 23
- d'entreprise 23
- d'exportation 140
- industrielle 47
Ligne de crédit 928
- de projet 560
Limitation de crédit 116, 920
- de dette 903
- de dividende 783
Limite de placement 532
- libre 511
"Linkage" 77
- en arrière 78
- en aval 79
Liquidation 828
- d'un compte 256
Liquidité 1227
Liste de contrôle 610
- des valeurs dorées 290
- d'opportunité d'investissements
     1073
Loi sur l'association et participation
     152
- sur les banques 153
- sur les contrats 151
- sur les sociétés 156
- sur les titres et actions 155
- sur l'investissement du capital
     étranger 157
Maison de banque 385
- de commission des exportations 450
- de consultation 968
- de crédit commercial 425
- de placement fermé 424
- d'escompte 449
- financière de vente à tempérament
     451
Maison-mère 384
Manipulation 291
Manque de liquidité 1214
Marchand de titres 419
Marché actif 295
- à la baisse 296
- après Bourse 305
- de l'acheteur 297
- de nouvelles émissions 304

Marché des changes 300
- d'escompte 299
- des devises 300
- des hypothèques 302
- des monnaies 301
- des titres 293
- de vendeur 831
- du capital 298
- du comptant 306
- du disponible 306
- étroit 303
- hors cote 305
- hypothécaire 302
- libre 305
- monétaire 298
- noir 6
Marge de profit 830, 846
- de sécurité 292, 741
Maximation de profit 847
Membre d'un syndicat de garantie
     465
Méthode de rendement 750
- de valeur actuelle 671
- du chemin critique 1026
Méthodes de la comptabilité du prix
     de revient 1044
Migration industrielle 48
Mise de fonds 895
Mission de banque 1005
- de collection des faits 1006
- de reconnaissance 1008
- d'évaluation 1004
- préparatoire de projet 1007
Mobilisation des ressources 566
Modernisation 835
Monnaie faible 121
- forte 119
- surestimé 120
- surévaluée 120
Motif fiscal 193
Mouvement de personnel 1020
Multiple imposition 201
Multiplicateur 172
Multi-prévision 1060
Nantissement 773
Nationalisation 173
Négociable en banque 309
Niveau de rendement 1257
Nombre indice 40
Non-cumulatif 312
Obligation chirographaire 267

FRANÇAIS

Obligation convertible 263
- de conversion 263
- fixe 264
- hypothécaire 266
- irremboursable 265
- non amortissable 265
Obligations amortissables 245
- au porteur 230
- convertibles 234
- d'adjustement 228
- de consolidation 235
- de conversion 234
- de profit 238
- en séries 247
- garanties 237
- garanties par des effets 232
- garanties par une hypothèque de seconde priorité 236
- légales 240
- nominatives 246
- nouvelles 239
- remboursable sur demande 231
- remboursables 245
Observation en cours d'emplois 1096
- sur le tas 1095
Offre agrégé 745
- pour vente 841
Opérateur 1042
Opération à cheval 371
- de banque 469
- de consolidation 916
Opérations de prêt 528
- du marché ouvert 174
Ordonnance de paiement de dividendes 784
Ordre d'achat 809
- fermé 810
- ouvert 811
Ordres à appréciation 272
Organisation de l'industrie 460
- des compétences et des functions 990
- de compétences et du personnel 991
- schématique 1010
Orientation en cours d'emplois 1100
Paiement contractuel 1233
- de coupon d'intérêt 261
- du comptant 360
Paiements différés 1188
Papier commercial 224

Papier de complaisance 222
Parc industriel 43
- industriel fonctionnel 45
- industriel spécialisé à un seul commerce 46
- industriel subordonné 44
Parité 175
- indirecte 82
Partage des actions 359
Part de marché 665
Participation au capital originaire 493
- au profit 686
Passif courant 926
- non exigible 924
Patronage 178
Patron-Manager 1011
Pays en voie de développement 17
Période de gestation 655
- de récupération 669
Permis d'exportation 140
Personnel de contrôle 1022
- de surveillance 1022
- étranger 1021
- expatrié 1021
- sur le terrain 985
PERT 1026
Perte de capital 1160
Petite caisse 1234
- exploitation 62
Placement 313, 522
- autonome 74
- de père de famille 278
- privé 314
- symbolique 527
Plafond de taux d'intérêt 515
Plan de construction 614
- de développement 19
- d'investissement 524
Planification de profit et système budgétaire 1110
- des carrières professionnelles 1039
- du budget 1156
Plans de modèle 666
Pléthore du marché 804
Plus-value d'actif 864
Point à jeu égal 599
- "breakeven" 599
- "cut-off" 632
Politique d'acquisition 556

Politique d'approvisionnement 556
- de commerce extérieur 142
- de formation 1130
- de la fixation des prix 1104
- de placement 525
- désinflationniste 125
- de "switch" 375
- fiscale 141
- monétaire 166
- orientée au développement 36
Portefeuille d'emprunts 1229
- des effets 933
- d'investissement 1226
Poste de l'actif 863
Potential de vente 739
Pouvoir de crédit 881
Pouvoir-mandat 849
Précisions de soumission 856
Préférence de liquidité 165
Premier cours des obligations 317
Première de taux 283
Prestation de substitution de crédit 475
- de succédané de crédit 475
Prêt à clause restrictive 547
- à taux de faveur 500
- commercial 529
- de dures conditions 540
- en devise forte 541
- en devises 539
- en monnaie faible 545
- en monnaie locale 542
- garanti 544
- indigène 530
- inférieur 929
- lié 547
Prêt-nom 274
Prêt non-garanti 548
- personnel 543
- pour les indigènes 530
- rural 531
- subordonné 929
Prévision 1058
- à court terme 1062
- à long terme 1059
- de ressources et applications des fonds 608
- de vente 1061
Prime 315
Priorités d'investissements 73
Prise de position politique 552

Privilège de rétention 164
Prix compétitif 675
- coûtant 618
- de compte 673
- de demande 676
- de demande sociale 681
- de facteur 677
- de garantie 656
- de marché 679
- de marché mondial 682
- de réport 252
- d'ouverture 318
- du comptant des actions 369
- fictif 580
- imputé 678
- international 682
- prévu 674
Problème de vente-mixte 738
- opérationel 843
Procédé de décision 969
- technique 1106
Procédure d'approvisionnement 555
- de retrait de fonds 574
- d'incorporation 844
Procédures d'exécution de la loi 150
Processus de procédé de décision 970
Procuration 849
Production brute 667
- nette 668
- technique 1108
- totale 667
Productivité de capital 683
Produits communs 684
- conjoints 684
Profiles des industries 1068
Profit 1236
- brut 1237
- de marchand de titres 289
- d'exploitation 1239
- net 1238
- non distribué 1240
Programmation linéaire 1077
Programme de conseil 472
- de consultation 472
- de "crash" 774
- de formation entre banques 1131
- de formation inter-bancaire 1131
- de petit crédit 533
- d'orientation 1099

FRANÇAIS

Programme du développement des
  directeurs 1053
- institutionnel de formation 1069
Prohibition d'importation 143
Projections financières 652
Projet 689
- continuel 697
- "cut-off" 694
- de liquidation de soi-même 695
- fictif 696
Promotion de l'efficacité économique
  490
- de vente 854
- du marché de capital 470
- systématique de vente 1105
Proportion des facteurs 30
Propriété mixte 1013
Propriété privée 1014.
- publique 1012
Protection 178
"Pyramiding" 322
Rapport annuel 755
- financier 1057
Rationnement de capital 102
Réalisation des actions 339
- d'une unité d'exportation 26
Rebais 1244
- différé 1245
Recensement de la production
  industrielle 12
Récépissé de dépôt 254
Recettes en devises 653
Recherche appliquée 1033
- d'écoulement de marchandises 1094
- du marché 1093
- du procédé technique 1107
- et développement 1114
- opérationnelle 1098
Rectification de la valeur de
  l'inventaire 1071
Réduction 1190
- du capital 1251
Réescompter 324
Référence de banquier 591
Refinancement 565
Région arriérée 2
Régions de développement 18
Relation hyrarchique des
  compétences 989
Relevé comparatif 1249
- consolidé 1250

Remboursement 1244
Remise 1157
Rémunération du capital 730
Rendement de l'actif 729
- de la propriété 731
- de l'investissement 732
- de ventes 733
- d'un titre d'obligation 227
- économique 728
- financier 1208
- social 728
Rentabilité 687
- commerciale 688
Rente annuelle 1149
Rentes consolidées 258
Réorganisation 850
- d'une entreprise 768
Répartition d'actions 753
Réport 252
Réserves 938
- d'amortissement 940
- de prévoyance 939 '
- extraordinaires 941
- légales 943
- légales minimales 944
- libres 942
- pour éventualités 939
Ressources et applications des
  fonds 607
- et applications des fonds
  escomptées 609
Restriction de crédit 116
Restrictions imposées au mouvement
  des devises 132
- quantitatives de crédit 114
Revalorisation 117, 185
Revaluation de la monnaie 117
Revenu brut 1216
- de transfer 98
- d'exploitation 1218
- gagné 1215
- net 1217
- non-gagné 1220
- retenu 1203, 1219
Revenus nets 1202
Risque calculé 568
- de commerce 734
- de crédit 569
- d'entreprise 734
- économique 735
- financier 736

Risque politique 737
Ristorne 1244
Rotation de l'inventaire 819
- du stock 819
Roulement de portefeuille 1235
Sans coupon 799
- dividende 800
Savoir faire gestionnaire 1085
Secteur public 84
Secteurs non-organisés 89
- organisés 88
Sélection d'un projet 693
Séminaire régional 1034
Service des dettes 1185
- du contentieux 976
Services consultatifs techniques 572
- d'administration 1086
- d'assurance-crédit 474
- de développement de gérance 1082
- de gérance 1086
- de marché du capital 294
- de pré-financement 554
- de prêt 663
Simulation 1116
Situation d'un projet 692
Société 422
- affiliée 423
- anonyme 431
- anonyme avec un fonds d'investissements ouvert 435
- à responsabilité limitée 432
- associée 423
- commerciale 422
- coopérative de construction 420
- de contrôle 429
- de "factoring" 427
- de petit crédit 426
- de placement 430
- de portefeuille 430
- fiduciaire 461
- fiduciaire avec un fixe programme
  d'investissements 463
- fiduciaire fermée 462
- filiale 423
- financière 428
- financière de l'industrie et
  commerce 439
- financière pour la petite industrie
  436
- holding 429
- hypothécaire agricole 438

Société multinationale 434
- par actions 431
- publique à responsabilité limitée
  433
Sociétés de garantie 445
- financière 444
Solde de caisse 1161
- liquide 1161
Solvabilité 1246
- actuelle 1247
- technique 1248
Sources d'approvisionnement 845
- externes 743
- internes 744
Sous-capitalisation 947
Sous-émission 820
Sous-évaluation 206
Sous-membre d'un syndicat de
  garantie 466
Sous-prêt 546
Spécialiste 1118
Spécification de soumission 856
Spéculateur 321
- à la hausse 251
- de titres 362
Spéculation 357
Stabilisation des prix 177
Stabilité de cours de change 133
Stagflation 92
Standardisation 1119
Statisticien 1120
Statut de la Charte 964
- d'une industrie pilote 64
Statuts sociaux 756
Stimulant fiscal 193
Stimulants de l'exportation 139
- d'investissement 148
Stratégie de placement 526
Substitution des importations 513
Subvention de dépenses
  administratives 1251
- de frais de gérance 1251
Sur-capitalisation 931
Surenchères compétitives 760
Surtaxe 190
Surveillance de projets 571
Syndicat 458, 1101
- de banque 409
- de banquiers 409
Syndic officiel de faillite 842

FRANÇAIS

Système bancaire 217
- de citation 836
- de programme, planification et
  budget 1112
- de reportage 851
- de sous-traitant 93
- d'information 812
- d'information de la direction 1084
- d'information gestionnaire 1092
Talon 945
Tantièmes des administrateurs 350
Tarif de douane 122
- douanier 122, 127
- douanier compensateur 126
"Task force" 1023
Taux courant 709
- d'arrérages 1242
- d'arriérés 1242
- de capitalisation 901
- de concentrations 564
- de coûts-bénéfices 707
- de coûts d'exploitation 721
- de couverture de l'actif fixe 717
- de couverture de l'investissement
  718
- de crédit 561
- de crédit commercial 562
- de "cut-off" 710
- de dette-capital actif 713
- de dette-propriété 711
- de dividende 1200
- de financement des ressources
  internes 1243
- de l'épargne 87
- de liquidité 705
- d'emprunts 561
- de paiement des dividendes 722
- de portefeuille 723
- de prêt 563
- de productivité de capital 724
- de profitabilité 725
- de réescompte 180
- de rendement 699
- de rendement de capital 708
- de rendement de capital investi 700
- de rendement équitable 702
- de rendement escompté 701
- de rendement interne 703
- de rendement juste 702
- de rendement marginal 703
- de rendement marginal de capital 720

Taux de rendement social 704
- de réserve d'amortissement 714
- dérivé 715
- des actions ordinaires 935
- d'escompte 180
- d'escompte bancaire 179
- de sécurité de prêt 719
- de service des dettes 712
- de solvabilité 726
- d'exploitation 698
- d'intérêt 514
- d'intérêt de devises 517
- d'intérêt de pénalité 518
- d'intérêt du marché 280
- d'intérêt effectif 516
- d'intérêt excellent 283
- d'intérêt naturel 281
- d'intérêt net 284
- d'intérêt nominal 282
- d'intérêt pénal 518
- d'intérêt subventionné 519
- d'inventaire-vente 1241
- d'utilisation de la capacité 698
- dynamique 716
- moyen de rendement de capital 706
- statique 727
Taxation multiple 201
Taxe à l'importation 129
- de garantie 656
Technique d'évaluation et de
  contrôle de programme 1026
- industrielle 1067
Techniques de contrôle des coûts
  1046
Technologies d'intensité de capital
  95
- d'intensité de travail 97
- intenses en capital 95
- intermédiaires 96
Terme d'échéance 376
Tirer profit 319
Titre commerçable 310
- d'actions 341
- d'obligation 226
- d'option 342
- négociable 310
Titres au porteur 230
- de bourse 343
- de participation 243
- de priorité 225
- de spéculation 253

Titres d'une grande liquidité 308
- éligibles 336
- en séries 247
- exempt de taxe 248
- hypothécaires 241
- hypothécaires ouvertes 242
- marrons 253
- nominatifs 246, 368
- non notés 338
- notés 333
- perpétuels 244
Traite 216, 761
Traité 259
Traite payable à presentation 762
Tranche d'actions 326
Transaction de déport 213
- de "switch" 372
Transfert de biens 104
Travaux publics 86
Tripotage de bourse 325
Trust de valeurs 429
Unification 834
Unité captive 11
- centrale 100
- d'annexe 99
Usance 377
Usure 378
Valeur active 863
- actuelle 670
- ajoutée 746
- capitalisée 950
- comptable 948
- de liquidation 949
- de marché 951
- nominale 379

Valeurs 328
- actives d'une banque 865
- à revenu fixe 233
- convertibles 346
- de bourse 343
- de conversion 329
- de gouvernement 331
- de seconde main 335
- digérées 330
- disponibles 871
- dorées 278
- d'un tiers 335
- éligibles 336
- fungibles 334
- immatérielles 870
- immobilisées 868
Valeurs intangibles 870
- irremboursables 332
- matérielles 877
- non amortissables 332
- non digérées 337
- remboursables sur demande 345
- tangibles 877
Ventes diluées 381
- du capital originaire 494
Vérification de la direction 1079
- des comptes 1152
- gestionnaire 1079
- opérationelle 1035
Versement de souscription 862
Viabilité financière 747
- générale 748
- technique 749
Vie économique 661
- utile 662
Zone de libre-échange 32

GERMAN

DEUTSCH

Abbruchswert 949
Abendkurse für Erwachsene 1055
Abgeleitete Nachfrage 635
- Verhältniszahl 715
Abkommen 259
Ablehnungsschreiben 825
Ablösungsfonds 914
Abrechnung 828
Abrechnungstag 340
Abrechnungstermin 340
Absatzforschung 1094
Absatzsteigerung 1105
Abschlagsdividende 789
Abschreibung 1192
Abschreibungsreserven 940
Absorptionsfähigkeit von
  Investitionen 71
Abtretungsurkunde 757
Abzug 1157, 1244
Afrikanische Entwicklungsbank 392
Aggregiertes Angebot 745
Agrarbankexperte 1019
Agrarentwicklungsbank 393
Agrarfinanzierung 497
Agrarindustrie 50
Agro-industrielles Unternehmen 383
Aktienbestand 933
Aktiendividende 364
Aktiengesellschaft 431
Aktienkapital 894
Aktienkonversion 363
Aktienmantel 341
Aktien mit multipler Stimm-
  berechtigung 351
- ohne Nennwert 352
Aktienpaket 326
Aktienspaltung 359
Aktienspekulant 362
Aktientausch 358
Aktientitel 341
Aktienumsatz 366
Aktienzuteilung 753
Aktive Börse 295
Aktiver Absatzmarkt 295
Aktivposten 863
- einer Bank 865
Akzeptbank 446
Akzeptkredit 775
Akzise 128
Allgemeine Durchführbarkeit 748
Alternative Investitionskosten 620

Alternative Kapitalkosten 619
- Kosten 625
Altmodische Geschäftsleitung 999
Amortisation des Vermögens-
  bestandes 1147
- einer Anleihe 1148
Amortisationsfonds 914
Amtlich nicht notierte Werte 338
- notierte Werte 333
Analyse der industriellen
  Entwicklungsmöglichkeit 1029
- der Leistungsfähigkeit 1028
- des kritischen Pfades 1026
Anfangsgeschäftskapital 1253
Anfangskurs von Schuld-
  verschreibungen 317
Angebotselastizität 641
Angefallene Zinsen 1223
Angeld 636, 664
Angemessene Ertragsrate 702
Angewandte Forschung 1033
Angleichsschuldverschreibungen 228
Anhäufung 207
Anlage 522
Anlagebank 398
Anlagefonds 464
Anlagegesellschaft mit fest-
  stehendem Investitionsprogramm
  463
Anlage-Informationszentrum 456
Anlagekapital 604, 868
Anlagekapitaldeckung 879
Anlagenachrichten 1072
Anlagevermögen 604, 868
Anlagevermögensertrag 729
Anlegung 313
Anleiheausschuss 992
Anleihe in harter Währung 541
- in Inlandswährung 542
- in lokaler Währung 542
- in weicher Währung 545
Anleihekapital 887
Anleihekomitee 992
Anleiheportefeuille 1229
Anleiheumwandlung 915
Anleihevertrag 829
Annexbetrieb 99
Annexer Industriepark 44
Annuität 1149
Anomalieswitchgeschäfte 373

Anomalieumstellung im
  Effektenengagement 373
Ansammlung 207
Anschaffungskosten 771, 1172
Anti-Inflation 20
Anti-Pollutionsvorkehrungen 24
Arbeitsintensive Technologien 97
Arbeitsplatzbewertung 1075
Arbeitsprozessplan 1024
Asiatische Entwicklungsbank 394
Auf Baisse gerichtetes Börsen-
  manöver 219
- dem Markt 210
- den Namen lautende Schuld-
  verschreibungen 246
Aufgelaufene Zinsen 1223
Aufgeld 252, 636
Aufgeschobener Nachlass 1245
Aufkaufen des Marktes 260
Auflösung 828
Auf professionelle Fertigkeit
  ausgerichtete Industrie 61
Aufsichtspersonal 1022
Aufwertung 185
Ausbildung auf dem Arbeitsplatz 1134
- auf dem Industriearbeitsplatz 1132
- im eigenem Land 1133
- in Drittländern 1135
Ausbildungsberater 1129
Ausbildungslücke 1128
Ausbildungspolitik 1130
Ausbildungsstätte der Regierung
  1127
Ausbildung von Management 1087
Ausfuhrlizenz 140
Ausführungsgarantie 551
Ausführungskriterien 1102
Ausfuhr von Waren zu
  Schleuderpreisen 796
Ausgabe 488
Ausgabebank 386
Ausgaben der Projektentwicklung
  645
Ausgabe von Obligationen 912
Ausgleichszoll 126
Ausländische Ausbildungshilfe 1054
Ausländisches Expertenpersonal
  1021
Auslandskapitalinvestitionsgesetz 157
Ausschlaggebende Interessen 817
Ausschliesslich Dividende 800

Ausschliesslich Extradividende 797
- Gewinnanteilschein 799
- Kapitalisierungsemission 798
Ausschuss 1101
Aussenhandelspolitik 142
Aussenstände 1138
Aussenstehende Anleihen 1228
- Bürgschaft 1213
Aussetzung 911
Ausstattungskredit 485
Auszahlung 488
Auszahlungsabteilung 973
Auszahlungsverhältnis 722
Automatisation 1036
Autonome Investierung 74
- Kapitalanlage 74
Autorisierte Aktien 367
"Backwash" Effekte 3
- Wirkung 3
Baissebörse 296
Baissespekulant 218
Baissier 218
Bank 385
Bankakzept 751
Bank-an-Bank Ausbildungsprogramm
  1131
Bankanstalt 385
Bankclearingstelle 447
Bankdiskont 215
Bankdiskontsatz 179
Bankenabrechnungsstelle 447
Bankengruppe 411
Bankenkonsortium 411
Bankfach 469
Bankfähig 309
Bankfähigkeit eines Projektes 590
Bankgeschäft 469
Bankgesetz 153
Bankhaus 385
Bankinstitut 385
Bankjurist 988
Bankkonsortium 409
Bankkredit 214
Bankmakler 414
Bankmission 1005
Bankmöglichkeiten 408
Bankrate 179
Bankreferenz 591
Banksatz 179
Banksyndikat 409
Banksystem 217

DEUTSCH

Banktratte 216
Bankverfassung 960
Bankwechsel 216, 751
Bankwesen 469
Barbestand 1161
Bardividende 1201
Bargewinnanteil 1201
Barkurs von Aktien 369
Barschaftsbasis 1162
Barverkehr 306
Barwert 670
Barzahlung 360
Bau-Arbeitsplan 614
Baugenossenschaft 420
Bedingte Verbindlichkeit 922
Befristete Einlage 269
Behördlich bestellter
  Konkursverwalter 842
Beobachtung auf dem Arbeitsplatz
  1096
Beratender Ingenieur 965
Beratung auf der Arbeitsstelle 1064
Beratungsprogramm 472
Berechnetes Risiko 568
Bereitstehende Güter 840
Bereitstellung von Kredit-
  substituten 475
Berichterstattungssystem 851
Berufsausbildung 1097, 1136
Berufsmässige Beratung 1043
Beschaffungsverfahren 555
Beschäftigungsanalyse 1025
Beschäftigungsausbildung 1076
Beschleunigte Abschreibung 1194
Beschränkender Faktor 827
Beschränkte Schuld 923
– Verbindlichkeit 923
Bestandliste 817
Bestätigungsbank 448
Bester Zinssatz 283
Bestes Profitgleichgewicht 598
Besteuerungsfähigkeit 199
Beteiligung am Grundkapital 493
Beteiligungsgeschäft 660
Betriebsausgaben 1207
Betriebsbudget 1231
Betriebseinkommen 1218
Betriebsgewinn 1239
Betriebsintensität 698
Betriebsjahr 1210
Betriebskapitalkredit 486

Betriebskoeffizient 721
Betriebskosten 1179
Betriebsstab 1009
Betriebsverlust 1232
Beurteilungselastizität 639
Bevölkerungsexplosion 83
Bevollmächtigter Angestellter
  eines Börsenmaklers 211
Bevorrechtigte Kosten 934
Bewertung der Geschäftsleitung 586
– der Kreditwürdigkeit 583
Bewertungsmission 1004
Bezugsrechtschreiben 852
Bilanz 1153
Bilanzanalyse 581
Billiges Geld 167
Blankoabgaben 339
Blankoverkäufe 339
Blockierte Vermögenswerte 869
Bodenkreditbank 399
Bonusaktie 344
Borgzinssatz 561
Börse 413
Börsenarbitrage 208
Börseneinführung 365
Börsengängige Werte 334
Börsenhändler 419
Börsenmakler 417
Börsenmanöver 381
– , auf Baisse gerichtetes 219
Börsennotiz 323
Börsenschiebung 325
Börsenwerte 343
Bruttodividende 788
Bruttoeinkommen 1216
Bruttoeinkünfte 1216
Bruttoertrag 1216
Bruttogewinn 1237
Bruttogewinnanteil 788
Brutto-Output 667
Brutto-Produktion 667
Bruttozinsen 1224
Buchforderungen 1138
Buchführung 1037
Buchhaltungsabteilung 971
Buchhaltungsgleichung 1145
Buchprüfung 1152
Buchsachverständiger 957
Buchschulden 1137
Buchwert 948
Budget 1156

199

Budgetbeschränkungen 101
Budgetkontrolle 1155
Budgetplanung 1156
Bürge 808
Bürgschaftsurkunde 189
Büro eines Schwindelmaklers 250
Büroverwaltung 998
Cash-flow 607
- Planung 608
Chefingenieur 1002
CIF 611
Commerzbank 388, 407
Computer 1042
Counterpartgeldmittel 105
"Cut-off" Projekt 694
- Punkt 632, 710
Dachgesellschaft 429
Darlehen für Einheimische 530
- in Devisen 539
Darlehensgeschäfte 528
Darlehenskapital 887
Darlehenskassenschein 205
Datenaufnahme-Mission 1006
Datenbank 1049
Debitoren 1138
Debitorenverkauf 427
Deckung 773
- des Schuldendienstes 633
Deckungsbewertung 582
Deckungsverhältnis des Kapital-
    anlagevermögens 717
Deckungsvorkehrungen 740
Defensive Emission 287
Defizit 1189
Deflation 16
Deflator 1050
Dem ermessen überlassene
    Aufträge 272
Deportgeschäft 213
Depotschein 254
Desinflationistische Politik 125
Devisenanleihe 539
Devisenauswirkung 654
Devisenbeschränkungen 132
Deviseneffekt 654
Deviseneinnahmen 653
Devisenmarkt 300
Devisenrisiko 570
Devisenverwaltung 131
Devisenzinssatz 517

Dezentralisierte industrielle
    Entwicklung 15
Diagnose der Geschäftsleitung 1083
Diagnosestudien auf dem Arbeits-
    platz 1065
Difizitäre Finanzierung 123
Direkte Kosten 1169
- Regierungsemission 149
Direktionsausschuss 963
Direktionskomitee 963
Direktorentantiemen 350
Direkt-primäre Nutzen 592
Diskontieren 271
Diskontierte Ertragsrate 701
Diskontiertes Cash-flow 609
Diskontierte Wechsel 221
Diskontmakler 415
Diskontmarkt 299
Diskontobank 449
Diskontsatz 179, 180
Diskontwechsel 221
Diversitätsfaktor 782
Dividende 1198
Dividendenauszahlungsschein 785
Dividendenbegrenzung 783
Dividendendeckung 1199
Dividendenrate 1200
Dividendenverfügung 784
Dividendenzahlungsverhältnis 722
Dokumentation 794
Dokumentenkredit 479
Doppelbesteuerung 200
"Dumping" 796
Durch Effektenlombard gesicherte
    Schuldverschreibungen 232
Durchführbarkeitsuntersuchung 646
Durch Gesamthypothek gesicherte
    Schuldverschreibungen 236
- im Range nachstehendes Pfand-
    recht gesicherte Schuld-
    verschreibungen 239
Durchschnitt, im 212
Durchschnittliche Kapitalertrags-
    rate 706
Durchschnittskosten 1168
Dynamische Verhältniszahl 716
Effekten 328, 343
Effektenengagementumstellung 372
Effektenhändler 419
Effektenmarkt 293

DEUTSCH

Effektive Nachfrage 634
Effektiver Zinssatz 516
Eigener Wechsel 320
Eigenkapital 891
Eigenkapitalertrag 731
Eigentumsübertragung 203
Einbehaltener Gewinn 1240
Einen Verlust ausweisen 271
Eingesetztes Kapital 888
Eingezahltes Kapital 895
Einheitsbankbetrieb 412
Einkaufskosten 771
Einkommenselastizität 642
Einkommensverteilung 37
Einlage auf feste Kündigung 269
Einlösbare Schuldverschreibungen
  245
Ein-Mann Geschäft 1011
Einrichtungen zur Förderung der
  Geschäftsleitung 1082
Einschliesslich Dividende 777
- Zinsen 778
Einschränkende Abmachung 107
Einstweilige Ausgaben 644
Einzelheiten der Lieferungsangebote
  856
Emissionsbank 386
Emissionsfirma 465
Emissionsgarantie 573
Emission wie im Kostenanschlag
  285
Empfindlichkeitstest 742
Enger Markt 303
Entscheidungsfällung 969
Entscheidungsfällungsprozess 970
Entwicklung der Geschäftsführung
  1081
- des Unternèhmertums 491
Entwicklungsausgaben 134
Entwicklungsbank 391
Entwicklungsbankfachmann 961, 982
- mit integrierten Wissensgebieten
  1041
Entwicklungsbudget 1159
Entwicklungsfinanzierung 503
Entwicklungsfördernde Aktivitäten
  487
Entwicklungsgebiete 18
Entwicklungsländer 17
Entwicklungsprogramm 19
Entwicklungssteuer 196

Entwicklungsunkostenkonto 1141
Entwicklungsverwaltung 981
Entwicklung von Fachleuten 1109
Erklärung über die einzuschlagende
  Politik 552
Ermächtigung 380
Erneuerungsschein 945
Eröffnungskurs 318
Ersatzkosten 1178
Erschöpfung 1190
Ersparnisse von Körperschaften 186
Erster Tageskurs 318
Erstklassige Wertpapiere 225
Ertrag einer Schuldverschreibung
  227
Ertragsfähige Vermögenswerte 867
Ertragsmethode 750
Ertragsniveau 1257
Ertragsrate 699
- des Investitionskapitales 700
Ertragsrechnung 1144
Erwarteter Preis 674
Erweitertes technisches Programm
  802
Erweiterung der industriellen
  Aktivitäten 21
Etatbeschränkungen 1ʊ1
Eurodollars 275
Eventuell eintretende Verbindlich-
  keit 922
Ex-Bezugsrecht 801
Exklusive Dividende 800
- Superdividende 797
Experte mit allgemeinem Fach-
  wissen 1063
Exportanreize 139
Exportfinanzierungsunterstützung
  495
Exportgüterindustrie 55
Export-Importbank 397
Exportindustrie 55
Exportkreditgarantie 137
Exportkreditversicherung 138
Exportlizenz 140
Exportnachrichten 984
Exportprämie 136
Exportrealisierungseinheit 26
Exportvermittlungsbank 450
Externe Kosten 622
- Mittel 743
Externer Buchprüfer 958

Externe Wirtschaftseffekte 27
Fachmann 1118
Faktorei 427
Faktorenverhältnis 30
Faktorkosten 623
Faktorpreis 677
Fällige Verbindlichkeit 926
Fälligkeit 1230
- einer Anleihe 832
Fälligkeitsbasis 1146
Fallstudie 1040
Feasibilitystudie 646
Feldbeobachtung 1095
Feldpersonal 985
Fertigkeitsausbildungsmöglichkeiten 90
Feste Aktiven 868
- Belastung 766
- Bruttokapitalanlage 918
- Schuldverschreibung 264
Festverzinsliche Schuld-
   verschreibungen 233
Filialbankbetrieb 410
Filialbankwesen 410
Finanzabkommen 106
Finanzberatung 1056
Finanzberichterstattung 1057
Finanzbewertung 585
Finanzerklärung 1209
Finanzfachmann 986
Finanz-Feasibilitystudie 648
Finanzielle Bewertung 585
- Durchführbarkeit 747
- Durchführbarkeitsstudie 648
- Erklärung 1209
- Infrastruktur 69
Finanzieller Ertrag 1208
Finanzielles Risiko 736
Finanzierung des Agrarsektors 497
Finanzierungsgesellschaft 428
Finanzierungsgesellschaften 444
Finanzierungsinstitute 444
Finanzierung von Aussenständen 496
- von gemeinnützigen Unternehmen 508
Finanzjahr 1210
Finanzkapazität 651
Finanzpolitik 141
Finanzprojektionen 652
Finanzrisiko 736
Finanzverwaltung 1089

Firmenwertkonto 861
Fixe Belastung 766
- Kosten 1170
Fixer Wechselkurs 182
Fixgeschäfte 339
Flexibler Wechselkurs 181
Flüssige Anlagen 871
- Mittel 871
Flüssiges Geld 167
Follow-up Personal 1022
Förderung der wirtschaftlichen
   Leistungsfähigkeit 490
Forderungen 1138
Forschung und Entwicklung 1114
Freie Reserven 942
Freier Wechselkurs 183
Freigrenze 511
Freihandelszone 32
Freiverkehr 305
Freiverkehrsmarkt 305
Fristtratte 763
Fristwechsel 763
Fundierte Belastung 766
- Schuld 905
- Staatsanleihen 258
Fundierungsschuldverschreibungen 235
Fungible Werte 334
Funktioneller Industriepark 45
Fusion 754
Galoppierende Inflation 66
Garant 808
Garantiedeckung 657
Garantieerklärung 189
Garantiegebühr 656
Garantiegesellschaften 445
Garantierte Schuldverschreibungen 237
Garantiescheine 237
Gebietserhebung 589
Gebietsstudien 589
Gebietsuntersuchungen 589
Gebühr für eine finanzielle
   Verbindlichkeit 1166
Gebundene Anleihe 547
Gebundener Kredit 547
Gedeckte Anleihe 544
- Verbindlichkeit 925
Gefälligkeitsakzept 222
"Gefangene" Produktionseinheit 11
Gegen-Garantie 473

DEUTSCH

Gegentransaktion 371
Gegenwartswert 670
Gegenwartswertfaktor 672
Geldabwertung 124
Geld auf tägliche Kündigung 307
Geldentwertung 124
Geldkurs von Aktien 369
Geldmarkt 301
Geldnahe Werte 308
Gemeinsame Finanzierung 504
- Kosten 1174
Gemeinschaftsgründung 660
Gemeinschaftsprodukte 684
Gemischtes Eigentumsrecht 1013
Generelle Realisierbarkeit 748
Genossenschaftsbank 389
Geometrisch-degressive
   Abschreibung 1195
Gesamtkosten 1182
Geschäftseinkommen 1218
Geschäftsführende Bank 400
Geschäftsführungskenntnis 1085
Geschäftsgewinn 1239
Geschäftsinhaber-Manager 1011
Geschäftsjahr 1210
Geschäftsleitende Bank 400
Geschäftsleitender Direktor 1001
Geschäftsleitungsberatung 1080
Geschäftsleitungsbuchführung 1078
Geschäftsrisiko 734
Geschäftsverlust 1232
Geschäftswert 806
Geschlossener Auftrag 810
Gesellschaft 422
- mit beschränkter Haftung 432
Gesellschaftsgründer 613
Gesellschaftskapital 885, 894
Gesellschaftsklausel 758
Gesellschaftssatzungen 756
Gesellschaftsvertrag 756, 833
Gesetzesdurchführungsverfahren 150
Gesetzliche Hindernisse 160
- Minimum-Reserven 944
- Reserven 943
Gesetzlicher Reservefonds 943
Gesetz über Beteiligung und
   Partnerschaft 152
- über die Gesellschaften 156
Gesicherte Schuld 925
Ges.m.b.H. 432
Gestationsperiode 655

Gewährsmann 808
Gewinn 1236
Gewinnanteil 1198
Gewinnanteilschein 785
Gewinnobligationen 238
Gewinnspanne des Börsenmaklers
   289
Gewinn und Verlustrechnung 1144
Gewöhnliche Dividende 792
Gezeichnetes Kapital 895
Glashausindustrie 57
Glattstellung eines Konto 256
Gleitklausel 1204
Gratisaktie 344
Greifbare Vermögenswerte 878
Grenze für Grundkapitalinvestierung
   532
Grenzkosten 1176
Grundkapital 885, 890, 894, 909
- ohne Stimmrecht 910
Gründungsvertrag 765
Gutgehendes Geschäft 805
Gutschein 327
Halbfertigfabrikate 35
Halbfertigprodukte 35
Handelsakademie 1038
Handelsbank 388, 407
Handelsbilanz 5
Handelsdarlehen 529
Handelsgesellschaft 422
Handelsgesetz 158
Handelskammer 421
Handelskredit 476, 1184
Handelskreditgesellschaft 425
Handelsorganisation 460
Handelsrentabilität 688
Handelsrisiko 734
Handelsspanne 830
Handelswechsel 224, 761
Handgeld 636
Harte Anleihe 540
- Währung 119
Hausindustrie 54
Haussespekulant 251
Haussier 251
Heimatindustrie 54
"Heisse" Emission 288
"Heisses" Geld 169
Herstellungskosten 621
Hilfskapital 886
Historische Kosten 1172

Höchstgrenze des Zinssatzes 515
Höchstkapazität 601
Holdinggesellschaft 429
Hypothek 170
Hypothekarkredit 482
Hypothekenbank 399
Hypothekenbrief 163
Hypothekenbriefe 241
Hypothekendokument 837
Hypothekenmarkt 302
Hypothekenpfand 170
Hypothekenpfandbrief 266
Hypothekenscheine 241, 242
Ideeller Wert einer Handelsfirm 806
Immaterielle Aktiva 870
Importersatz 513
Importkontingent 144
Importsperre 143
Importsteuer 129
Importverbot 143
Im Zuge einer Sanierung ausgegebene
  Schuldverschreibungen 228
Indexzahl 40
Indirekte Devisenkosten 624
- Kosten 1173
- Parität 82
- Steuer 202
Indirekt-sekundäre Nutzen 593
Industriebedingte Wanderbewegung 48
Industrieberatung 1066
Industrieentwicklungsbank 395
Industrieentwurfszentrum 41
Industrieerziehung 42
Industrieförderungsinstitut 49
Industriegelände 43
Industrie in den Kinderschuhen 57
Industrielle Ausbildung 42
- Konzessionierung 47
Industrie mit Pionierrang 64
Industriepark 43, 46
Industrieproduktionsindex 38
Industrieproduktionszensus 12
Industrieprofile 1068
Industrietechnik 1067
Industrie- und Handelsfinanzierungs-
  gesellschaft 439
Induzierte Investierung 75
In einem einzigen Handelsgewerbe
  spezialisierter Industriepark 46
Inflation 65
Inflationslücke 67

Informationssystem 812
- der Geschäftsführung 1084
Infrastruktur 68
Inhaberpapier 310
Inhaberschuldverschreibungen 230,
  233
Inklusive Bezugsrechte 779
- Bonus 776
- Dividende 778
- Prämie 776
- Zinsen 778
Installierte Kapazität 601
Institutionelle Finanzierung 146
- Investoren 452
- Kapitalanleger 452
Institutionelles Ausbildungsprogramm
  1069
- Kapital 605
Interamerikanische Entwicklungs-
  bank 396
Interbankaires Ausbildungsprogramm
  1131
Interessen der Geschäftsführung 993
Interimschein 327
Internationale Entwicklungs-
  vereinigung 454
- Finanzierungsgesellschaft 455
Internationaler Preis 682
Internationales Anbotemachen 760
Interne Ertragsrate 703
- Mittel 744
Interner Buchprüfer 959
- Zinssatz 703
Inter-Projektkoordinierung 816
Intersektorielle Analyse 1030
In Umlauf gesetztes Kapital 889
Inventarumsatz 819
Inventar-Verkaufsverhältnis 1241
Inventarverwaltung 1070
Investierbare Geldmittel 70
Investierbares Kapital 70
Investierung 522
- in Grundkapital 492
Investierungsgesellschaft 430
- mit geschlossenem Anlagefonds
  424
Investierungsnachrichten 1072
Investitionsanreize 148
Investitionsbank 398
Investitionsbankfachmann 962
Investitionsdeckungsverhältnis 718

DEUTSCH
Investitionsertrag 732
Investitionsertragsanalyse 579
Investitionsgarantie 147
Investitionsgeschäft 523
Investitionsklima 72
Investitionsleiter 954
Investitionsmakler 418
Investitionsplan 524
Investitionspolitik 525
Investitionsportefeuille 1226
Investitionsprioritäten 73
Investitionsstrategie 526
Investitions- und geschäftsleitende
  Bank 401
Investitionsverwalter 987
Investitionszuteilungskriterien 659
Investmentfonds 464
Investorvertrauen 76
Jahresbericht 755
Jahresrente 1149
Juristische Hilfe 159
- Person des Privatrechtes 440
Kalkuliertes Risiko 568
Kapazitätsbenützungsrate 698
Kapital, in Umlauf gesetztes 889
- , noch nicht zur Einzahlung
  aufgerufenes 896
Kapitalabhebungsverfahren 574
Kapitalabschreibung 1255
Kapitalanlagegesellschaft mit in der
  Höhe unbegrenztem Investmentfonds
  435
Kapitalanlegervertrauen 76
Kapitalausgaben 1205
Kapitalbeteiligung 884
Kapitalbildung 9
Kapitalbudget 1159
Kapitalertrag 730
Kapitalerertragsrate 708
Kapitalerzeugung 1164
Kapitalflucht 8
Kapitalgüter 33
Kapitalherabsetzung 1254
Kapitalintensive Industrie 52
Kapitalintensive Technologien 95
Kapitalisierter Wert 950
Kapitalisierung 899
Kapitalisierungsemission 900
Kapitalisierungsverhältnis 901
Kapitalkonto 1139

Kapitalkosten 603
Kapitalleichte Industrie 53
Kapitalmarkt 298
Kapitalmarktdienste 294
Kapitalmarktförderung 470
Kapitalmobilisierung 566
Kapitalproduktivität 683
Kapitalrationierung 102
Kapitalrückgewinnungsfaktor 602
Kapitalschaffung 1164
Kapitalschwache Körperschaft 946
Kapitalspesen 1165
Kapitalstruktur 899
Kapitalverlust 1160
Kapitalvermögen 930
Kapitalwertzunahme 1158, 1256
Kapitalzufluss 10
Kassenbasis 1162
Kassensaldo 1161
Kassenzu- und Abfluss 607
Katalog von Investitionsgelegen-
  heiten 1073
Katalytische Funktion 471
Kaufauftrag 809
Käufermarkt 297
Kaufmännisches Management 994
Kaufnote 103
Kennziffer 40
Klausel der Zielsetzung einer
  Gesellschaft 838
Kleinaktien 229
Klein-Anleiheprogramm 533
Kleinbetrieb 62
Kleine Kasse 1234
Kleingewerbe 62
Kleingewerbefinanzierungs-
  gesellschaft 436
Kleinkreditverein 426
Kleinobligationen 229
Kommissionsgebühr 257
Kompetenzdelegation 1051
Kompetenzhyrarchie 989
Kompetenz- und Funktions-
  organisation 990
Kompetenz- und Personal-
  organisation 991
Konkurs 759
Konkursordnung 154
Konkursrechtliche Bestimmungen
  154
Konkursverfahren 759

Konnossement 764
Konsolidierte Finanzerklärung 1250
- Schuld 905
Konsolidierungsoperation 916
Konsortium 458
Konsortiumfinanzierung 501
Konstruktions-Arbeitsplan 614
Konsulentenfirma 968
Konsulentengruppe 967
Konsumentenberatung 13
Konsumentenkredit 477
Konsumgüter 34
Kontenüberziehung 550
Kontinuierliches Projekt 697
Kontrakt 259
Kontraktuelle Zahlung 1233
Kontrollabteilung 974
Kontrollierender Aktienbesitz 817
Kontrollierte Industrie 60
Kontrolliste 610
Kontrollpersonal 1022
Konventionelle Finanzierung 502
Konversionsaktien 346
Konversionsanleihe 536
Konversionsemission 286
Konversionspapier 263
Konversionspapiere 234
Konversionsrecht 853
Konvertierbare Effekten 329
Konzentrationsgrad 564
Konzentrationsintensität 564
Konzertzeichner 362
Koordinationsstelle 382
Körperschaft des bürgerlichen
  Rechtes 440
- des öffentlichen Rechtes 441
Körperschaftssteuer 195
Korrespondenzbank 390
Kostenanschlag 617
Kostenberechnung 1047
Kosteneffizienz 616
Kosten-Ertragsanalyse 575
Kosten-Gewinnanalyse 575
Kostenkalkulation 1047
Kostenkontrolle 1045
Kostenkontrolltechniken 1046
Kosten-Nutzenverhältnis 707
Kostenpreis 618
Kostenpreisberechnung 1047
Kostenüberzug 770
Kosten und Vertrag 772

Kosten, Versicherung und Fracht 611
Kostenverteilungsanalyse 1027
Kostenvoranschlag 617
Kreditabteilung 972
Kreditanalyse 576
Kreditaufschub 478
Kreditbasis 880
Kreditbeschränkung 920
Kreditbrief 824
Kreditfähigkeit 630, 881
Kreditfonds 1212
Kreditgarantie 113
Kredit gegen automatisch
  verlängerbaren Kreditbrief 483
- gegen Prolongationsakzept 483
- gegen Sicherheit 479
Kreditinflation 112
Kreditintensität 883
Kreditkapazität 880
Kreditknappheit 116
Kreditkontrolle 108
Kreditlimitierung 920
Kreditlinie 928
Kreditmanagement 1088
Kreditmöglichkeiten 111
Kreditoren 1137
Kreditrahmen 928
Kreditrisiko 569
Kreditschöpfung 110
Kreditstand 630
Kreditverschiebung 115
Kreditversicherungsdienste 474
Kreditwürdigkeit 631
Kredit zur Finanzierung von
  Abzahlungsgeschäften 480
Kreuzsektorenanalyse 577
Kritischer Pfad 1026
Kumulative Dividende 786
Kumulativer Gewinnanteil 786
Kündbare Aktien 345
- Obligationen 231
- Schuldverschreibungen 231
Kundenakzept 752
Kundenunternehmung 769
Kundenwechsel 224
Kundschaft 806
Kursmakler 417
Kursnotiz 323
Kurzfristige Finanzierung 509
Kurzfristiger Schatzwechsel 204
- Warenkredit 467

DEUTSCH

Kurzfristiges Barvoratsvolumen 1163
Kurzfristige Verbindlichkeit 926
- Vorhersage 1062
Kybernetik 1048
Lagerumsatz 819
Ländliche Darlehen 531
Landwirtschaftliche Hypotheken-
  gesellschaft 438
Langfristige Durchschnittskosten
  1175
- Finanzierung 505
- Schuld 924
- Verbindlichkeit 924
- Vorhersage 1059
Langfristig umsetzbare Vermögens-
  werte 875
Laufende Aktivposten 866
Laufendes Flüssigkeitsverhältnis 709
- Konto 1140
- Liquiditätsverhältnis 709
Laufzeit 376
Leihkapitalintensität 919
Leihkapitalquote 919
Leihzinssatz 562
Leistungsfähigkeitsanalyse 1028
Leistungsgarantie 551
Leistungskriterien 1102
Letzter Kurs 316
Lieferungsangebotdokumente 855
Limitierender Faktor 827
Limitierung der Grundkapital-
  investierung 532
Lineare Abschreibung 1196
Lineares Programmieren 1077
Linearprogrammierung 1077
"Linkage" 77
Liquidation 828
Liquidationswert 949
Liquidität 1227
Liquiditätspräferenz 165
Liquiditätsrate 705
Liste von hochwertigen Wert-
  papieren 290
- von Investitionsgelegenheiten 1073
Lohn-Sicherheitsverhältnis 719
Mahnsystem 836
Maklergebühr 249
- im Börsensaal 416
- im Parkett 416
Maklerprovision 249
Managementausgaben 1206

Managementberatung 1080
Managementbuchführung 1078
Managementdienste 1086
Management einer eingetragenen
  Gesellschaft 995
- Feasibilitystudie 649
Managementinteressen 993
Managerinformationssystem 1092
Manipulation 291
Marginale Kapitalertragsrate 720
Marktanteil 665
Marktbewertung 587
Marktforscher 1003
Marktforschung 1093
Marktforschungsabteilung 977
Markt für Neuemissionen 304
Marktorientierte Industrie 59
Marktpreis 679
Marktverwaltung 1090
Marktwert 951
Marktzinssatz 280
Maschinenkredit 485
Maschinenteilfinanzierung 499
Maschinen- und Material-
  beschaffungspolitik 556
Maschinen- und Materialbe-
  schaffungsquellen 845
Maximalkapazität 601
Mehrfachbesteuerung 201
Mehrfacher Wechselkurs 184
Mehrwert 746
Methode des Gegenwartswertes 671
Methoden der Kostenbuchhaltung
  1044
Mitglied eines Emissionssyndikats
  465
Mitteilung über einen fälligen
  Betrag 273
Mittelfristige Finanzierung 506
Mittlere Geschäftsleitung 996
Modellpläne 666
Moderne Geschäftsleitung 997
Modernisierung 835
Multinationale Gesellschaft 434
Multipler Wechselkurs 184
Multiple stimmberechtigte Aktien
  351
Multiplikator 172
Mündelsichere Schuldver-
  schreibungen 240
- Wertpapiere 278, 336

Musterpläne 666
Mutterbetrieb 100
Muttergesellschaft 384
Mutterhaus 384
Nachfinanzierungskontrolle 553
Nachfrageanalyse 578
Nachfrageelastizität 638
Nachfragepreis 676
Nachfrage und Angebot 220
Nachlass 1157
Nachzugsaktien 349
Namensaktien 368
Nationalbank 406
Nationale Nutzen 595
Nationalisierung 173
Natürlicher Zinssatz 281
Nebengesetze 964
Nebenproduktindustrie 51
Negative Investition 1197
Nennwert 379
Nettobetriebskapital 1252
Nettoeinkommen 1217
Nettoeinkünfte 1217
Nettoertrag 1217
Nettogeschäftskapital 1252
Nettogewinn 1238
Nettonutzen 596
Nettooutput 668
Nettoproduktion 668
Nettovermögen 872, 930
Nettozinssatz 284
Netzplananalyse 1026
Neudiskontieren 324
Neudiskontierungssatz 180
Nicht einlösbare Schuldverschreibung 265
- einlösbare Werte 332
- erarbeitetes Einkommen 1220
Nichtfundierte Belastung 767
Nichtkumulativ 312
Nichtkumulative Dividende 790
Noch nicht bis zum Höchstbetrag in Anspruch genommene Hypotheken-scheine 242
- nicht zur Einzahlung aufgerufenes Kapital 896
Nominaler Zinssatz 282
Nominalkapital 885, 890
Nominalkonto 1142
Nominalwert 379
Normung 1119

Notreserven 939
Notrücklagen 939
Nutzen durch Veredlungsverfahren 597
- durch Weiterverarbeitung von Produkten 597
Nützliche Lebensdauer 662
Nutzschwelle 599
Obligationsanleihe 537
Offener Auftrag 811
Offenes Konto 1143
Offenmarktgeschäfte 174
Offenstehendes Konto 1143
Offentliche Arbeiten 86
- Auslagen 81
- Emission 821
Offentlicher Sektor 84
- Treuhänder 858
- Versorgungsbetrieb 85
Offentliches Eigentum 1012
- Unternehmen 443
Offentliche Zeichnungseinladung 848
Offentlich-rechtliche Körperschaft 441
Ohne Bezugsrecht 801
- Dividendenbonus 797
- Kupon 799
Okonomische Bewertung 584
- Feasibilitystudie 647
Okonomischer Ertrag 728
Operationelle Abteilung 978
- Prüfung 1035
Operationelles Problem 843
Operationsresearch 1098
Optionsdividende 791
Optionskapital 606
Ordentliche Dividende 792
Organisationsplan 1010
Organisierte Sektoren 88
Orientierung auf dem Arbeitsplatz 1100
Orientierungsprogramm 1099
Parallelfinanzierung 507
Parität 175
Paritätskurs 175
Pekuniäre externe Wirtschafts-effekte 28
Personalkredit 543
Personalumschlag 1020
PERT 1026
Pfand 612

DEUTSCH
Pfandbrief 262
Pfandbriefe 233
Pfandrecht 164
Planung der Berufslaufbahnen 1039
- des Kassenzu- und Abflusses 608
Plazierung 313
Politisches Risiko 737
Portefeuilleturnus 1235
Portefeuilleverwaltung 1103
Portfolioverhältnis 723
Postsparkasse 403
Prämie 315
Preisaufschlag 830
Preisfestsetzungspolitik 1104
Preiskontrolle 176
Preisnachlass 1244
Preisnotierung 323
Preisstabilisierung 177
Preis- und Produktionsindex 39
Primazinssatz 283
Prioritätsaktien 355
Privatbank 404
Private Alternativkosten 626
- Anlegung 314
- Auslagen 80
Privateigentum 1014
Private Plazierung 314
Privates Unternehmen 442
Produktionskapital 892
Produktionskosten 621
Produktionskostenanalyse 1032
Produktionsprozessforschung 1107
Produktionsverwaltung 1091
Produktivität des Kapitales 683
Produktivitätsintensität des
   Kapitales 724
Produktrentabilitätsanalyse 1031
Profit 1236
Profitbeteiligung 686
Profitbuchführung 1111
Profiterwartung 685
Profitieren 319
Profitmaximierung 847
Profitplanung und Budgetsystem 1110
Profitrate 725
Profitrechnung 1111
Profitspanne 846
Programmevaluierung und Kontrolle
   1026
Programmfinanzierung 557
Programm-Planungs und Budget

System 1112
Projekt 689
Projektabteilung 979
Projektauswahl 693
Projektbegutachter 1018
Projektbewertung 691
Projektdirektor 1015
Projektfinanzierung 558
Projektformulierung 559
Projektidentifizierung 512
Projektingenieur 1017
Projektkosten 690
Projektleiter 1015
Projektlinie 560
Projektlokalisierung 692
Projektnationalökonom 1016
Projektvorbereitungsmission 1007
Protektion 178
Prototyp Industriezentrum 63
Provision 257
Prüfung der Geschäftsführung 1079
Quantitative Kreditbeschränkungen
   114
Rabatt 1244
Rahmenvorhersage 1060
Rasch umsetzbare Vermögenswerte
   874
Ratenkaufkredit 480
Ratenzahlungsfinanzierungsbank 451
Rechnungsjahr 1210
Rechnungspreis 673
Rechnungsprüfer 957
Rechtsabteilung 976
Reduzierung 1190
Refinanzierung 565
Regierungsausgaben 135
Regierungseffekten 331
Regionalentwicklung 1
Regionalseminar 1034
Regulierte Industrie 60
Reiner Zinssatz 284
Reingewinn 1202
Reinverdienst 1201
Reinvermögen 872, 930
Rekordprogramm 774
Rentabilität 687
Rentabilitätsrate 725
Rentenanleihen 244
Reportgeschäft 252
Reservekapital 893
Reservekapitalisierung 902

Reserven 938
Revolvierender Fonds 913
Risikokapital 898
Risikostreuung 489, 567
Rückständiges Gebiet 2
Rückwärts "Linkage" 78
Rückzahlbare Schuldverschreibungen 245
Rückzahlungsperiode 669
Saldierung eines Konto 256
"Sandwich" Kurse 1115
Satzungen 964
Schattenpreis 680
Schattenprojekt 696
Schätzer 956
Schatzschein 205
Scheinverkäufe 381
Schiffsfrachtbrief 764
Schleuderausfuhr 796
Schlüsselindustrie 58
Schlusskurs 316
Schlussschein 103
Schneller geschäftlicher Aufschwung 7
Schuldbegrenzung 903
Schulden 1137
Schuldendienst 663, 1185
Schuldendienstverhältnis 712
Schulden mit erster Priorität 907
- mit letzter Priorität 906
Schuldentilgungsfonds 914
Schuldinstrumente 268
Schuldschein 255
Schuldverschreibung 226
Schuldverschreibungen, auf den Namen lautende 246
- , durch Effektenlombard gesicherte 232
- , durch Gesamthypothek gesicherte 236
- , durch im Range nachstehendes Pfandrecht gesicherte 239
- , im Zuge einer Sanierung ausgegebene 228
- mit Gewinnbeteiligung 243
Schwarzer Markt 6
Schwebende Belastung 767
- Schuld 904
Seefrachtbrief 764
Selbständige Niederlassung 955

Selbstfinanzierungsrate 1243
Selbstkostenberechnung 1047
Selbstkosten eines Produktes 1171
Selbstkostenpreis 618
Selbstkostenpreisfestsetzung 1211
Selbst-liquidierendes Projekt 695
Selektive Kreditkontrolle 109
Serienanleihen 247
Sich automatisch abdeckende Vorschüsse 467
- durch Gegentransaktionen sichern 279
Sicherheit 612
Sicherheiten 328
Sicherheitsbewertung 582
Sicherheitsgrenze 741
Sicherheitsspielraum 292
Sicherheitsvorkehrungen 740
Sich stets erneuernder Fonds 913
Sichtkredit 535
Sichttratte 762
Sichtwechsel 762
Simulation 1116
Simulationsspiele 1117
Sofortkauf 361
Solvenz 1246
Solvenzverhältnis 726
Sonderaktien 347
Sonderbelegschaft mit Spezialaufgaben 1023
Sondervorzugaktien 348
Sonstige Vermögenswerte 876
Soziale Alternativkosten 628
- Ertragsrate 704
- Kosten 627
Sozialer Ertrag 728
- Nachfragepreis 681
Sparbank 405
Spar-Investitionslücke 188
Sparkasse 405
Sparrate 87
Spar- und Anleihegenossenschaft 457
Sparverein 459
Spekulant 321
Spekulation 357
Spekulationspapiere 253
Spezialbearbeiter 1118
Spezialist 1118
Spezifikation der Submissionsofferte 856

DEUTSCH

Spitzenwerte 225
Staatsbank 406
Staatseigentum 1012
Stagflation 92
Stammaktien 353, 908
Stammaktienintensität 935
Stammkapital 894, 909
Standardisierung 1119
Standardkosten 1180
Startbetriebskapital 1253
Statistiker 1120
Statistische Qualitätskontrolle 1113
Statisches Verhältnis 727
Statuten 756
Stellagegeschäft 371
Stellgeschäft 371
Stellvertretung 849
Steueranreiz 193
Steuer auf nicht ausgeschüttete
  Gewinne 198
- auf nicht verteilte Gewinne 198
Steuerbefreiung 191
Steuerfreie Dividende 793
- Wertpapiere 248
Steuerfrei gezahlte Dividende 793
"Steuerhimmel" 192
Steuerkraft 199
Steuerpolitik 141
Steuerzusatz 190
Stimmenhäufung 780
Stimulierende Gesetzgebung 161
Strafzinssatz 518
Strohmann 274
Studie 1121
Stundung 807
Subanleihe 546
Submissionsoffertedokumente 855
Substitutionselastizität 640
Substitutionskosten 1178
Subventionierte Finanzierung 510
Subventionierter Kapitalismus 94
Subvention von Verwaltungsausgaben
  1251
Switchabschnitt 374
Switchgeschäft 372
Switchkupon 374
Switchpolitik 375
Symbolinvestierung 527
Symbolische Investierung 527
Syndikat 458, 1101
Systemanalyse 1124

Systemanalysenexperte 1125
Talon 945
Tätigkeitsanalyse 1025
Tätigkeitsausbildung 1076
Tätigkeitsbeschreibung 1074
Tatsachenaufnahme-Mission 1006
Tatsächliche Nachfrage 634
- Zahlungsfähigkeit 1247
Technische Abteilung 975
- Beratungsdienste 572
- Bewertung 588
- Durchführbarkeit 749
- Durchführbarkeitsstudie 650
- Feasibilitystudie 650
- Herstellung 1108
Technischer Prozess 1106
Technisches Verfahren 1106
Technische Zahlungsfähigkeit 1248
- Zahlungsunfähigkeit 814
Technologische externe Wirtschafts-
  effekte 29
Teilzahlungskredit 481
Termingeschäft 276
Teueres Geld 168
Tiefeninterview 1052
Tilgung 936
Tilgungsdatum 937
Tochtergesellschaft 423
Traditionelle Geschäftsleitung 999
Transfereinkommen 98
Tratte 761
Treuhandgesellschaft 461
Treuhandgesellschaft mit
  geschlossenem Anlagefonds 462
Trockener Wechsel 320
Typisierung 1119
Überalterung 839
Überbrückungsfinanzierung 534
Überemission 822
Überkapazität 600
Überkapitalisierung 931
Überschüssige Reserven 941
Überschwemmung des Marktes 804
Überseeausbildung 1135
Übertragbar 309
Übertragungskosten 629
Übertragungsurkunde 757
Übertragung von Wertpapieren 857
Überwachter Kredit 484
Überwachung von Projekten 571
Überwertete Währung 120

Überzeichnung 932
Umgruppierung 850
Umlaufsvermögen 866
Umorganisation eines Unternehmens 768
Umsatz 859
Umschuldungsanleihe 536
Umschuldungsrecht 853
Umwandlung einer Anleihe 915
Unantastbare Vermögenswerte 870
Unbelastetes Anlagevermögen 873
- Kapital 897
Unfundierte Schuld 904
Ungedeckte Anleihe 548
Ungedeckter Gläubiger 860
Ungedeckte Schuld 927
Ungeordnete Anleihe 929
Ungesicherte Gläubiger 860
Ungesicherte Schuldverschreibung 267
- Verbindlichkeit 927
Unorganisierte Sektoren 89
Unsichere Forderungen 1187
Unteranleihe 546
Unterbewertung 206
Unteremission 820
Unter-Emissionsfirma 466
Unterentwickeltes Gebiet 2
Unterkapitalisierung 947
Unterlieferantsystem 93
Unternehmen mit hoher Leihkapital-quote 917
Unternehmensberater 966
Unternehmenserhebung 1123
Unternehmensfreiheit 23
Unternehmensuntersuchung 1123
Unternehmer 643
Unternehmerentwicklung 491
Unternehmerfreiheit 23
Unterstellter Preis 678
Unterstellte Zinsen 1225
Untersuchung 1121
Unverteilter Gewinn 1240
Unvorhergesehene Ausgaben 615
Unzulänglichkeitslücke 658
Usance 377
Variable Kosten 1183
Verauslagung 488
Verbindlichkeiten 1137
- eines Unternehmens 921
Verbrauchsabgabe 128

Verbrauchssteuer 128
Verbreitungseffekt der Industrialisierung 91
Verdientes Einkommen 1215
Vereinbarung über Wertpapier-termingeschäfte 277
Vereinigung 754
Verfügbare Mittel 871
Verfügbarkeit von Kapital 1227
Vergleichende Finanzerklärung 1249
Vergleichsurkunde 781
Vergleichsvertrag 781
Vergütung für Abschreibung 1193
- für Reduzierung 1191
Verhältnis der Amortisations-reserven zu Originalkosten des Kapitalanlagevermögens 714
- der Zahlungsrückstände 1242
- von langfristigen Schuld-verpflichtungen zu Eigenkapital 711
- von Schuldverpflichtungen zu Aktivvermögen 713
Verkäufe auf Baisse 339
Verkäufermarkt 831
Verkäufe von Grundkapital 494
Verkaufsangebot 841
Verkaufsertrag 733
Verkaufsförderung 854, 1105
Verkaufskosten 1167
Verkaufs-mix Problem 738
Verkaufspotential 739
Verkaufsvorhersage 1061
Verkehrspapier 310
Verminderung der Devisenreserven 31
Vermögensübertragung 104
Vermögenswert 863
Vermögenszuwachs 864
Vermögenszuwachssteuer 194
Verpflichtungen 1137
Verschachtelung 322
Verschiedene Aktiva 876
Verschmelzung 754, 834
Verschuldung 1221
Versicherungsdeckung 815
Vertrag 259
Vertragliche Verpflichtung 145
Vertragsgesetzgebung 151
Vertrag über die Errichtung einer Gesellschaft 833
Vertretungsmacht 849

DEUTSCH

Vertriebsagentur 468
Vervielfältigung der Industrie-
  produkte 21
Verwaltete Geldmittel 549
Verwaltung einer Geschäftsstelle 998
Verwaltungsdirektorium 1000
Verwässertes Aktienkapital 370
Verzichtete Exporte 25
Verzichtsbrief 826
Verzichtsschreiben 826
Verzugskosten 1177
Volksaktien 229
Volleingezahlte Aktien 354
Vom Käufer beherrschter Markt 297
- Markt aufgenommene Wertpapiere
  330
- Markt noch nicht aufgenommene
  Wertpapiere 337
Von der Höhe der Forderung und dem
  Umfang des belasteten Grundstücks
  unabhängige Hypothek 171
- der Regierung garantierte Dividende
  787
Vorbereitende Ausgaben 644
Vorgeschlagener Kandidat 311
Vorhersage 1058
Vor-Investierungsdienste 554
Vorläufige Dividende 789
Vormission 1008
Vorstand 1000
Vorwärts "Linkage" 79
Vorzugsaktien 355
Vorzugs-Beteiligungsaktien 356
Vorzugsfinanzierung 500
Wachstumsorientierte Politik 36
Wahlaktie 342
Wahrscheinlichkeitsanalyse 580
Währungsabwertung 124
Währungsaufwertung 117
Währungskonvertierbarkeit 118
Währungspolitik 166
Wandelaktien 346
Wandelobligationen 234
Wandelschuldverschreibung 263
Wandelschuldverschreibungen 234
Warenakzept 752
Warenbestellung 809
Warenkredit 476
Warenwechsel 224, 761
Wechselagent 417
Wechseldiskont 180

Wechselkredit 775
Wechselkurskontrolle 130
Wechselkursstabilität 133
Wechselmakler 415
Wechselseitige Sparkasse 402
Weiche Anleihe 500
- Währung 121
Weltbank 453
Weltmarkpreis 682
Wertberichtigung des Inventars 1071
Werte aus zweiter Hand 335
- von dritter Seite 335
Wertfestsetzung des Inventars 1071
Wertminderung 1192
Wertpapierabteilung 980
Wertpapiere 328, 343
- mit geringem Nominalwert 229
Wertpapiergesetzgebung 155
Wertpapiermarkt 293
Wertpapierverwässerung 270
Wertverlust 1192
Wettbewerb-Bieten 760
Wettbewerbspreis 675
Wiederbeschaffungskosten 1178
Winkelbörse 250
Wirtschaftliche Bewertung 584
- Demokratie 22
- Durchführbarkeitsstudie 647
- Indikatoren 637
- Lebensdauer 661
Wirtschaftsabteilung 983
Wirtschaftschule 1038
Wirtschaftsdemokratie 22
Wirtschaftserhebung 1122
Wirtschaftsforschungsabteilung 983
Wirtschaftskonsulent 952
Wirtschaftsrisiko 735
Wirtschaftsuntersuchung 1122
Wucher 378
Zahlung des Zinsscheines 261
Zahlungsaufschiebung 1188
Zahlungsbilanzdefizit 4
Zahlungsfähigkeit 1246
Zahlungsfähigkeitsverhältnis 726
Zahlungsunfähigkeit 813, 1214
Zeichnungsbetrag 862
Zeit- und Bewegungsstudie 1126
Zeitwechsel 223
Zeitwert 670
Zensus der industriellen Produktion
  12

Zentralbank 387
Zinsangleichssteuer 197
Zinsen während der Konstruktions-
    periode 1222
Zinssatz 514
Zinssatzspanne 520
Zollrückvergütungsmöglichkeiten 795
Zollsatz 122
Zolltarif 127
Zollverzeichnis 122
Zubringerindustrie 56
Zulieferersystem 93
Zum Nennwert 209
Zur Einzahlung aufgerufenes Kapital
    882
- Parität 209
Zurückbehaltener Gewinn 1203, 1219
Zusammenschluss 834
Zusammenwirkende Faktoren 14
Zusatzkosten 1181
Zusatzkredit 498

Zusätzlich herbeigeführte Nutzen 594
Zuteilungsbenachrichtigung 823
Zuteilungsschein 823
Zuwendung 1150
Zuwendungskonto 1151
Zwangsersparnisse 187
Zwangssparbeträge 187
Zwangssparen 187
Zwangsverwalter 842
Zwangsvollstreckung aus einer
    Hypothek 803
Zwangswirtschaftliche Preisbildung
    176
Zweifelhafte Aussenbestände 1186
- Forderungen 1186
- Schulden 1186
Zweiggesellschaft 423
Zwischenbilanz 1154
Zwischenschein 327
Zwischentechnologien 96